Routledge Guide

The Routledge Guidebook to Hegel's *Phenomenology of Spirit*

The *Phenomenology of Spirit* is Hegel's most influential and important work, and unlocking this text is essential to understanding Hegel's philosophical system. *The Routledge Guidebook to Hegel's Phenomenology of Spirit* explores the major themes in Hegel's classic work and aids the reader in understanding this key text, examining:

- The context of Hegel's thought and the background to his writing
- Each section of the text in relation to its goals, meaning and significance
- The reception the book has received since its publication
- The relevance of Hegel's ideas to modern philosophy.

With an introductory overview of the text, end-of-chapter summaries and further reading included throughout, this guidebook is essential reading for anyone wishing to get to grips with Hegel's contribution to Western philosophy.

Robert Stern is Professor of Philosophy at the University of Sheffield, UK. He is the author of *Hegel, Kant and the Structure of the Object* (1990) and *Hegelian Metaphysics* (2009).

ROUTLEDGE GUIDES TO THE GREAT BOOKS
Series Editor: Anthony Gottlieb

The *Routledge Guides to the Great Books* provide ideal introductions to the work of the most brilliant thinkers of all time, from Aristotle to Marx and Newton to Wollstonecraft. At the core of each Guidebook is a detailed examination of the central ideas and arguments expounded in the great book. This is bookended by an opening discussion of the context within which the work was written and a closing look at the lasting significance of the text. The *Routledge Guides to the Great Books* therefore provide students everywhere with complete introductions to the most important, influential and innovative books of all time.

Available:

Aristotle's Nicomachean Ethics Gerard J. Hughes
Locke's Essay Concerning Human Understanding E. J. Lowe
Heidegger's Being and Time Stephen Mulhall
Plato's Republic Nickolas Pappas
Wittgenstein's Philosophical Investigations Marie McGinn
Wollstonecraft's A Vindication of the Rights of Woman Sandrine Bergès

Forthcoming:

De Beauvoir's The Second Sex Nancy Bauer
Descartes' Meditations on First Philosophy Gary Hatfield
Galileo's Dialogue Maurice A. Finocchiaro
Hobbes' Leviathan Glen Newey
Mill's On Liberty Jonathan Riley

Routledge Guides to the Great Books

The Routledge Guidebook to Hegel's *Phenomenology of Spirit*

Robert Stern

Routledge
Taylor & Francis Group

LONDON AND NEW YORK

First edition published in the Routledge Philosophy Guidebook series in 2001
This edition published 2013
by Routledge
2 Park Square, Milton Park, Abingdon, Oxon OX14 4RN

Simultaneously published in the USA and Canada
by Routledge
711 Third Avenue, New York, NY 10017

Routledge is an imprint of the Taylor & Francis Group, an informa business

British Library Cataloguing in Publication Data
A catalogue record for this book is available from the British Library

Library of Congress Cataloging in Publication Data
Stern, Robert, 1962–
The Routledge guidebook to Hegel's Phenomenology of spirit / Robert Stern.
p. cm. – (The Routledge guides to the great books)
Prev. ed. pub.: Routledge philosophy guidebook to Hegel and the Phenomenology of
spirit, 2002.
Includes bibliographical references (p.) and index.
1. Hegel, Georg Wilhelm Friedrich, 1770 1831. Phänomenologie des Geistes. I. Stern,
Robert, 1962– Routledge philosophy guidebook to Hegel and the Phenomenology of
spirit. II. Title. III. Title: Guidebook to Hegel's Phenomenology of spirit.
B2929.S65 2012
193–dc23
2012021215

ISBN: 978-0-415-66445-5 (hbk)
ISBN: 978-0-415-66446-2 (pbk)
ISBN: 978-0-203-09420-4 (ebk)

Typeset in Garamond
by Taylor & Francis Books

Printed and bound in Great Britain by the MPG Books Group

CONTENTS

PREFACE AND ACKNOWLEDGEMENTS

'A great man condemns posterity to the necessity of explicating him' (NA: 574). Written as an isolated aphorism, it is unclear whether in making this claim, Hegel was thinking of himself or others: but there is no doubt that in his case, this necessity still holds. As a great thinker, Hegel continues to exert an enormous influence on our time; so in order to comprehend ourselves, we must continually strive to come to terms with his thought, and to understand it anew.

This book is a contribution to this process, intended to shed light on the *Phenomenology of Spirit* for those who are approaching this work for the first time, and who are looking for some way through the labyrinth. I have therefore endeavoured to make my commentary as clear as possible, and to relate it closely to the text. Of course, as Hegel perhaps foresaw, a rich tradition of interpretation has grown up around the *Phenomenology*, particularly since the 1930s (see Chapter 8); but for reasons of space and accessibility, I have not been able to reflect critically on other interpretations in any detail here, although I have provided references and further reading. I have also assumed that my audience will primarily be English-speaking, so I have used standard translations where available, making amendments when necessary (see the Bibliography for further details).

I have been helped in this project by many individuals. I would first like to thank Tim Crane and Jo Wolff for inviting me to undertake it (and for waiting for me until I was able to do so). I am particularly grateful to those members of staff and post-graduates at the University of Sheffield who participated in a reading group on the *Phenomenology*, accompanied by a draft of my commentary, who led me to clarify my thoughts and writing in a number of ways: Leif Wenar, Dominique Kuenzle, Mark Day, and Kathryn Wilkinson were particularly helpful (and stalwart) in this regard. I am also grateful to the two classes of students who took my course on the *Phenomenology*, and who acted as a testing ground for the suitability of my text for its intended audience. Other individuals who have offered helpful comments and guidance at various times include: Gary Browning, Matthew Festenstein, Terry Pinkard, Nicholas Walker, Robert Wokler, and Heather Worden. I owe an especially large debt to those who acted as readers of the manuscript for Routledge: Fred Beiser, Stephen Houlgate, Ken Westphal, and Jo Wolff. All of them made a number of suggestions and constructive criticisms, which have improved the final book (although, of course, not all dis-agreements between us on matters of interpretation have been settled, and none of them should be held responsible for the views expressed here). Finally, Routledge also provided considerable support on the editorial side, where Muna Khogali and Tony Bruce were efficient and encouraging throughout.

Hegel may have anticipated the drive for explication that his work would provoke; he certainly anticipated its dangers, emphasizing in the Preface of the *Phenomenology* how hard fair-minded explication can be:

> This concern with aim or results, with differentiating and passing judgement on various thinkers is therefore an easier task than it might seem. For instead of getting involved with the real issue, this kind of activity is always away beyond it; instead of tarrying with it, and losing itself in it, this kind of knowing is forever grasping at something new; it remains essentially preoccupied with itself instead

of being preoccupied with the real issue and surrendering to it. To judge a thing that has substance and solid worth is quite easy, to comprehend it is much harder, and to blend judgement and comprehension in a definitive description is the hardest thing of all.

(PS: §3, p. 3)

As a thinker who has suffered more than most from superficial criticism, Hegel was right to think that others would find it easier to attack him than to take the trouble to understand him fully; and as I can testify from personal experience, he was also right to think that the 'hardest thing of all' is to succeed in doing what any commentary such as this must try to do, namely to 'blend judgement and comprehension in a definitive description' (and, in my case, all within a limited compass). I am especially grateful to my family (including its newest member), who have helped make this difficult task so much easier.

The author and the publisher wish to thank Oxford University Press for kind permission to reprint from: *G. W. F. Hegel: The Phenomenology of Spirit* translated by A. V. Miller (1977).

SERIES EDITOR PREFACE

"The past is a foreign country," wrote British novelist, L. P. Hartley: "they do things differently there."

The greatest books in the canon of the humanities and sciences can be foreign territory, too. This series of guidebooks is a set of excursions written by expert guides who know how to make such places become more familiar.

All the books covered in this series, however long ago they were written, have much to say to us now, or help to explain the ways in which we have come to think about the world. Each volume is designed not only to describe a set of ideas, and how they developed, but also to evaluate them. This requires what one might call a bifocal approach. To engage fully with an author, one has to pretend that he or she is speaking to us; but to understand a text's meaning, it is often necessary to remember its original audience, too. It is all too easy to mistake the intentions of an old argument by treating it as a contemporary one.

The *Routledge Guides to the Great Books* are aimed at students in the broadest sense, not only those engaged in formal study. The intended audience of the series is all those who want to understand the books that have had the largest effects.

AJG
October 2012

Author Preface to the New Edition

There are three main changes to this new edition. First, I have added a section to the first chapter, in which I offer a brief summary of the *Phenomenology* as a whole, which I hope will help orientate the reader. Second, at the end of each chapter, I have again added a brief summary of the chapter of the text that has been discussed, which I also hope will help the reader follow what has gone on previously. Finally, I have included a last chapter on the reception of the *Phenomenology* and its impact, which I hope will help the reader better understand the divergent ways in which the book has been interpreted and taken up, and its significance within philosophy. I am grateful to three advisers from Routledge, who inspired these changes.

Another, less substantive, change is to use paragraph numbers as well as page numbers to refer to the *Phenomenology*. Although these section numbers do not appear in German editions of the book, they are used in the Miller translation which forms our text here; and I believe that they will also be used in forthcoming translations by Terry Pinkard for Cambridge University Press, and Nicholas Walker for Oxford University Press. My hope is therefore that as well as making it easier to find quotations in the Miller translation, the numbers will also enable readers to find the relevant passages in these new translations, when they are published.

Finally, I have updated the bibliography. However, I have resisted the temptation to make any substantive changes to the text itself.

I am grateful to Routledge for inviting me to include this guide to the *Phenomenology* in their new series, thus giving me the chance to make these alterations, which I hope will be of benefit to new readers, and of interest to old ones.

INTRODUCTION

Immediately after Hegel's death in 1831 there emerged two schools, known as the Young (or Left) Hegelians and the Old (or Right) Hegelians, who offered radically different readings of Hegel's political philosophy. The Left Hegelians (such as Feuerbach, Marx, and Engels) saw in Hegel a utopian vision of freedom, community, and the triumph of the human spirit, while the Right Hegelians saw in Hegel a theocratic defence of the Prussian state, support for the status quo of absolute monarchy, and a quietistic conservatism. Since then, thinkers from across the political spectrum have viewed Hegel as an ally, while he is also taken as an enemy by others on both the left and the right.

This feature of Hegel-reception is not confined to his political philosophy, but is repeated across the board. Thus, for some he is a Romantic critic of the Enlightenment and a source of anti-rationalism in modern thought, whilst for others he is an opponent of Romanticism and a defender of the authority of reason; similarly, for some he is a theological philosopher seeking to uphold Christian orthodoxy, while for others he is a radical atheist setting out to undermine religious faith; and, for some he is a thinker in the Kantian tradition, following out the latter's idealism, while for others he is Kant's most effective opponent, replacing Kant's failed philosophical endeavour with something new of his own. Thus, the story of Hegel's reception is far from simple: he has been taken up from all sides, and attacked from all sides, as the assessment of his position has shifted in contrary directions.

How is it that Hegel can be open to such contrasting interpretations? What makes his thought so protean, that his constituency of friends and foes is so heterogeneous? Why are allegiances to Hegel so changeable, so that at one time he can be appropriated by one side and then at another time by its opposite? These are questions that are raised by the *Phenomenology* as much as by any of Hegel's works, and they deserve some response.

An obvious place to look for an answer is in the nature of Hegel's writings themselves, and their notorious style. A first suggestion might be that through mere stylistic ineptitude, Hegel made his works so hard to understand that his readers could see in them whatever they wanted to find, leaving his writings unusually open to diverse appropriations. Now, it is of course true that it can be formidably difficult to read Hegel, and partly for no more than stylistic reasons: while he can write clearly and even well, his prose can also be dense, obscure, and overburdened with technical terminology and neologisms. But there is more to it than this. For testing though it often is, Hegel's writing is rarely unintelligible. A more substantial stylistic difficulty is not with comprehension *per se*, but in properly locating Hegel's own position within the work. For, in the *Phenomenology* in particular, Hegel takes up an unusual and highly distinctive stance towards his audience: the authorial voice is muted; the discussion is left 'unsignposted', so we are not told where we are going or what Hegel's final objectives are; other philosophers, texts, and historical episodes are alluded to but not explicitly identified; and positions are advanced in a way that may make them seem final, which then turn out to be provisional in the light of criticisms that appear much later on. Thus, even when it is clear enough what Hegel is saying, it is not always clear in what spirit it is being said, and how far it represents Hegel's actual view, so this remains elusive and open to contrasting interpretations. It often requires considerable exegetical sensitivity to establish whether Hegel is ultimately seeking to defend some position, or attack it, and thus which side he is really on.

However, Hegel's elusiveness cannot be fully explained simply by matters of style and method, as these only really create problems for the uninitiated. A more substantial explanation can perhaps be given in terms of *context*; for how Hegel is categorized depends to an unusual degree on the background against which he is placed, and with whom he is juxtaposed. Thus, to take an example: for those who treat Voltaire, Diderot, or Hume as paradigmatic Enlightenment figures, Hegel will appear as an obviously anti-Enlightenment thinker, because he shares none of their atheism, cosmopolitanism, or scientific naturalism; but in a more German context and against the background of critics of the Enlightenment like Jacobi, Herder, or Hamann, it is Hegel's commitment to the ideals of the *Aufklärung* that stand out. Similarly, while comparisons with Kant or the early Fichte may appear to show that Hegel was a conservative political thinker, against the background of other theorists of his time (such as Karl Ludwig von Haller) Hegel may be represented as a liberal. Changes in historical perspective can therefore bring about radical re-evaluations of Hegel's position, as his ideas are thereby cast in a new light.

Not only does the issue of finding the right historical context make it difficult to categorize Hegel properly: a third factor is the nature of Hegel's thought itself, and its *dialectical* character. By this I mean that it is a central feature of Hegel's philosophical perspective, as we shall see, that on many disputes he does not seek to resolve them by taking up one side or the other, but rather tries to recast the issue by showing how the dichotomy underlying the dispute is false, and that it is therefore possible to integrate elements from both positions. This means that his standpoint is very hard to categorize in traditional terms: for while some aspects may come from one position, others may come from its apparent opposite, so that both sides in the debate can find *some* support for their position in his work, making this liable to contrary appropriations. Thus, for example, for many Hegel is identified as a Christian philosopher, where evidence from this appears to come from his hostility to the crude atheism of the Enlightenment; but Hegel's conception of Christianity is distinctive in that it attempts to undercut this Enlightenment critique of religious faith (which involves charging Christianity with irrationalism, dubious historical authenticity, and authoritarianism) by incorporating elements of this critique into a revised conception of Christian doctrine, so that his theism is designed to be compatible with the kind of humanism to which it is traditionally opposed. Hegel's position will therefore always prove unstable when the attempt is made to fit it within the traditional framework, as it appears that both sides have an equal right to claim him as an ally. Likewise, Hegel makes himself vulnerable to attack from those who use categories such as 'liberal', 'humanist', or 'rationalist' in a more simplistic way than is appropriate here: for, by attempting to incorporate other elements into these doctrines, Hegel can appear to be departing from them. Thus, for example, many humanists will take Hegel's positive remarks about religion to show he is a Christian philosopher who thereby *repudiates* humanism, while in fact Hegel is trying to subvert just this antithesis, and bring together both Christian and humanist elements in a way that does not undermine either side; but this makes him vulnerable to attack from those who do not recognize any possibility for compromise on this issue. As a result, by attempting to find room for what has been called 'the Hegelian middle', Hegel has made his position very hard to characterize in a stable way, for in his struggle to do justice to both sides, he may be claimed or attacked by either.

In what follows, I will attempt to make sense of this 'Hegelian middle', by showing how it is generally wrong to see Hegel as straightforwardly occupying *either* one side *or* the other on many issues; rather, he is usually to be seen as attempting to undermine this opposition by showing that these two options form a false dichotomy, and that the best option lies in some sort of compromise between them. Thus, although Hegel is a critic of the Enlightenment in some aspects, it is simplistic to see him as an *anti*-Enlightenment thinker; likewise, although he sees some fundamental problems in the outlook of modernity, this does not make him a conservative; and although he attempts to go beyond a crude atheism, this does not make him a theist. The challenge in understanding Hegel is to do justice to this many-sidedness; for, as Hegel insisted, it is always tempting to simplify matters and return to rigid oppositions. The cost, however, is that we will greatly reduce the space on our conceptual map, and will end up oscillating between readings of Hegel and treatments of the issues themselves, which fail to do justice to the true complexity of the situation. By better respecting the dialectical nature of Hegel's outlook, I believe, we may finally arrive at a more stable and lasting assessment of his thought, and reach a proper understanding of the ambitious nature of what he was trying to achieve.

In the rest of the book, I therefore attempt to trace out Hegel's dialectical handling of a series of issues, as these are presented in the *Phenomenology*. In the first chapter, I set the *Phenomenology* in the context of Hegel's life and works, and characterize his dialectical method in more detail, while showing how the Preface and the Introduction to the *Phenomenology* can be used to shed some light on Hegel's intentions for the book as a whole. In subsequent chapters, I then deal with each chapter of the *Phenomenology* in turn, following through the discussion as it progresses from 'Consciousness' to 'Absolute Knowing', as Hegel tries to teach us how dialectical thinking is possible, and what it might ultimately achieve. In conclusion, I consider the fascinating reception that the book has received.

ABBREVIATIONS

The following abbreviations are used for references to works by Hegel and Kant. For full details of works cited, and methods of citation, see the bibliography at the end of the volume.

WORKS BY HEGEL

AW	'Aphorisms from Hegel's Wastebook'
BP	*The Berlin Phenomenology*
CJI	*The Critical Journal of Philosophy*, 'Introduction: On the Essence of Philosophical Criticism Generally, and its Relationship to the Present State of Philosophy'
DFS	*The Difference Between Fichte's and Schelling's System of Philosophy*
EL	*Hegel's Logic: Part One of the Encyclopedia of the Philosophical Sciences*
EN	*Hegel's Philosophy of Nature: Part Two of the Encyclopedia of the Philosophical Sciences*
ES	*Hegel's Philosophy of Mind: Part Three of the Encyclopedia of the Philosophical Sciences*
ETW	*Early Theological Writings*

FK	*Faith and Knowledge*
HL	*Hegel: The Letters*
ILHP	*Introduction to the Lectures on the History of Philosophy*
ILPWH	*Lectures on the Philosophy of World History; Introduction: Reason in History*
JS I	*Jenaer Systementwürfe I: Das System der speculativen Philosophie*
JS II	*Jenaer Systementwürfe II: Logik, Metaphysik, Naturphilosophie*
JS III	*Jenaer Systementwürfe III: Naturphilosophie und Philosophie des Geistes*
LA	*Hegel's Aesthetics: Lectures on Fine Art*
LHP	*Lectures on the History of Philosophy*
LPR	*Lectures on the Philosophy of Religion*
NA	'Notizen und Aphorismen 1818–31'
NL	*Natural Law: The Scientific Ways of Treating Natural Law, Its Place in Moral Philosophy, and Its Relation to the Positive Sciences of Law*
PH	*The Philosophy of History*
PR	*Elements of the Philosophy of Right*
PS	*Phenomenology of Spirit*
PW	*Political Writings*
RH	*Reason in History: A General Introduction to the Philosophy of History*
RSP	'The Relationship of Scepticism to Philosophy'
SEL	*'System of Ethical Life' (1802/3) and 'First Philosophy of Spirit' (Part III of the System of Speculative Philosophy 1803/4)*
SL	*Science of Logic*

WORKS BY KANT

CPrR	*The Critique of Practical Reason*
CPR	*The Critique of Pure Reason*
GMM	*Groundwork of the Metaphysics of Morals*
RP	*What Real Progress Has Metaphysics Made in Germany Since the Time of Leibniz and Wolff?*

1

THE *PHENOMENOLOGY* IN CONTEXT
(*PHENOMENOLOGY*, PREFACE AND INTRODUCTION)

HEGEL AND HIS TIMES

It is often said of Hegel (1770–1831) that he lived an uneventful life at an eventful time. Certainly his biography is relatively humdrum compared to that of Kierkegaard or Marx, for example. However, its uneventfulness can be exaggerated: he did, after all, have an illegitimate son at a young age; know many of the leading intellectual figures of his period, including Goethe, Schelling, and Hölderlin; and have a career with contrasting lows and highs, from a long period of relative anonymity up until his late forties, to national and growing international renown by the time of his death less than two decades later. It may be that Hegel's life has generated little interest because the character who lived it has been seen as rather unprepossessing: Hegel the man is commonly viewed (even by some of his admirers) as dogged, conformist, bombastic, and careerist. However, once again this assessment must be treated with caution, as he also clearly had his virtues, including loyalty, intellectual integrity, fortitude in the face of adversity, an awkward charm, and a capacity for joy, humour, and deep emotion, hidden behind the rather forbidding exterior that looms out at us from the portraits we have of him. Thus, while perhaps prone to irritate, offend, and puzzle some of those with whom he came into contact, he was also capable of inspiring devotion and reverence, and abiding affection. His life and character are certainly more complex and interesting than is often assumed. (For a thorough study, see Pinkard 2000a.)

Nonetheless, it is probably right that priority in considering Hegel's work should be given to the times in which he lived, rather than to his life and character: for his work was more obviously shaped by this, than by biographical circumstances or the nature of his personality. Despite the apparent abstractness of much of his writing, Hegel was deeply engaged with the political and historical events around him, to which he sought to respond in philosophical terms. This is the meaning of his famous image of the owl of Minerva: the sacred bird of Minerva (or Athena), the goddess of wisdom, flies at dusk, after the happenings of the day, for only then can philosophy reflect on what has occurred, and fulfil its role as 'the *thought* of the world' (PR: Preface, p. 23).

Now, while it may be misleading to emphasize the ordinariness of Hegel's life, it is not misleading to emphasize the extra-ordinariness of his times: these were indeed remarkable, on several levels. First, at the historical and political level, Hegel and other thinkers of his generation witnessed the French Revolution, the bloody aftermath of the Terror, the rise and fall of Napoleon, and the July Revolution of 1830, whilst living through the demise of the Holy Roman Empire and the reorganization of political and social life in many German states, as the tide of liberal reform ebbed and flowed around them. The events in France were of particular importance to all German intellectuals of this period. Even as a student, Hegel formed part of a clandestine political club to discuss the revolution of 1789 (giving rise to the story that he joined others in planting a 'Tree of Liberty' to mark the event), while he claimed that he always took a toast throughout his life to celebrate the falling of the Bastille on 14 July (in 1820, less than one year after the passing of the repressive Karlsbad Decrees, he startled his companions by buying them the best champagne so that they could do likewise). It is therefore no surprise that Hegel gave the Revolution a prominent place in his discussion of freedom and modernity in the *Phenomenology*, as well as in his other works on history and social philosophy.

Second, Hegel lived in a period of philosophical as well as historical and political upheaval, where it seemed that new and exciting possibilities for thought were opening up, and where competing conceptions of these possibilities were emerging. Hegel was a major figure in the movement of German Idealism, which runs roughly from the publication of the first edition of Immanuel Kant's *Critique of Pure Reason* in 1781, to the eclipse of Hegelianism in the 1840s, a movement that some see as rivalling classical Greek philosophy for originality and significance. German Idealism was inaugurated by Kant's 'critical philosophy', with its attempt to set metaphysics on 'the secure path of a science' (CPR: Bxviii), and to balance the competing perspectives of determinism in natural science and freedom in morality. However, Kant's successors came to feel that his actual achievement was to leave philosophy vulnerable to scepticism, while failing to overcome this central dualism between freedom and determinism, morality and the scientific picture, the autonomous subject and the natural self. They therefore sought to go 'beyond Kant', in seeking to find another philosophical system that would achieve what he had set out to do, and on a comparable scale, encompassing the natural sciences, the arts, and history, as well as epistemology, metaphysics, ethics, political philosophy, and philosophy of religion. (See Ameriks 2000a for a helpful overview of German Idealism as a movement.)

Third, Hegel lived in a remarkable cultural period, situated at a kind of crossroads between the Enlightenment and Romanticism. Thus, on the one hand he was fully aware of the range of new ideas the Enlightenment had brought to the sciences, political life, ethics and religion, as well as the reaction to those ideas by a variety of critical forces. On the other hand, he was also exposed to the more recent developments associated with Romanticism, which offered a distinctive approach to the issues raised by the debate between the Enlightenment and its critics, with its own organicist conception of nature, redemptive picture of history, and faith in the power of art. Hegel may be seen as taking up many of the concerns raised by the Romantics such as Schiller, Novalis, and others, but in a way that sought to give a new direction to the basic ideas of the Enlightenment (such as 'reason' and 'progress') rather than setting them aside. In Hegel's work, therefore, we find the confluence of the two major intellectual currents of his era.

With these events and issues in the background, it is hardly surprising that Hegel's philosophy has a depth and complexity not often seen in calmer times, when the waters of intellectual and political life run more still. It is at this point in history that many of the paradigms of modern thinking were to be formed; and Hegel was to begin his own contribution to shaping them with the writing of the *Phenomenology*.

THE PLACE OF THE *PHENOMENOLOGY* IN HEGEL'S LIFE AND WORKS

The publication of the *Phenomenology* in 1807 marks the beginning of Hegel's 'mature' philosophy: everything written and published before then is classified among his early or preparatory writings. The *Phenomenology* is taken to mark a watershed in Hegel's intellectual development for three reasons.

First, it was through this work that Hegel started to emerge as a distinctive figure within the movement of post-Kantian German Idealism, as he began to set himself apart from other philosophers of this period. In his publications prior to the *Phenomenology*, Hegel seemed content to follow the lead of his more precocious friend and mentor F. W. J. Schelling (1775–1854). Hegel's association with Schelling began in their student days, when both attended the Protestant Seminary at the University of Tübingen (together with Friedrich Hölderlin (1770–1843), who would much later come to be regarded as one of Germany's greatest poets, and who also influenced Hegel in this period). While Hegel's stolid virtues earned him the nickname 'the Old Man' from his classmates at Tübingen, and while he was slow to establish his reputation, Schelling's rise was meteoric: his *System of*

Transcendental Idealism (1800) was quickly seen as moving beyond the post-critical philosophy of J. G. Fichte (1762–1814), in the same radical manner that Fichte himself had tried to take Kant's critical philosophy further forward. Both Schelling and Hegel had shared the dismal fate of leaving Tübingen to become private tutors in wealthy families (Hegel in 1793 and Schelling in 1795); but while Schelling was appointed a professor at the University of Jena in 1798 at the age of 23, and was well known as the author of the *System of Transcendental Idealism* as well as other works, Hegel remained a private tutor until 1801, when a legacy from his father at last enabled him to follow Schelling to Jena, at the latter's invitation. There he qualified as a *Privatdozent* (unsalaried university teacher) with a thesis on natural philosophy, a subject close to Schelling's concerns; after obtaining his licence to teach, the two began running courses together. Hegel's first published work under his own name appeared that year, under the unwieldy but descriptive title of *The Difference Between Fichte's and Schelling's System of Philosophy*.[1] In 1802 Hegel joined Schelling in editing a philosophical periodical, the *Critical Journal of Philosophy*, to which he contributed his second major publication, 'Faith and Knowledge', as well as writing the long introduction to the first issue, entitled 'The Essence of Philosophical Criticism Generally, and its Relationship to the Present State of Philosophy in Particular'. In these essays, Hegel seemed to identify himself as a follower of Schelling, and clearly put forward his friend's position as the best hope for post-Kantian philosophy. Other publications of this period that appeared in the *Critical Journal* – 'The Relationship of Scepticism to Philosophy' (1802) and 'On the Scientific Way of Dealing with Natural Law' (1802–3) – are less explicitly Schellingian in subject matter and argument, but they are not particularly distinctive taken on their own. Schelling left Jena in 1803, going first to the University of Würzburg, and then on to Munich in 1806; with Schelling's departure, Hegel began to be more openly critical of his friend's position, and to achieve a greater distance from it (for details, see Lukács 1975: 423–48). However, Hegel's rather modest reputation at this stage meant he found it harder than Schelling to move on from Jena, and he was eventually forced to leave academia altogether, becoming a newspaper editor in Bamberg in March 1807. In the same year, he published the *Phenomenology*, which he hoped would revive his academic career, by establishing him as a thinker in his own right. (As Pinkard 2000a: 403 notes, however, it took some time before the originality of the *Phenomenology* came to be clearly recognized, as 'ten years after [its] publication … [Hegel] was still trying to convince much of the literary public that his philosophy was an advance on Schelling's and not just another version of it'. See ibid.: 256–65 for an account of how the *Phenomenology* was first received.)

But the *Phenomenology* represents a watershed not just because here some critical distance between Hegel and Schelling can clearly be identified for the first time in Hegel's published writings; it is also the first work in which Hegel began at last (aged 37) to lay out his own distinctive approach to the problems that had concerned his predecessors and so to adopt an outlook that is recognizably 'Hegelian'. Thus, the position Hegel puts forward in the *Phenomenology* on a variety of issues is the one he will go on to defend in the remainder of his mature publications, while in his pre-*Phenomenology* writings his ideas were still in a state of flux. There is therefore a considerable degree of intellectual continuity between this work and those that follow: first, the *Science of Logic*, which appeared in three parts, in 1812, 1813, and 1816 respectively, written after Hegel had moved from Bamberg to become headmaster of a gymnasium in Nuremberg in 1808; second, the *Encyclopedia of the Philosophical Sciences*, the first edition of which he published in one volume in 1817 after his appointment as professor at the University of Heidelberg, and which became a three-volume work by the time of its third edition in 1830; third, the *Philosophy of Right* of 1821, published three years after Hegel's move from Heidelberg to the professorship at the University of Berlin in 1818; and finally his lectures on aesthetics, philosophy of religion, philosophy of history, and history of philosophy, which were published as works edited by his students after his death in 1831. Neither in his pre-Jena writings of 1793 to 1801 (which focus more on ethical and religious questions, and issues of contemporary politics) nor in the published Jena writings of 1801 to 1806 (which focus on critiques of other thinkers) is it possible to see anything more than the seeds of what was to be a fully developed philosophical position in the *Phenomenology* and the rest of the works that followed it. The *Phenomenology* is thus the initial step in the intellectual journey that was to take Hegel from the obscurity of his early career in Jena and Bamberg, where he struggled to make any kind of mark, to the eventual triumph of his period in Berlin, where 'what does Hegel think about it?' was the first question of the chattering classes (see Pinkard 2000a: 612).

A third reason why the *Phenomenology* is considered the first of Hegel's mature writings is that it is also given a *systematic* place in his thought, in a way that the earlier works are not. Hegel was most insistent about the need for system-building, declaring that '[a]part from their interdependence and organic union, the truths of philosophy are valueless, and must then be treated as baseless hypotheses, or personal convictions' (EL: §14, p. 20). The first published version of Hegel's system as a whole, with its division into Logic, Philosophy of Nature, and Philosophy of Spirit (*Geist*),[2] is the edition of the *Encyclopedia of the Philosophical Sciences* that appeared in 1817, while the earlier *Science of Logic* is a detailed elaboration of the first part of the system, and the later *Philosophy of Right* develops some of the ethical and political issues dealt with in the third part, under the section 'Objective Spirit'. But Hegel had begun his attempt to articulate a rigorously articulated philosophical system after his move to Jena in 1801, so that although this project was not finalized at the time (and continued to develop through the various editions of the *Encyclopedia*), Hegel was already thinking in a systematic way when he came to compose the *Phenomenology*. Thus, while the *Phenomenology* was published some years before the *Encyclopedia* system appeared, it was written while Hegel was working on its predecessors, and so is shaped by the same concerns and fundamental ideas. (The Jena lecture materials and unpublished notes in which Hegel made these early attempts to work out a satisfactory philosophical system are now to be found in the *Jenaer Systementwürfe* (Jena System Drafts) from 1803 to 1804, 1804 to 1805, and 1805 to 1806: see JS I, JS II, and JS III.)

Moreover, the *Phenomenology* reveals Hegel's systematic concerns not just because he was already thinking in this way while in

Jena; he also felt at this time that any system he was to complete would need some sort of introduction, a role which the *Phenomenology* was designed to fill. Initially, Hegel planned to publish an introduction to his system of around 150 pages, together with a 'Logic' as the first part of his system, in a single volume at Easter in 1806; but this never appeared, and instead he quickly completed the *Phenomenology* as a much longer and independent work. His first title for this work was a 'Science of the Experience of Consciousness'[3] (which was the title originally envisaged for the projected earlier, shorter introduction to the system), but after the proof stage he altered the title to the one we now have. However, the publisher of the first edition saw fit to include both titles so that it first appeared as 'System of Science: First Part: the Phenomenology of Spirit', with a further title inserted between the 'Preface' and the 'Introduction', which in some copies read 'Science of the Experience of Consciousness' and in others read 'Science of the Phenomenology of Spirit', also as a result of confusion on the part of the publisher created by Hegel's vacillations. As well as trying to signal its place within his system in its title, Hegel's 'Preface' also highlighted the *Phenomenology*'s role as a necessary introductory work, as being required if we are to see things in the way that Hegel's fully developed philosophical science demands:

> Science on its part requires that self-consciousness should have raised itself into this Aether in order to be able to live – and [actually] to live – with Science and in Science. Conversely, the individual has the right to demand that Science should at least provide him with the ladder to this standpoint, should show him this standpoint within himself ... When natural consciousness entrusts itself straightway to Science, it makes an attempt, induced by it knows not what, to walk on its head too, just this once; the compulsion to assume this unwonted posture and go about in it is a violence it is expected to do to itself, all unprepared and seemingly without necessity. Let Science be in its own self what it may, relatively to immediate self-consciousness it presents itself in an inverted posture; or, because this self-consciousness has the principle of its actual existence in the certainty of itself, Science appears to it not to be actual, since self-consciousness exists on its own account outside of Science ... It is

this coming-to-be of *Science as such* or of *knowledge*, that is described in this *Phenomenology* of Spirit.

(PS: §§26–27, pp. 14–15)

In constituting a 'ladder' designed to take us towards the standpoint of the kind of philosophical system which Hegel was working on in Jena and which came to be articulated later in the *Encyclopedia*, the *Phenomenology* therefore has a claim to be considered as vital to a proper understanding of Hegel's mature systematic work, in a way that his previous publications do not.

However, whilst everyone recognizes that the *Phenomenology* marks a turning-point in Hegel's philosophical career, in terms of its originality, its depth and sophistication, and its systematic significance, certain remarks by Hegel himself have led some to warn that we should not expect to fit the *Phenomenology* into his final philosophical outlook without remainder (where some go on to claim that that final outlook introduced certain deplorable elements that are thankfully missing in the *Phenomenology* as an earlier work, while others go on to disparage the *Phenomenology* as a misleading guide to Hegel's ultimate position). This dispute has come about for several reasons. First, while Hegel certainly stresses the *Phenomenology*'s systematic importance in the work itself and in its various titles and subtitles, in later presentations of the system he appears to downplay this role (for example, commenting of a projected second edition of the *Phenomenology* that he did not live to complete, that it would no longer be called the 'first part' of the system of science: cf. SL: 29). In the second place, the third part of the *Encyclopedia*, the *Philosophy of Spirit*, contains a long section in which the earlier parts of the *Phenomenology* (the three chapters on Consciousness, Self-Consciousness and parts of that on Reason) reappear in much the same form, suggesting perhaps that the *Phenomenology* was now supposed to lose its status as a self-contained and independent work. Third, some commentators have been puzzled that Hegel should have supplied the *Encyclopedia* itself with its own introductory apparatus in §§26–78 of the *Logic*, if the *Phenomenology* was meant to serve that role.

Behind these matters of scholarship (which are hardly conclusive: cf. Forster 1998: 547–55, Stewart 2008), there is a deeper and more significant concern, namely, that the haste in which the *Phenomenology* was written inevitably lends to the work an unconsidered and ungoverned quality (typified in confusions surrounding the title page, Preface, and table of contents), which disqualifies it as a settled statement of Hegel's position. The story of the *Phenomenology*'s composition in this respect is the stuff of philosophical legend. Hegel was forced to finish the book in great haste because his friend Friedrich Immanuel Niethammer had promised to pay the publisher's costs if he failed to supply the completed manuscript by 18 October 1806. As Hegel was rushing to meet this obligation, Napoleon moved to capture Jena, and Hegel entrusted part of the manuscript to a courier who rode through French lines to the publisher in Bamberg. Although he completed the manuscript (except the Preface) the night before the battle for the city, he did not dare to send the last instalment, and so missed his deadline (although he was not held responsible for the delay, as this had occurred due to an act of war). Given the extraordinary circumstances of its composition, the question naturally arises how far the work can be presumed to provide us with a coherent and properly worked out account of Hegel's position. Hegel himself seems to have recognized that at the very least, the *Phenomenology* needed reworking, and hence planned a second edition, which he began preparing immediately prior to his death – although the fact that at this late stage he still felt a second edition was needed perhaps itself suggests that for him the *Phenomenology* had never lost its status as an important work with its own unique role in the system. Hegel expressed his sense of dissatisfaction concerning the text as we have it in a letter to Niethammer on 16 January 1807, written after reading through the proofs: 'I truly often wished I could clear the ship here and there of ballast and make it swifter. With a second edition to follow *soon* – if it pleases the gods! – everything shall come out better' (HL: 119–20). Given Hegel's own apparent qualms, there has always been some support for the view – expressed with varying degrees of sophistication and scholarly subtlety – that the *Phenomenology* cannot be taken as a unified and properly structured work, and so should not be taken as a reliable statement of Hegel's final view. (Cf. the famous remark in Haym

1857: 243, that 'the *Phenomenology* is *a psychology brought to confu-sion and disorder by history, and a history brought to ruin by psychology*'. For a helpful brief discussion of this issue, with further references to the current scholarship, see Pippin 1993: 53–56.)

It is certainly the case that perhaps the greatest challenge to any reading of the *Phenomenology* is to show how it can be under-stood as a coherent and well-ordered work, and to fit its bewil-dering range of topics into a satisfactory and unified philosophical conception. While recognizing that the *Phenomenology* is far from flawless (which, as we have seen, Hegel himself accepted), I would nonetheless claim that it still has an underlying unity of purpose and method, which can be brought to light once its overall approach is clarified. It is to be hoped that this unity will become clearer as we proceed through the work, once we grasp how Hegel understood the *Phenomenology*'s role as an introduction to the system, and what he intended that system as a whole to accomplish.

HEGEL'S SYSTEM

'In everything that is supposed to be scientific, reason must be awake and reflection applied. To him who looks at the world rationally the world looks rationally back; the two exist in a reciprocal relationship' (ILPWH: 29/RH: 13; translation adap-ted). These comments, made in the course of his discussion of the philosophy of history, may stand as an epigraph for Hegel's phil-osophy as a whole, in telling us much about the aspirations of that philosophy, and how he hoped those aspirations would be achieved.

Hegel's aim, as this comment makes clear, is to help us see that the world is rational, by getting us to look at it in the right way; for, Hegel holds, the world *is* rational, and the goal of human inquiry is to 'bring this rationality to consciousness', that is, to become aware of this rationality, and hence achieve a fully adequate comprehension of reality. (Cf. PS: §7, pp. 4–5, where Hegel speaks of philosophy as 'opening up the fast-locked nature of substance, and raising this to self-consciousness ... by bringing consciousness out of its chaos back to an order based on thought

[and] the simplicity of the Notion'. Cf. also PR: Preface, p. 12, 'nature is *rational within itself*, and ... it is this *actual* reason present within it which knowledge must investigate and grasp conceptually – not the shapes and contingencies which are visible on the surface, but nature's eternal harmony, conceived, however, as the law of essence *immanent* within it'.) In claiming that the world is rational in this respect, Hegel means many things, but mainly he means that it is such that we can find deep intellectual and practical *satisfaction* in it: there is nothing in reality *as such* that is aporetic to reason, which is truly incomprehensible, contradictory, or inexplicable, and there is nothing in reality which makes it inherently at odds with our purposes and interests. As the world itself is rational in this way, once we can see that this is so, the world will thereby have shown itself to us in the right manner, and we will have achieved absolute knowledge, which represents the highest form of satisfaction; until that point is reached, Hegel calls our knowledge 'finite' or 'conditioned', in so far as this rational insight has not yet been attained.

Now, as Hegel also makes clear in this comment, whether we attain this state of absolute knowledge does not just depend on the world and the fact that it is rational: it also depends on *us*, on how we *look* at the world. If we are unable to view the world correctly, therefore, it will not appear satisfactory to reason: that is, the world will appear to contain elements that are incomprehensible, contradictory, and alien, in a way that may lead us into despair. However, Hegel's project is not the purely conservative or quietistic one of reconciling us to the world no matter what difficulties we see in it; rather, Hegel aims to give us a way of resolving those difficulties by finding a new way of looking at things, to show us the world as it intrinsically is when these difficulties are removed (cf. Hardimon 1994: 24–31). Thus, Hegel believes that the greatest contribution philosophy can make is to help us overcome our despair, by providing us with fresh ways of thinking about reality, thereby bringing us back to our sense that the world is a rational place, one in which we can truly feel 'at home'; for, as he puts it in the *Philosophy of Right*, '"I" is at home in the world when it knows it, and even more so when it has comprehended it' (PR: §4Z, p. 36). (Cf. also EL: §194Z, p. 261,

'The aim of knowledge is to divest the objective world that stands opposed to us of its strangeness, and, as the phrase is, to find ourselves at home in it: which means no more than to trace the objective world back to the notion – to our innermost self.')

In order to achieve this goal, as Hegel says, 'reason must be awake and reflection applied': that is, philosophy must take a reflective stance, by identifying and guarding against those forms of thought that lead us to adopt an intellectual or practical conception of the world that prevents it appearing rational to us in the way it should, when we are looking at it properly. Philosophy must therefore set out to correct those outlooks which create the puzzles that stop us from seeing reason in the world, by showing how these outlooks arise as a result of some sort of distortion which can be overcome, thereby enabling the puzzles to be resolved and the world to look back to us in a rational way once again. If philosophy does not fulfil this role, then we may become convinced either that the world is not rational as such, or that even if it is, it can never look that way to us, and so can never be a 'home' to creatures like ourselves. Hegel sees both these options as (literally) counsels of despair: but both will remain options until philosophy has shown that we can achieve a perspective from which the world is made fully satisfactory to reason. Only then, Hegel argues, will we have overcome our estrangement from the world and thus have achieved freedom:

> The ignorant man is not free, because what confronts him is an alien world, something outside him and in the offing, on which he depends, without his having made this foreign world for himself and therefore without being at home in it by himself as in something his own. The impulse of curiosity, the pressure for knowledge, from the lowest level up to the highest rung of philosophical insight arises only from the struggle to cancel this situation of unfreedom and to make the world one's own in one's ideas and thought.
>
> (LA: I, p. 98)

We have seen, therefore, that Hegel takes it that we are responsible for creating the kind of intellectual and social environments that lead us to find the world intellectually and socially alien, as the world itself is and should be a 'home' to us. But given this, how does Hegel think these alienating conceptions come about? Hegel claims that such mistaken conceptions arise because we are inclined to think in a 'one-sided' or oppositional way: we believe that something is *either* finite *or* infinite, one *or* many, free *or* necessitated, human *or* divine, autonomous *or* part of a community, and so on. The difficulty is, Hegel argues, that if we take things in this way, then reason will find it hard to make sense of things, as it will then look at reality in a way that abstracts from the complex interrelation of these 'moments', when in fact to see itself in the world, reason must grasp that there is no genuine dichotomy here. Thus, to take one example, by assuming that to act freely is to act in a way that is not constrained or fixed in any way, we are faced with the apparent absurdity of taking only arbitrary choices as autonomous actions, as it is only then that we could be said to be acting without anything specifically determining our behaviour; but if we then take autonomous actions to be of this kind, it is then hard to see freedom as being particularly desirable or significant (cf. EL: §§155–59, PS: §§362–69, pp. 218–22). At this point, we may well feel baulked by a puzzle so deep that we no longer know where to turn to find the satisfaction reason craves: but for Hegel, it is just here that 'reason must be awake and reflection applied'. That is, we must ask whether there is something intrinsically problematic about our starting point, and whether this has created our subsequent difficulties, namely, our assumption that freedom involves lack of constraint; for if the constraining factor is something we can 'internalize', then it appears that constraint and freedom can be made compatible and should not be opposed. Hegel argues that our initial dichotomy must therefore be broken down if the puzzle is to be resolved, '[f]rom which we may learn what a mistake it is to regard freedom and necessity as mutually exclusive' (EL: §158Z, p. 220): only then, Hegel suggests, will we come back to seeing the world as rational once again.[4]

In his desire to find some sense of intellectual and social harmony by overcoming the divisions and dichotomies that seemed to make this impossible, Hegel was clearly responding to the sense of dislocation shared by many of his contemporaries, both within his immediate circle (such as Schelling and Hölderlin) and beyond. This dislocation was felt at many levels, as it appeared that the Enlightenment had shaken old certainties but had put nothing substantial in their place. Thus, reason was seen as leading to scepticism, science to mechanistic materialism, social reform to bloody revolution, humanism to empty amoralism and crude hedonism, and individualism to social fragmentation. There was therefore a felt need on all sides to find a way forward, to 'begin again' in a manner that did not lead to these unhappy consequences. But for Hegel, as we shall see, it was crucial that this new direction should not involve the simple *repudiation* of reason, science, social reform, and so on. Instead, Hegel argues that the conceptual assumptions underlying the way these ideas had been developed required investigation, to show how they could be taken forward in a less limited and one-sided way; only once this had been achieved, he believed, could the ideas of the Enlightenment help us find satisfaction in the world, rather than cutting us off from it, for only then could we find a way of reconciling the demands of reason *and* religion, freedom *and* social order, scientific naturalism *and* human values, and so on. Unlike the irrationalists and conservatives of the counter-Enlightenment, who questioned the critical power of reason, and unlike the Romantics, who turned to art and aesthetic experience as a cure for the ills of modernity, Hegel's position is therefore distinctive in continuing to give philosophy the exalted role of restoring our sense of intellectual and spiritual well-being, albeit a philosophy that thinks in a new, non-dualistic, way. As Hegel puts it in the 'Difference' essay of 1801: 'When the might of union vanishes from the life of men and the antitheses lose their living connection and reciprocity and gain independence, the need of philosophy arises' (DFS: 91).

It is because of his insistence that we must learn how to break down the opposition between certain fundamental concepts (such as freedom and necessity, one and many, and so on), that Hegel's thought is characterized as *dialectical*. Hegel himself uses this term quite rarely, and his only prolonged discussion of what he means by it is in Chapter VI of his *Encyclopedia Logic*, entitled 'Logic Further Defined and Divided'. In this short chapter, Hegel distinguishes three stages in the development of thought, which he identifies as '(a) the Abstract side, or that of understanding; (b) the Dialectical, or that of negative reason; (c) the Speculative, or that of positive reason' (EL: §79, p. 113). The first stage, of understanding, is characterized as that faculty of thought which treats its concepts as apparently discrete and (in Hegel's terms) 'finite'; it therefore 'sticks to fixed determinations and the distinctness of one determination from another: every such limited abstract it treats as having a substance and being of its own' (EL: §80, p. 113; translation modified). Hegel acknowledges that we will always find it tempting to think of things in this way, as we seek to order the world into distinct and self-identical aspects, and up to a point this can bring great intellectual and practical benefits: the mistake the understanding makes, however, is to forget that these aspects are abstractions made against the background of a more complex interdependence. This mistake is brought home to the understanding in the second or dialectical stage of thought, which is 'the inherent self-sublation of these finite determinations and their transition into their opposites' (EL: §81, p. 115; translation modified): 'its purpose is to study things in their own being and movement and thus to demonstrate the finitude of the partial categories of understanding' (EL: §81Z, p. 117). Hegel argues that it is here that scepticism finds its natural place, for when the understanding is forced to see that its conceptual divisions lead it into incomprehension, it may come to doubt that we can ever arrive at a satisfactory grasp of how things are (cf. McGinn 1993, Valberg 1992: 197–218). However, he insists that the results of the dialectical stage are not merely 'negative' in this way: rather, they lead on to the third and final stage of *reason*, which 'apprehends the unity of the determinations in their opposition – the affirmation, which is embodied in their dissolution and their transition' (EL: §82, p. 119; translation modified). Thus, after we have been forced to rethink our concepts in such a way as to break down the 'abstract "either–or"' of the understanding (EL: §80Z, p. 115), we will then arrive at a new conceptual standpoint, from which it can be seen that these concepts can be brought together, thereby overcoming the sceptical aporia of the dialectical stage. According to Hegel, without this conceptual transformation, it will be impossible for us to see the world without apparent incoherence; only once we have identified and surpassed the rigid conceptual dichotomies of the understanding will we be able to conceive of reality in a way that is satisfactory to reason. Thus, as Hegel puts it, '[t]he battle of reason is the struggle to break up the rigidity to which the understanding has reduced everything', while 'the metaphysic of understanding is dogmatic, because it maintains half-truths in their isolation': the 'idealism of speculative philosophy carries out the principle of totality and shows that it can reach beyond the inadequate formularies of abstract thought' (EL: §32Z, pp. 52–53).

Hegel's outlook here may therefore be likened to those who claim that when we are faced with apparently intractable intellectual problems, we should not try to answer them 'head on', by taking up one side or the other, but should rather step back and apply ourselves 'reflectively' (as Hegel puts it), and ask how it is the problem has arisen in the first place; once we see that the problem has its source in a set of one-sided assumptions, if we can overcome that one-sidedness, then the problem will simply dissolve and we can escape the 'oscillation' between one unsatisfactory stance and its equally unsatisfactory opposite. (Cf. AW: 2, translation modified, 'The questions which philosophy fails to answer, are answered by seeing that they should not be so posed in the first place.') However, where Hegel differs from many more recent philosophers who otherwise share this 'therapeutic' approach with him (cf. Wittgenstein 1968, Austin 1962) is that he does not take this approach in order to champion the superiority of 'ordinary language' or our 'pre-philosophical outlook' against the snares and delusions of philosophy and its 'forgetting' of our common-sense conception of things. Rather, for Hegel, it is the other way round, as the outlook of the understanding forms the natural starting point of our thoughts, so that it is only with the intervention of further philosophical reflection that we can see our way through the problems that this generates. Far from thinking that common sense or our ordinary pre-philosophical scientific, political, or religious beliefs should just be 'left alone', Hegel claims that they must be reflected on philosophically if we are to make the 'discovery ... that gives philosophy peace' (Wittgenstein 1968: §133); for, Hegel maintains, these beliefs are in fact saturated with philosophical assumptions, and are unstable on their own. Thus, though in a sense Hegel takes some of the central problems of philosophy to be pseudo-problems (in that they are generated by our way of looking at the world, rather than inherent in the world itself, and so should be resolved 'reflectively' rather than via further inquiry), he nonetheless holds that they can only be dealt with by turning *to* philosophy, and not *away* from it, as only philosophy and not 'natural conscious-ness' is capable of the kind of dialectical thinking that is required to overcome the puzzles that 'natural consciousness' itself generates:

> What man seeks in this situation, ensnared here as he is in finitude on every side, is the region of a higher, more substantial, truth, in which all oppositions and contradictions in the finite can find their final resolution, and freedom its full satisfaction. This is the region of absolute, not finite, truth. The highest truth, truth as such, is the resolution of the highest opposition and contradiction. In it validity and power are swept away from the opposition between freedom and necessity, between spirit and nature, between knowledge and its object, between law and impulse, from opposition and contradiction as such, whatever forms they may take. Their validity and power *as* opposition and contradiction is gone. Absolute truth proves that nei-ther freedom by itself, as subjective, sundered from necessity, is absolutely a true thing nor, by parity of reasoning, is truthfulness to be ascribed to necessity isolated and taken by itself. The ordinary consciousness, on the other hand, cannot extricate itself from this opposition and either remains despairingly in contradiction or else casts it aside and helps itself in some other way. But philosophy enters into the heart of the self-contradictory characteristics, knows them in their essential nature, i.e. as in their one-sidedness not absolute but self-dissolving, and it sets them in the harmony and unity which is truth. To grasp this Concept of truth is the task of philosophy.
>
> (LA: I, pp. 99–100)

Thus, Hegel sees that the role of philosophy is to lead ordinary consciousness away from the oppositional thinking of the understanding, in order to overcome the kind of conceptual tensions that make the world appear less than fully intelligible to us; once this is achieved, we will overcome the intellectual and practical difficulties that have arisen because we do not look at the world rationally, at which point the world will look back at us in a rational manner.

Now, obviously, showing that reason can enable us to feel 'at home in the world' by freeing us from the apparent opposition between concepts like freedom and necessity, one and many, finite and infinite, and so on is an enormous and ambitious undertaking, which aims at nothing less than the dissolution of all the traditional 'problems of philosophy' and the aporias that these oppositions generate. It is this undertaking which forms the basis of Hegel's *Encyclopedia* system, beginning with the *Logic*.[5] In the *Logic*, Hegel sets out to show how the various categories of thought are dialectically interrelated, in such a way that the conceptual oppositions responsible for our perplexities can be resolved, once we rethink these fundamental notions. Hegel suggests that of great importance in this respect is how we conceive of the categories of universal, particular and individual (which he calls the categories of the 'notion' or 'concept'),[6] for (he holds) it is only when the opposition between these categories is overcome that the tension in our conceptual scheme can be resolved, to be superseded by a more unified and rational world-picture. Hegel focuses on these categories, and especially on the relation between universal and individual, because he holds that they are central to our way of thinking, and are thus very pervasive. (Cf. PR: §258, p. 276, 'Considered in the abstract, rationality consists in general in the unity and interpenetration of universality and individuality.') At the metaphysical level, we oppose the universality of the ideal to the individuality of the real, and so generate the debate between Platonists on the one hand and nominalists on the other; we oppose the universality of essence to the individuality of existents, and so generate the debate between essentialists and existentialists; we oppose universal properties to individual entities, and so generate the debate between predicate realists and predicate nominalists; we oppose the universality of form to the individuality of matter, and so generate the debate between conceptual realists and conceptual idealists; and we oppose the universality of God to the individuality of man, and so generate the debate between theists and humanists. At the epistemological level, we contrast the universality of thought with the individuality of intuition, and so generate the debate between rationalists and empiricists. And at the moral and political level, we distinguish the community as universal from the citizen as individual, and so generate the debate between communitarianism and liberalism; we distinguish the universal interest from the individual interest, and so generate the debate between the egoist and the altruist; we distinguish the universality of the general good from the particularity of the individual agent, and so generate the debate between the utilitarian and the Kantian; we distinguish the universality of law from the freedom of the individual, and so generate the debate between the defender of the state and the anarchist; and we distinguish the universality of rights and natural law from the particularity of local traditions and customs, and so generate the debate between the cosmopolitan who thinks that all societies should be ruled in the same way, and the communitarian who thinks divergent cultural histories should be respected.[7]

Hegel therefore claims that crucial issues of metaphysics, epistemology, ethics, and political and religious thought are all associated with the ways in which the categories of universal, particular, and individual are conceived, such that apparently insuperable philosophical difficulties will be generated unless these categories are brought together or 'mediated' in the right way. Thus, when Hegel talks of the failure of 'the understanding' to overcome the opposition between these categories, he can point to a whole series of divisions in our view of the world, between abstract and concrete, ideal and real, one and many, necessity and freedom, state and citizen, moral law and self-interest, general will and particular will, reason and tradition, God and man. Hegel believed that the division between universal and individual lies behind all these dichotomies; but at the same time, he believed that we do not have to set these categories apart, but can see things as *combining* individuality with universality, the one aspect depending on the other (cf. EL: §164, pp. 228–29, SL: 605).[8] Because Hegel thought that these are the categories that can be best integrated in this way, in his *Logic* Hegel works through other sets of categories (such as being and nothingness, quantity and quality, identity and difference, whole and part, one and many, essence and appearance, substance and attribute, freedom and necessity), to show that with these categories certain residual dichotomies remain. It is therefore only once we arrive at the categories of universal, particular, and individual that truly dialectical thinking becomes possible for us; the aim of philosophical reflection is thereby achieved.

Having reached the categories of thought in the *Logic* which Hegel thinks will enable us to 'look at the world rationally', in the next two books of the *Encyclopedia* Hegel moves on to show that this then enables the world to look rationally back at us, in such a way that reason can find satisfaction in it. In the *Philosophy of Nature*, Hegel considers the natural world in this regard, trying to show that where we find conceptual difficulties in our understanding of nature (for example, in the notion of 'action at a distance'), this can be resolved through a more dialectical approach. As Hegel puts it in his discussion of heat,

> [t]he task here is the same as that throughout the whole of the philosophy of nature; it is merely to replace the categories of the understanding by the thought-relationships of the speculative Notion, and to grasp and determine the phenomenon in accordance with the latter.
>
> (EN: II, §305, p. 88)

Likewise, in the *Philosophy of Spirit*, Hegel considers the human world at the levels of anthropology, phenomenology of mind, psychology, ethics, politics, art, religion, and philosophy, where again his aim is to demonstrate here that the value of his dialectical method rests on the categorial investigations of the *Logic*. Hegel does not doubt the far-reaching significance of that investigation for all these fields of inquiry, in so far as all involve conceptual assumptions that must be made dialectical if the damaging one-sidedness in our thinking is to be avoided:

> metaphysics is nothing but the range of universal thought-determinations, and is as it were the diamond-net into which we bring

everything in order to make it intelligible. Every cultured consciousness has its metaphysics, its instinctive way of thinking. This is the
absolute power within us, and we shall only master it if we make it
the object of our knowledge. Philosophy in general, as philosophy,
has different categories from those of ordinary consciousness. All
cultural change reduces itself to a difference of categories. All revolu-
tions, whether in the sciences or world history, occur merely because
spirit has changed its categories in order to understand and examine
what belongs to it, in order to possess and grasp itself in a truer,
deeper, more intimate and unified manner.

(EN: I, §246Z, p. 202)

THE ROLE OF THE *PHENOMENOLOGY*

We have therefore seen in a general way what Hegel wanted his
philosophical system to achieve, and how he hoped it would achieve
it: by enabling us to think dialectically and so to resolve certain
'blindspots' in how we take the world to be, it will allow the
world to look back in a rational way, to manifest its rational structure
to us. The question now arises: what role is there for the *Phenomenology*
within this enterprise, and how does that role come about?

As we have already seen, Hegel himself characterizes the *Phenomenology* as an introduction to the system, and now it can be
made clearer why such an introduction is needed, and how it
might proceed. Hegel takes it that in order for his system to
succeed in showing how we can find rational satisfaction in the
world, we must enter into a process of conceptual therapy (undertaken in the *Encyclopedia*); but he recognizes two preliminary difficulties here. The first is that we may feel no need for this
therapy, because we do not see the problem for which this therapy is the solution, or because we do not see that non-dialectical
thinking is the source of the problem, or because we think the
problem is intrinsically irresoluble. The second difficulty is that
we just may not know how to go about making the kind of dialectical revisions that Hegel believes are required to follow
through the transitions of the *Logic*.

As an introduction to the system, the *Phenomenology* therefore
has two fundamental tasks, one motivational and the other

pedagogic. The motivational task is to make us see why we are *required* to undertake the kind of reflective examination of our categories that takes place in the *Logic*. Hegel points out that though we *use* categories all the time (such as being, cause and effect, force) we do not usually recognize that the categories we adopt in this way have a vital influence on how we view and act in the world, and thus we do not see the importance of critically reflecting on them:

> everyone possesses and uses the wholly abstract category of *being*. The sun *is* in the sky; these grapes *are* ripe, and so on *ad infinitum*. Or, in a higher sphere of education, we proceed to the relation of cause and effect, force and its manifestation, etc. All our knowledge and ideas are entwined with metaphysics like this and governed by it; it is the net which holds together all the concrete material which occupies us in our action and endeavour. But this net and its knots are sunk in our ordinary consciousness beneath numerous layers of stuff. This stuff comprises our known interests and the objects that are before our minds, while the universal threads of the net remain out of sight and are not explicitly made the subject of our reflection.
>
> (ILHP: 27–28)

Hegel thinks that the best way of getting us to move to the *Logic*, and to turn from merely *using* categories to affording them the rightful 'honour of being contemplated for their own sakes' (SL: 34) is to make vivid to us exactly how important it is to think dialectically, by showing what goes wrong for a consciousness when it does not. Thus, as we shall see, the *Phenomenology* operates by tracing the development of a consciousness through various ways of thinking about the world (including itself and other consciousnesses), where this consciousness is faced by apparently intractable difficulties in making the world a 'home', until at last it comes to recognize that what underlies these difficulties is its failure to think dialectically: at this point, it is ready to make the transition to the *Logic*, where instead of merely being shown why conceptual therapy matters, we undergo the therapy itself, by making 'thoughts pure and simple our object' (EL: §3, p. 6). The *Phenomenology* therefore portrays consciousness in three modes, where at first it is blithely oblivious to any potential problem and so is characterized by a self-confident 'certainty'; it is then faced with a problem, but is unable to resolve it given the conceptual resources at its disposal; it then succumbs to despair, and reifies the problem by treating it as unresolvable, as inherent in the world. Only when all these three stances are exhausted, will consciousness be ready to reflect on the particular assumptions that are causing it the difficulty; and only when all these assumptions have been shown to be problematic, will consciousness be ready to undergo the kind of profound analysis of the categories of thought that is proposed within Hegel's speculative philosophy:

> Quite generally, the familiar, just because it is familiar, is not cognitively understood. The commonest way in which we deceive either ourselves or others about understanding is by assuming something as familiar, and accepting it on that account; with all its pros and cons, such knowing never gets anywhere, and it knows not why. Subject and object, God, Nature, Understanding, sensibility, and so on, are uncritically taken for granted as familiar, established as valid, and made into fixed points for starting and stopping. While these remain unmoved, the knowing activity goes back and forth between them, thus moving only on their surface ... Hence the task nowadays consists ... in freeing determinate thoughts from their fixity so as to give actuality to the universal, and impart to it spiritual life.
>
> (PS: §31 and §33, pp. 18–20)

Hegel thus characterizes his approach in the *Phenomenology* as '[a] scepticism that is directed against the whole range of phenomenal consciousness [which] renders the Spirit for the first time competent to examine what truth is', by forcing consciousness to question 'all the so-called natural ideas, thoughts, and opinions, ... ideas with which the consciousness that sets about the examination [of truth] *straight away* is still filled and hampered, so that it is, in fact, incapable of carrying out what it wants to undertake' (PS: §78, p. 50).

However, ordinary consciousness may resist this 'task' of speculative philosophy not merely because it finds no need for it (the motivational problem); it may do so because (as Hegel recognizes) it finds it too counter-intuitive and intellectually demanding, as its conceptual certainties are overturned and it is required to 'walk on its head' (the pedagogic problem):

> The mind, denied the use of its familiar ideas, feels the ground where it once stood firm and at home taken away from beneath it, and, when transported into the region of pure thought, cannot tell where in the world it is.
>
> (EL: §3, p. 7)

Hegel therefore gives the *Phenomenology* a role here too, helping consciousness gradually to question those conceptual certainties and thus to move to a position where it can see what it might mean to give them up. Thus, as it proceeds through the *Phenomenology*, consciousness does come to set aside some of its 'familiar ideas', so that by the end it is prepared for the kind of explicit examination of those ideas that is achieved in the *Logic*. This is the pedagogic function of the *Phenomenology*: it helps ordinary consciousness face up to the fact that it can no longer take the apparently obvious distinctions of the understanding for granted, and so makes speculative philosophy possible for it.

The *Phenomenology* is therefore written in a distinctive style, in so far as it has a story to tell from two points of view: the point of view of ordinary consciousness, which is undergoing this experience of moving from confident 'certainty' to despair, to renewed certainty as it revises its position and sees things in a different way; and the point of view of Hegel (and us) as *observers* of this consciousness, who already occupy the speculative standpoint, and who can therefore see, in a way that consciousness itself cannot, what is going wrong for it and why. Thus, Hegel will often 'step back' from merely describing the experience of consciousness itself, to comment on what is *really* going on, or to anticipate how eventually consciousness will come to resolve a particular problem, when at that point in the narrative this is not apparent to consciousness itself. For consciousness itself, therefore, the *Phenomenology* is a *via negativa*, as it responds to some failed position with another position that is equally one-sided, and so equally doomed to collapse. But at the same time *we* (as phenomenological observers) learn a great deal from seeing what is going wrong, and when (at the end of the *Phenomenology*) consciousness is ready to adopt our standpoint, then it too will be in a position to learn these lessons for itself.

Given this conception of the *Phenomenology*, it is therefore possible to see why the *Phenomenology* forms an introduction to the system set out in the *Encyclopedia* and associated works, and why also material from it is repeated *within* that system, in the *Philosophy of Spirit*: for in the *Phenomenology* we just experience the difficulties caused by our non-dialectical use of the categories, while in the *Philosophy of Spirit* which *follows* the *Logic* in the system, we are able to understand those difficulties more explicitly in the light of the categorial discussion of the *Logic*, and so diagnose them fully in a way that is not yet possible in the *Phenomenology* itself.

As well as linking the *Phenomenology* to the rest of Hegel's system, and particularly the *Logic*, in a natural way, I hope that another advantage of this emphasis on the dialectic will become clear as we proceed: namely, it will allow us to treat the *Phenomenology* itself as a unified work, but without having to distort the text in order to do so. One difficulty is that the *Phenomenology* discusses consciousness both at the level of the individual, and at the social level (most particularly in Chapter VI on 'Spirit', in its treatment of the Greek world and the Enlightenment, for example), where some commentators have seen this as problematic (for references and further discussion, see Pippin 1993: 55–56). But, on my account there is nothing particularly troubling here: for, as Hegel himself stresses (cf. EN: I, §246Z, p. 202), just as we can see that individuals employ categories in how they think about the world, so too do cultures and world-views in which individuals participate, in the sense that these can also be characterized as involving certain categorial assumptions (as when Hegel says, for example, that the Greeks lacked the modern concept of 'the person'). From the perspective of my reading, therefore, it is hardly surprising that the discussion operates at both the individual and the cultural–historical level. This in my view explains why in Chapter VI, Hegel feels able to make his notorious move from 'shapes merely of consciousness' to 'shapes of a world'

(PS: §441, p. 265). Another difficulty that has faced many commentators is that they have sought for unity by seeing the *Phenomenology* as focused on one problem or issue: for example, that
Hegel is here offering a theory of knowledge, designed to overcome the familiar problems of scepticism, relativism, and sub-
jectivism; but then they have struggled to integrate more
obviously ethical or social parts of the text into this reading (cf.
Pippin 1989: 154–63, where he tries to give an epistemological
account of the master/slave section, which in my view is more
naturally read as addressing issues in social philosophy; and
Rockmore 1997, which starts by treating epistemological issues
as fundamental, but then fails to locate such issues in large parts
of the text). Once again, however, on my approach this problem
does not arise: for, on this approach, what unifies the *Phenomenology* is the consistency of its diagnostic *method*, which is then
applied to a number of *different* problem areas. Once this is
accepted, there is no need to look for *one* key issue, or to treat the
Phenomenology as a contribution to *one* area of philosophy (as a
contribution to epistemology *or* ethics, *or* philosophy of religion,
or whatever): rather, the unity of the work comes from its attempt
to show that a similar difficulty is common to a range of concerns,
which all show the same kind of distortion in our thinking
(cf. Nagel 1986, who takes the problem of reconciling subjective
and objective standpoints to underlie fundamental issues in
ethics, political philosophy, epistemology, and metaphysics).
Thus, in answer to Haym's question, how one work can include a
discussion of sense perception and also 'the madness of Diderot's
musician ... [and] the fanaticism of Marat and Robespierre'
(Haym 1857: 241), we can reply (rather prosaically, perhaps) that
all reveal dialectical limitations at different levels and to different
degrees.

Finally, I hope that my approach may shed some light on the
notorious problem of explaining Hegel's transitions in the *Phenomenology*, from one form of consciousness to the next. Some
readings require these transitions to be extremely rigorous. For
example, those readings that treat the *Phenomenology* as a transcendental argument are committed to the view that each new
form of consciousness is introduced as a necessary condition for

the possibility of the previous form of consciousness. (Cf. Taylor 1972, Norman 1981: 121, Neuhouser 1986, Pippin 1989, Stewart 2000. I myself have followed Taylor in arguing that Hegel's treatment of 'perception' contains some interesting transcendental claims about the content of perceptual experience (see Stern 2000: 164–75; Stern forthcoming); but I am doubtful that this procedure can be made to fit the *Phenomenology* as a whole.) On other readings, Hegel is seen as aiming to establish his position as uniquely coherent by showing *all* other possible world-views to involve some sort of incoherence, and that this requires him to be *exhaustive* in moving through these world-views, so that every transition must involve the smallest possible alteration from one perspective to the next. (Cf. Forster 1998: 186, '[T]he "necessity" of a transition from a shape of consciousness A to a shape of consciousness B just consists in the complex fact that while shape A proves to be implicitly self-contradictory, shape B preserves shape A's constitutive conceptions/concepts but in a way which modifies them so as to eliminate the self-contradiction, and moreover does so while departing less from the meanings of A's constitutive conceptions/concepts than any other known shape which performs that function.') The advantage of readings of this sort is that they take seriously the things Hegel says in some of his programmatic remarks, for example that 'the goal' as well as the 'serial progression' from one form of consciousness to the next is 'necessarily fixed' (PS: §80, p. 51). The difficulty, however, is that it is hard for these readings to show that the rigour they demand is actually to be found in the development of the *Phenomenology* (as Forster, for example, implicitly concedes, when he comments that the text might need to be 'reconstructed' in order to fit the method he proposes for it: see Forster 1998: 187. Cf. also K. R. Westphal 1998b: 94–95). Faced with this difficulty, other commentators have gone to the opposite extreme, and denied that there is any real method at all underlying the order in which the forms of consciousness develop. (Cf. Kaufmann 1965: 171, 'And the *Phenomenology* is certainly *unwissenschaftlich*: undisciplined, arbitrary, full of digressions, not a monument to the austerity of the intellectual conscience and to carefulness and precision but a wild, bold, unprecedented book that invites comparison with some great literary masterpieces.') Readings of this kind have the advantage of not trying to hold Hegel to a methodological ideal that he failed to meet; but on the other hand they make a nonsense of Hegel's own claims for the systematic nature of his work, and ignore the kind of structure that *can* be found in it.

Now, on my approach we can take the transitions seriously, but are not committed to these being more rigorous than a realistic interpretation of the actual text allows. On this approach, there is indeed a 'necessary progression and interconnection of the forms of the unreal consciousness' (PS: §79, p. 50), in the sense that its fundamental limitations force consciousness to face certain difficulties, and to handle these difficulties in a particular way. Consciousness will therefore find itself caught up in a characteristic movement: starting from one position, it comes to see that that position leads to problems that are unresolvable from that standpoint. Consciousness will therefore be plunged into despair, as it now finds no satisfaction in the world, but only puzzlement and frustration. However, Hegel claims that consciousness cannot remain content with this sense of dissatisfaction, as 'thought troubles its thoughtlessness, and its own unrest disturbs its inertia' (PS: §80, p. 51); it must therefore move to a fresh standpoint, in order to recover its sense of being 'at home in the world'. It will therefore adopt a new perspective by questioning some of the assumptions of the position from which it began. However, as a merely 'unreal' (natural, ordinary, unspeculative) consciousness, it does so in a one-sided or undialectical manner, and so arrives at another position which (*because* of this one-sidedness) is no more workable; so it then plunges into despair once again, only then to question the assumptions of *this* position in an incomplete manner, and so on. Thus, for example, after finding sense-certainty to be inadequate, consciousness moves to perception, which no longer thinks of objects as mere individuals, but instead thinks of them as bundles of property-universals; but this makes it difficult to capture the unity of the object as an individual, so it regards these universals as instantiated in a substratum; but this makes it difficult to see how the substratum relates to the properties, so it moves to a conception of objects as the appearance of a holistic structure of interconnected forces; but this sets up a problematic dualism between a world of sensible phenomena and the super-sensible beyond of theoretical understanding; so consciousness rejects this beyond and instead sees the world as something it can master through action; and so on. Or, to take some examples from later in the *Phenomenology*: Hegel argues that problems with Greek ethical life lead consciousness to question the perspective of the Greeks and to introduce new notions of individuality and freedom, but these concepts are themselves developed one-sidedly, in a way that leads to fresh difficulties highlighted in various ways through the chapters on 'Reason' and 'Spirit'. Likewise, he argues that while modern consciousness has become dissatisfied with a certain kind of dogmatic religious belief, it moves beyond that in a limited way, thereby introducing the kind of Enlightenment standpoint that is merely materialistic and utilitarian. Thus, in all these transitions, Hegel wants us, as phenomenological observers, to see that the moves consciousness makes are inevitable given its dialectical limitations; likewise, we are supposed to see that these limitations mean that it cannot properly escape the difficulties of one standpoint when it moves to another, because it does so in a merely one-sided manner. Only at the end of the *Phenomenology*, when the 'natural' consciousness we have been observing at last feels this dissatisfaction for itself, will it be ready to reflect on the categorial assumptions that have led it to this impasse, thereby finally understanding the need for the kind of philosophical self-examination required in order to achieve 'absolute knowing'. Thus, at the end of the *Phenomenology*, consciousness can see that far from the world itself being irrational or alien, 'what seems to happen outside of it, to be an activity directed against it, is really its own doing' (PS: 21); at that point it is ready to begin the kind of categorial examination that we find in the *Logic*, and the preparatory role of the *Phenomenology* is at an end.

OVERVIEW OF THE TEXT

Before we begin to look at Hegel's complex work in detail, a brief overview of the text and its basic structure may be helpful.

The *Phenomenology* begins with a Preface followed by an Introduction. While it offers some classic but gnomic summaries of
Hegel's outlook, some account of his methodological commit-
ments, and some pungent challenges to his rivals, the Preface is
less a guide to the reader, and more a test of her nerve. The
Introduction proceeds more straightforwardly. Here Hegel considers an issue that greatly concerned him, and which he sum-
marized elsewhere in the question 'with what must science
begin?' (SL: 67) if it is to be the kind of systematic investigation
he wants to make it. He rejects the call to start by assessing our
cognitive capacities, as he thinks this will inevitably lead to
unwarranted sceptical doubts about the adequacy of these capacities. Instead, he proposes to look at claims that consciousness
makes about the world (including itself), to see how stable they
prove to be, or whether they in fact collapse into the opposing
viewpoint in a dialectical manner. By following this investigation
through, we will move closer to a more stable outlook that is not
subject to these pressures, and thus to a form of knowledge that
we are entitled to treat as absolute.

For this process to work, we need to begin with the simplest
outlook that is available to us, as otherwise we might neglect
some possible form of consciousness or world-view which could
then come back to challenge our final position. Hegel characterizes this simple outlook as 'sense-certainty' in the opening
section of the first chapter on consciousness, where in this chapter
he is focusing on the accounts consciousness gives of things
around us, rather than of ourselves as subjects. Sense-certainty is
basic in this way because it operates with a very simple picture of
objects as just individual things, and therefore of knowledge as
involving merely immediate experience without any use of concepts. However, Hegel argues that the only view sense-certainty
can then in fact have of objects is as abstract universals, so that
the position overturns itself, and is forced to adopt a more
sophisticated position, in which universals are now used to characterize individuals, as properties. This then leads to a position
which Hegel calls 'perception'. But problems in grasping the
relation between individuals and their properties result in an
oscillation between substance/attribute views of these objects (as

'One' substratum underlying many properties) and bundle views (of the object as an 'Also' or collection of such properties). Consciousness then arrives at the idea of universal forces and laws, and thus makes an important step towards the scientific world-picture; but at this stage, this picture opens up a split between the world as we experience it, as containing individual things, and a scientific model in which that individuality is dissolved at a different level, in a flux of forces.

Faced with these puzzles in understanding the world that encompasses it, consciousness now turns to consider itself, and thus moves from Consciousness to Self-Consciousness. Here again Hegel begins with a simple position, which takes the self to be of unique significance as an individual, and thus takes its freedom to consist in the unlimited exercise of this individuality. At the same time, it is forced to recognize the world as containing other subjects and not just objects, as only in such subjects can it find a way to exercise its authority in a manner that involves more than just an endless process of destruction – for other subjects can submit to its will, without having to be entirely negated in the process. This, then, leads to a life-and-death struggle between subjects, which reaches a temporary resolution when one subject submits to the other, in the relation of slave to master. However, Hegel argues, the master's position is not in fact satisfactory, as in so far as he now exercises his authority over a subject that is considered worthless in his eyes, this authority is empty and meaningless. Meanwhile, Hegel suggests, through engaging with the world for the master in work, the slave manages to gain a sense of how it can relate to external reality in a different way, by overcoming its otherness without needing to destroy it; instead, it finds that the objects it labours on can come to embody its projects and be made into a vehicle for its ideas.

Hegel then moves on to a form of rationalism that he identifies with Stoicism (the first of the many positions that he will connect with outlooks from history, albeit often in a loose and allusive – and therefore elusive – way). This may either be seen (negatively) as a retreat by the individual into the inner citadel of its free intellect after the failure of both the master and the slave to find a more practical kind of freedom, or (positively) as the result of the slave's realization that in understanding the world it can get beyond its individuality and find a more lasting satisfaction. This tension then leads to Scepticism, as the inner retreat cuts consciousness off from the very world that it is trying to understand, so that it then attempts to live with mere 'appearances'. In the last section of the Self-Consciousness chapter, this turns into a division between us finite individual human beings on the one hand, and a higher form of universality on the other, seen as an unchanging divine being cut off from the contingency and particularity of the world in which we live, a gap that we can only hopelessly try to bridge by attempts at overcoming our individual bodily natures, and by the mediation of priests.

This tension resolves itself in another revival of rationalism, which moves from seeking satisfaction in the beyond to seeking it once again in the world around it, through the power of reason. This therefore forms the theme of the next chapter. It begins with a critique of the attempt by idealism to see things as the product of the mind, where, because the mind involves universal concepts, individuality is said to come from an extra-mental 'thing-in-itself' (as in Kant) or 'external impetus' (as in Fichte) that at the same time lies *outside* the mind, and so is rendered unknowable. Consciousness therefore turns to a more realist form of rationalism, which seeks to find rational structures in nature, of which the individual is also taken to be part. Hegel suggests, however, that consciousness has trouble in finding any such rational order here, where the natural world proves hard to classify into kinds, and our own thoughts and behaviour do not follow clear universal laws. Having been disappointed in this way by theoretical rationality, consciousness now turns to a more practical standpoint, which at first prioritizes individuality over universality, and so seeks to find pleasure, to follow its own convictions, and to pursue its own virtues. However, as these positions lead to failure, consciousness moves to a more rationalistic and universalistic standpoint, first trying to follow apparently self-evident moral rules, and then (when these rules prove difficult to apply) to employ the universalizability test of Kantian ethics to tell it how it should act. But, Hegel argues, such formal tests turn out to be empty and are thus unable to provide us with any adequate moral guidance outside the concrete practices of an ethical community; he therefore introduces such a community in the next chapter on Spirit.

Beginning at the furthest remove from the Kantian picture, Hegel starts with the ethical community of the ancient Greeks, where individuals identify themselves in an immediate and unquestioning manner with the universal laws and customs that comprise the norms of their society. He argues that in this society, the sides of universality and individuality begin by complementing one another, for example in the harmonious relation between the *polis* and the family, or the human law and the divine law. However, using the story of *Antigone* as emblematic, Hegel shows how this harmony breaks apart, in a way that leads us back to the more dualistic outlook of modernity. The individual now sees himself as opposed to nature and so *self*-creating; no longer takes there to be any harmony between its own individual interests and the general interest of society; and to be opposed to religion in a way that culminates in the atheistic Enlightenment. Fundamentally, the individual is looking for freedom, but in an inadequate form, as can be seen in the anarchy of the Terror that resulted from the French Revolution, where individuals sought to represent the universal or general will, but were unable to do so without seeming to reduce it to their own particular ends, with the result that they had to be swept aside in a chaos of perpetual revolution. Equally, Hegel argues, a similarly dualistic picture underlies modern ethics as exemplified by Kant, who posits a division between the rational and the desiring self, which he then tries unsuccessfully to bridge by offering his practical postulates of immortality and of God, as grounding at least some hope that the division might be overcome in the hereafter. In moving to the less self-alienated standpoint of conscience, consciousness is nonetheless still unable to avoid moral relativism, which then becomes a kind of empty quietism, whereby no action seems worth doing, and the individual is reduced to an abstraction.

Finally, Hegel turns to consider religion, which we have seen has already figured at many places earlier in the dialectic. Hegel's aim is to provide the groundwork for a view of religion that can avoid the pathologies that he has considered previously (for example, in the Unhappy Consciousness, or in the religious life of Antigone), and which can ultimately be made compatible with philosophy. He therefore tries to show how religious thought has developed, from earlier forms of nature religion, to increasingly individualized and personified conceptions of the gods held by the Greeks, to Christianity, in which God becomes man, and the universal is therefore made particular in the individual, in a way that philosophy alone can fully comprehend. With this, Hegel makes the step to the brief concluding chapter on Absolute Knowing, which has little content of its own, but just recaps on what has gone before, and points us forward to the *Logic*, in which the dialectical categorial relations underlying the *Phenomenology* are more fully explored.

Set out in this abbreviated form, it is perhaps easy to see why commentators and critics have been baffled by the structure of the work. However, as I hope the table below brings out, once the book is looked at with the dialectic of universal and individual in mind, it can be seen how much this shapes the analysis that Hegel offers, in a way that will be developed further in what follows.

Consciousness	Sense-certainty	Treats objects as bare individuals, and aims at knowledge that does not involve concepts – but ends up with empty universality
	Perception	So treats objects as bare individuals plus universal properties ('One'), or bundles of universal properties ('Also') – but cannot combine the individuality of the object with the universality of properties
	Force and the Understanding	So treats objects as individual appearances of underlying universals (such as forces or laws) – but ends up with a two-tiered conception of reality
Self-Consciousness	Desire	Conceives of itself as bare individual 'I' or subject
	Life and Death Struggle	But then cannot recognize any shared universality with other individuals, leading to conflict

	Master/Slave Dialectic	One individual wins the conflict (master) because the other gives way (slave). But the master remains in the individuality of desire, while the slave attains ability to abstract from this individuality in work	
	Stoicism	Unsatisfactory nature of the master/slave relation leads to withdrawal from individuality, to seek universality in the rational order of world	
	Scepticism	But this underlying rational order cannot be reached, only the individuality of appearances	
	Unhappy Consciousness	Leads to division between eternal and universal reason (God) and finite individual creatures (man)	
Reason	Idealism	Dualism of Unhappy Consciousness replaced by seeing subject as the source of universal forms, rather than coming from a transcendent other; but individuality still originates from outside, based on the unknowable ground of particular experiences, leading to a limit on our cognition	
	Observing Reason	So move to more realist positions, that attempt to find universal forms and laws in nature, in thought, and in what governs our behaviour; but this rational order is elusive	
	Active Reason	So move from seeking the universal forms in nature to following individuality, in the attempt to conduct life on an individualistic basis: seeking pleasure, following the law of one's heart, and individual virtues	
	Practical Reason	But the individual recognizes the need for more universal laws and principles to govern its behaviour, leading to Kantian ethics. But this universality proves to be empty	
Spirit	The Ethical Order	Turn from moderns to Greeks, to give moral life more content, where the Greeks at first appear to have balanced universality and individuality; but then the inherent instability of their position is illustrated by *Antigone*, where both sides clash	
	Culture	Return to moderns, and consideration of how individuals relate to the universal social order, culminating in analysis of the Terror as resulting from the attempt by individuals to represent in themselves the universal will of the people	

	Morality	Consideration of Kantian moral postulates, as an attempt to bridge the gap between the universality of morality and the empirical nature of the individual. Individual then turns to his own conscience as a moral guide, and from there to the forgiveness of the individual, which takes us to religion
Religion	Natural Religion	Starts with concept of divine as universal natural forces, but divine is progressively made concrete and individual
	Art Religion	Gods seen as increasingly human and individualized
	Revealed Religion	God made manifest in individual man (Jesus), but also universal spirit (holy ghost)
Absolute Knowing		Consciousness ready to move on to the *Logic*: having experienced this dialectic of categories, can now turn to their examination

Of course, many complexities and nuances will have to be brought into this outline (where I have added some headings that do not appear in Hegel's text itself, while modifying some section titles). But having presented this overview, we can now therefore turn to that text, beginning with the Preface and the Introduction.

THE PREFACE AND THE INTRODUCTION

Given that Hegel thinks that the ordinary consciousness will be ready and able to face up to the ordeal of dialectical thinking (to 'take on … the strenuous effort of the Notion' (PS: §58, p. 35)) only after it has been through the chastening experience of the *Phenomenology*, it is not so surprising that he holds that any attempt to tell us what such thinking involves before we have had that experience would be wasted effort: we would inevitably misunderstand what was required, and be unable to grasp what is demanded of us. The Preface and the Introduction to the *Phenomenology* are therefore notorious for failing to assist its readers by telling them anything in advance about the conclusions to be reached, as those conclusions will only be properly grasped at the end of the work, and not the beginning: 'the real issue is not exhausted by stating it as an aim, but by carrying it out, nor is the result the actual whole, but rather the result together with the process through which it came about' (PS: §3, p. 2). Thus, as many commentators have complained, Hegel seems to set out deliberately to make the preliminaries to the *Phenomenology* hard to understand until one has been through the work as a whole, so that they are more suitably read at the end rather than at the outset; this seems particularly true of the Preface, which only came to be written after the work was complete, so that it serves more as a coda to the text (or perhaps even to Hegel's entire system) than as a preamble. (As Hegel remarked rather superciliously, 'The usual royal road in philosophy is to read prefaces and book reviews, in order to get an approximate idea of things' (AW: 4). This is a shortcut he seems determined to deny us.)

THE PREFACE

Nonetheless, though the Preface does not give much away concerning the content of the *Phenomenology*, and is certainly far from transparent and fully explicit, it is still highly relevant to Hegel's main theme, which is that we must satisfy reason in our conception of the world, and further that philosophy as a speculative science can help reason find that satisfaction: 'The true shape in which truth exists can only be the scientific system of such truth. To help bring philosophy closer to the form of Science, to the goal where it can lay aside the title "*love* of knowing" and be *actual* knowing – that is what I have set myself to do' (PS: §5, p. 3). Much of the Preface is therefore taken up with polemicizing against his contemporaries who (Hegel believes) have failed to achieve what he sets out to do, either because they have held that satisfaction can only be attained by abandoning reason in favour of faith, or because they have mistaken the kind of world-view in which true intellectual satisfaction can be found.[9]

With regard to the first group, he launches a scathing attack on those who argue that consciousness must seek immediate awareness of the divine and abandon thought altogether, if it is to feel at home in the world; these critics of philosophy (such as

F. H. Jacobi (1743–1819)) blame it for undermining former certainties through its excessive rationalism, for which it must now make amends by committing itself to 'edification rather than insight' (PS: §7, p. 5). Hegel is scornful of what seems to him to be a merely anti-philosophical mysticism:

> The 'beautiful', the 'holy', the 'eternal', 'religion', and 'love' are the bait required to arouse the desire to bite; not the Notion, but ecstasy, not the cold march of necessity in the thing itself, but the ferment of enthusiasm, these are supposed to be what sustains and continually extends the wealth of substance ... Such minds, when they give themselves up to the uncontrolled ferment of [the divine] substance, imagine that, by drawing a veil over self-consciousness and surrendering understanding they become the beloved of God to whom He gives wisdom in sleep; and hence what they in fact receive, and bring to birth in their sleep, is nothing but dreams.
>
> (PS: ¶7 and ¶10, pp. 5–6)

Hegel declares that thankfully the period of such irrationalism has passed, and that 'ours is a birth-time and a period of transition to a new era' (PS: §11, p. 6). However, he also states that when it first appears on the scene, this renewed commitment to reason is flawed by a certain intellectual immaturity, as this new way of thinking is 'no more a complete actuality than is a newborn child; it is essential to bear this in mind. It comes on the scene for the first time in its immediacy or its Notion ... Science, the crown of a world of Spirit, is not complete in its beginnings' (PS: §12, p. 7). The result of such immaturity, Hegel says, will be that it is claimed that rational insight is said to be 'the esoteric possession of a few individuals', whereas in fact (as the *Phenomenology* is intended to show) '[t]he intelligible form of Science is the way open and equally accessible to everyone' (PS: §13, p. 7). Moreover, in the early stages of its development this programme has taken a shape that has made it an easy target for its critics, as it has sought to satisfy reason with a 'monochromatic formalism' in which philosophy tries to pin down the bewildering variety of phenomena in a few simple schemas, and hence ends up declaring that 'all is one'. Hegel states that we are right to be dissatisfied with this outcome, and to be successful philosophy must provide us with a deeper form of rational insight than this:

> To pit this single insight, that in the Absolute everything is the same, against the full body of articulated cognition, which at least seeks and demands such fulfilment, is to palm off its Absolute as the night in which, as the saying goes, all cows are black – this is cognition naively reduced to vacuity.
>
> (PS: §16, p. 9)

However, although he accepts that some of the contemporary critics of philosophy have a point in attacking the philosophical sciences in their current state, he nonetheless insists that this is because in this state they are not properly developed, and that further philosophical progress will show that such attacks are premature:

> Science in its early stages, when it has attained neither to completeness of detail nor perfection of form, is vulnerable to criticism. But it would be as unjust for such criticism to strike at the very heart of Science, as it is untenable to refuse to honour the demand for its [i.e. Science's] further development.
>
> (PS: §14, p. 8)

This section of the Preface, and a later one on the same topic (PS: §§50–51, pp. 29–31), are clearly designed to alert the reader to the fact that Hegel's position is not to be aligned with Schelling's identity-philosophy and its associated philosophy of nature. Rather, while Hegel acknowledges Schelling's importance as a pioneer in giving contemporary philosophy a renewed intellectual optimism and respect for reason, he also plainly wishes to warn his readers that such optimism cannot find its fulfilment in the work of Schelling and his followers, for although Schelling tries to avoid irrationalism, his conception is too formulaic and empty to make the world properly comprehensible to us. If reason is to find satisfaction, Hegel argues, it must preserve the distinctions that Schelling simply collapses, but in such a way that these distinctions become unproblematic:

Whatever is more than such a word, even the transition to a mere proposition, contains a *becoming-other* that has to be taken back, or is a mediation. But it is just this that is rejected with horror, as if absolute cognition were simply being surrendered when more is made of mediation than in simply saying that it is nothing absolute, and is completely absent from the Absolute. But this abhorrence in fact stems from ignorance of the nature of mediation, and of absolute cognition itself ... Reason is, therefore, misunderstood when reflection is excluded from the True, and is not grasped as a positive moment of the Absolute.

(PS: §§20–21, pp. 11–12)

Hegel diagnoses Schelling's mistake here as based on a desire for a form of intellectual satisfaction that is blissfully unaware of the problems faced by ordinary finite understanding, modelled on 'the life of God and divine cognition ... [where] that life is indeed one of untroubled equality and unity with itself, for which otherness and alienation, and the overcoming of alienation, are not serious matters' (PS: §19, p. 10); but Hegel argues that this is a mistake, for the divine intellect must be able to work through these problems if such intellectual satisfaction is not just to be 'insipid'. For philosophy to succeed against edification, for reason properly to answer its irrationalist critics, Hegel claims we must move from the identity-philosophy of Schelling to the properly dialectical outlook of his own speculative system; in this way, Hegel seized the torch of progressive thinking from his friend and former colleague, and began a rift between the two that was never to heal.

In this section of the Preface, Hegel comes out with some of his most notoriously dark sayings, namely that 'everything turns on grasping and expressing the True, not only as *Substance*, but equally as *Subject*' (PS: §17, p. 10), and that 'The True is the whole' (PS: §20, p. 11). As Hegel himself points out (PS: §17, pp. 9–10), it is only through 'the exposition of the system itself' that he can properly justify these claims, or even render them fully intelligible; but the fact that they come in the course of his skirmish with Schelling (or perhaps, as Hegel himself always insisted, with Schelling's less able followers) makes them somewhat easier to interpret. For, as we have seen, it is clear that what troubled Hegel about Schelling's approach was its tendency towards monism, that is, to the view that 'all is one' (PS: §16, p. 9). In claiming, therefore, that 'the True' is not only substance, but also subject, Hegel may be taken as rejecting this monistic position, on the grounds that it collapses the subject/object distinction, whereas (in Hegel's view) the subject can be both distinguished from the world *and* find itself in it:

> This Substance is, as Subject, pure *simple negativity*, and is for this very reason the bifurcation of the simple; it is the doubling which sets up opposition, and then again the negation of this indifferent diversity and of its antithesis [the immediate simplicity]. Only this self-*restoring* sameness, or this reflection in otherness within itself – not an *original* or *immediate* unity as such – is the True.
>
> (PS: §18, p. 10)

In declaring that 'The True is the whole' (PS: §20, p. 11), Hegel thus associates himself with holism as against monism; for while he rejects atomism or radical dualism, he is happy to accept 'identity-in-difference', whereas (in his view) the Schellingian takes reality to be fundamentally self-identical and lacking in differentiation. Hegel calls *Spirit* the subject that embodies this relation of identity-in-difference to the world, by finding itself in its 'other', so that while it is not cut off from the world (radical dualism), it is not indistinguishable from it either (monism):

> The spiritual alone is the *actual*; it is essence, or that which has *being in itself*; it is that which *relates itself to itself* and is *determinate*, it is *other-being* and *being-for-self*, and in this determinateness, or in its self-externality, abides within itself; in other words, it is *in and for itself*.
>
> (PS: §25, p. 14)

(It is a matter of some dispute as to whether Hegel was right to associate Schelling with monism here, and to claim that Schelling's doctrine of 'intellectual intuition ... fall[s] back into inert simplicity' by submerging subject into substance (PS: §17, p. 10): see Bowie 1993: 55–56. It is also frequently argued that Hegel himself fails to show how this doctrine of 'identity-in-difference' avoids either incoherence or itself ending up as monistic as the position he is criticizing: cf. James 1909, Russell 1956: 21.)

Hegel then goes on to consider at some length why his dialectical outlook cannot be grasped by consciousness immediately, and so why we cannot proceed to it directly 'like a shot from a pistol', in the way that the Schellingian system 'begins straight away with absolute knowledge, and makes short work of other standpoints by declaring that it takes no notice of them' (PS: §27, p. 16). Hegel here makes clear what is distinctive about the therapeutic nature of his approach: consciousness has to see that its own way of understanding the world has failed, before it can grasp the significance of Hegel's way of looking at things:

> But the life of Spirit is not the life that shrinks from death and keeps itself untouched by devastation, but rather the life that endures it and maintains itself in it. It wins its truth only when, in utter dismemberment, it finds itself.
>
> (PS: §32, p. 19)

Hegel therefore contrasts his approach to that adopted by history and mathematics, where the outcome of these inquiries can be understood and defended without going through any such 'labour of the negative' (PS: §19, p. 10): he argues that this is the wrong model to use for his form of therapeutic inquiry, where here 'truth therefore includes the negative also, what could be called the false, if it could be regarded as something from which one might abstract' (PS: §47, p. 27). As a consequence, he rejects the mathematical method as inappropriate for philosophy, observing in his defence:

> If this comment sounds boastful or revolutionary – and I am far from adopting such a tone – it should be noted that current opinion itself has already come to view the scientific regime bequeathed by mathematics as quite *old-fashioned* – with its explanations, divisions,

axioms, sets of theorems, its proofs, principles, deductions, and conclusions from them.

(PS: ¶48, p. 28)

(As Harris 1997: I, p. 154, n. 31 remarks, by 'current opinion' Hegel probably means Kant and Jacobi, judging by his comment at SL: 816 that they had 'exploded' the Spinozistic approach of arguing *more geometrico* as a philosophical method.) On the other hand, he warns that in rejecting the 'pedantry and pomposity of science' we should not be tempted towards the anti-rationalistic 'non-method of presentiment and inspiration, or by the arbitrariness of prophetic utterance, both of which despise not only scientific pomposity, but scientific procedure of all kinds' (PS: §49, p. 29).

Hegel therefore claims that his project puts him between two extremes: on the one hand 'the inadequacy of ordinary common sense' (PS: §70, p. 43) with its 'habit of picture-thinking' (PS: §58, p. 35), but on the other hand a purely esoteric and mystical philosophy that cannot be articulated (what he calls 'the uncommon universality of a reason whose talents have been ruined by indolence and the conceit of genius' (PS: §70, p. 43)); rather, Hegel says, his is 'a truth ripened to its properly matured form so as to be capable of being the property of all self-conscious Reason' (PS: §70, p. 43). He therefore criticizes a philosophy that is non-speculative in that it merely sets out to overturn common sense without putting anything in its place: such a philosophy mistakenly 'imagines that by establishing the void it is always ahead of any insight rich in content' (PS: §59, p. 36). On the other hand, he also stresses that genuine philosophical thought will always represent a challenge to non-philosophical consciousness, 'which makes comprehension difficult for it' (PS: §60, p. 36). To illustrate this, he focuses on the way in which the ordinary subject–predicate form is tested by philosophical propositions like 'God is being' or 'the actual is the universal', where the predicate is not being attributed to the subject in the normal way: 'The philosophical proposition, since it *is* a proposition, leads one to believe that the usual subject–predicate relation obtains, as well as the usual attitude towards knowing. But the philosophical content destroys this attitude and this opinion' (PS: §63, p. 39). Thus, though he does not doubt that the public is 'ripe to receive [the truth]' (PS: §71, p. 44), Hegel in the Preface warns the reader not to be misled into accepting a non-Hegelian view of what that truth is, but also not to expect grasping it to be easy: 'True thoughts and scientific insight are only to be won through the labour of the Notion' (PS: §70, p. 43).

THE INTRODUCTION

Like the Preface, the Introduction has a clear polemical intention in setting out to show how a new approach is needed after the false starts in philosophy prior to Hegel. Also like the Preface, the Introduction makes plain what Hegel takes to be the consequences of failure: unless philosophy can make good on its promise to find reason in the world, then the forces of anti-philosophy will triumph, heralding a return to sceptical irrationalism, to '[t]his conceit which understands how to belittle every truth, in order to turn back into itself and gloat over its own understanding, which knows how to dissolve every thought and always find the same barren Ego instead of any content' (PS: §80, p. 52). However, whereas in the Preface Hegel's polemic is rather narrow in seeing this irrationalism as arising out of the 'immaturity' and 'empty formalism' of the kind of philosophical position occupied by the post-Kantians, in the Introduction Hegel tries to deal with a more fundamental challenge, one that sees such irrationalism as stemming from nothing more than a 'natural assumption' (PS: §73, p. 46) concerning the method of philosophical inquiry. Hegel accepts that once this 'natural assumption' is made, then sceptical irrationalism follows; he therefore aims to show that it is in fact not 'natural' at all, and that instead it should be treated as an unwarranted imposition.

Hegel sets out the problematic assumption at the start of the Introduction: namely, that before we set out to find 'reason in the world', we must first step back and examine whether our intellects have the capacity for this sort of understanding, where the fear is that otherwise we may find ourselves embarking on a hopeless project with no prospect of success. In a passage that

Hegel cites elsewhere (FK: 68–69), John Locke famously recommended this procedure, which requires that we 'take a Survey of our own Understandings, examine our own Powers, and see to what Things they [are] adapted' (Locke 1975: 47); and although Hegel cites Locke here, he could equally well have quoted the following passage from Descartes:

> Now, to prevent our being in a state of permanent uncertainty about the powers of the mind, and to prevent our mental labours being misguided and haphazard, we ought once in our life carefully to inquire as to what sort of knowledge human reason is capable of attaining, before we set about acquiring knowledge of things in particular.
>
> (Descartes 1985: 30)

In addition, Hegel sees Kant's critical project as sharing essentially the same outlook, according to which we must begin in philosophy by first investigating the scope of our intellectual capacities (cf. FK: 69, EL: §10Z, p. 14 and EL: §41Z, p. 66); and although Locke may not have been a sceptic or idealist, Hegel holds that Kant in the end was both, and in a way that was inevitable given his Lockean starting point. For, once we adopt this approach, we inevitably treat our thought as an 'instrument' or 'medium' with in-built limitations, and the idea naturally arises that our cognitive capacities *stand between* us and reality; it then comes to seem that the world as it is 'in itself' is inaccessible from our perspective, an 'evil' that we find we cannot remedy no matter how hard we reflect on the nature of this 'instrument' or 'medium' (PS: §73, pp. 46–47). The Kantian may seek to console us here by adopting a more relativistic conception of truth, and claim that this provides us with an adequate goal of inquiry; but Hegel is airily dismissive of such intellectual bad faith, claiming that

> we gradually come to see that this kind of talk which goes back and forth only leads to a hazy distinction between an absolute truth and some other kind of truth, and that words like 'absolute', 'cognition', etc. presuppose a meaning which has yet to be ascertained.
>
> (PS: §75, p. 48)

Now, in order to rebut this apparently inevitable slide into sceptical irrationalism, Hegel's aim here is to suggest that there is in fact nothing that obliges us to adopt the 'natural assumption' that we must begin by 'first of all [coming] to an understanding about cognition' (what could be called 'the critical epistemic method'). One argument for it might be that it is properly pre-suppositionless, as it does not assume anything about our capacity to investigate the world; but, Hegel claims, the adoption of this approach does not in fact make the critical epistemic method presuppositionless, as it still assumes something, namely that we have the ability successfully to 'step back' and investigate our cognitive capacities. So, as Hegel puts the point in the *Logic*, if it is claimed that the limitations of our intellect must be assessed before we can begin inquiring into the 'true being of things', then presumably before we can begin inquiring into the limitations of our intellects we must assess our capacity for such inquiry; and thus our capacity to achieve *that* must be assessed, and so on ad infinitum, for 'the examination of knowledge can only be carried out by an act of knowledge'. Thus, the aim of the critical epistemic theorist to investigate our cognitive capacities without also using them and so 'to seek to know before we can know' is nonsensical and absurd, 'as absurd as the wise resolution of Scholasticus, not to venture into the water until he had learned to swim' (EL: §10, p. 14). Faced with this difficulty, defenders of the 'natural assumption' may instead claim that their procedure is warranted, because otherwise we cannot be sure that our cognitive faculties are up to the job of arriving at knowledge; in the *Logic*, Hegel suggests that this was Kant's view: 'We ought, says Kant, to become acquainted with the instrument, before we undertake the work for which it is to be employed; for if the instrument be insufficient, all our trouble will be spent in vain' (ibid.). Hegel's argument against this view in the *Phenomenology* is straightforward: why should we *need* any assurance of this sort before beginning our inquiries? Why shouldn't we just start and see how far we get? Hegel thus recommends that rather than going in for any sort of preliminary investigation of our faculties, 'Science ... gets on with the work itself ... and mistrusts this very mistrust' (PS: §74, p. 47).

Now, it is important to remember that Hegel's target here is a view of the critical epistemic method that sees it as a 'natural assumption', one that claims that this inquiry into the nature of our cognitive capacities is an obvious and commonsensical starting point of any responsible philosophical endeavour, either because of a conviction that in this way we can guard against grasping 'clouds of error instead of the heaven of truth' (PS: §73, p. 46), or because of a 'fear' of taking anything for granted (PS: §74, p. 47). It is harder to see how Hegel's arguments here would tell against other ways of motivating the critical epistemic method, particularly those built around the claim that there is *positive* evidence that our cognitive capacities are limited, based on the apparent failure of our inquiries in certain areas (theology or metaphysics, for example). Given this evidence of our cognitive limitations, it might then be seen as sensible to see what it is about our cognitive capacities which produces those limitations, so that we do not try to overstep them in a way that would prove fruitless or misleading. Thus, it would seem, the critical epistemic method could be motivated not by an epistemic over-scrupulousness that gets things in the wrong order by questioning our capacities before it has sought to exercise them; rather, it could be motivated by a desire to make a reasonable inventory of our abilities faced with real evidence of their limitedness. (In terms of Hegel's analogy, therefore, this sort of critical theorist is not like someone who wants to learn to swim without getting wet, but instead like someone who, having nearly drowned, has got out of the water to reflect on how far his swimming abilities can be expected to take him.) It may seem that Hegel's arguments here do not really deal with this way of taking the critical epistemic method (although it could be said he tackles it elsewhere, for example in his attack on Kant's claim that the problems of metaphysical thinking show reason to be limited: cf. EL: §§45–52, pp. 72–86).

At this stage, however, it is not clear how much of a worry this should be to the Hegelian. For here Hegel is focusing on how a 'natural assumption' about philosophical inquiry *as such* can lead to sceptical irrationalism, and the claim that proper methodology requires that we should *start* with the critical epistemic method;

he is not concerned at this point to rule out the possibility that once we get on with the business of trying to understand the world, we may find that we encounter certain intractable difficulties which make it apparent that there are particular cognitive limitations we must accept. *If* this happens (and as we have already seen, for Hegel it is a very big 'if'), then proceeding as the critical epistemic theorist suggests may be sensible. Thus, while this point may undermine the force of his polemic here as a critique of Kant and perhaps others (if it can be shown that they adopted the critical epistemic method for the reasons just given, and not for the reasons Hegel criticizes), this still does not undermine his central philosophical point, that there is little reason to adopt the critical theorist's approach as a 'natural assumption' at the outset, *prior* to philosophical inquiry; and it is only if it *is* a 'natural assumption' that it is valuable to the sceptic's case, as only then would it seem to show that doubts about our capacity for knowledge arise as soon as we even begin to seek such knowledge, so that it is somehow self-defeating to seek to know reality. What is significant, therefore, is that Hegel undermines the status of the critical epistemic method as a 'natural assumption', even if some of its proponents (such as Kant) could have had other, philosophically more substantive, reasons for adopting it.

Nonetheless, Hegel argues that it would be a mistake to take the failure of the critical theorist's 'natural assumption' to show that we can just be sure that our view of the world is the correct one, or that we can proceed with whatever presuppositions we like. The difficulty is that different conceptions of the world may strike different inquirers as valid, so that unless we can show why one conception is to be preferred to the others, we could not claim that that conception has a right to be regarded as true. However, it would be wrong to expect proponents of these other conceptions to concede defeat without any argument (as this would be dogmatic); and it would be wrong to attempt to overcome other such conceptions by assuming things about the world that they do not accept (as this would be question-begging); we must therefore attempt to show that these other conceptions are inadequate *on their own terms*, and are thus *self*-undermining, so that in the end if and when we arrive at a conception that is not inadequate in this way, we will have reached a conception that has established its legitimacy in a non-dogmatic and non-question-begging way. This is what is known as Hegel's method of *immanent critique*: to establish that his conception is the one that is best able to make us feel 'at home in the world', Hegel first sets out to show that these other conceptions cannot overcome the problems and puzzles that arise for them, so that they cannot claim to give us the kind of rational satisfaction that is required.

Thus, as a preliminary to Hegel's systematic position, the *Phenomenology* has the task of bringing out how each non-dialectical viewpoint involves some sort of self-contradiction; it is thus a 'way of despair' for ordinary consciousness (PS: §78, p. 49), as it comes to see that its conceptions are inadequate:

> this path is the conscious insight into the untruth of phenomenal knowledge, for which the supreme reality is what is in truth only the unrealized Notion ... The series of configurations which consciousness goes through along this road is, in reality, the detailed history of the *education* of consciousness itself to the standpoint of Science.
>
> (PS: §78, p. 50)

Hegel claims that because each inadequate stage of consciousness 'suffers this violence at its own hands' (PS: §80, p. 51), he can persuade consciousness to accept his position in a non-dogmatic and non-question-begging way, by showing that consciousness moves towards it of its own accord, as it seeks to make good on its own internal problems. We therefore do not need to assume anything about the world at the outset, or to use such assumptions to criticize consciousness: rather, '[c]onsciousness provides its own criterion from within itself' by which its adequacy can be judged, 'so that the investigation becomes a comparison of consciousness with itself' (PS: §84, p. 53). Thus, Hegel famously declares, 'since what consciousness examines is its own self, all that is left for us to do is simply to look on' (PS: §85, p. 54). Consciousness will find itself in the position of seeing that how it took things to be is somehow incoherent, and so will be forced to revise its outlook accordingly, until ultimately a conception is reached where it is able to see how to free itself from these problems, at which point 'knowledge no longer needs to go beyond itself, where knowledge finds itself, where Notion corresponds to object and object to Notion' (PS: §80, p. 51). However, while consciousness will move forward immanently in this way, without our having to motivate or impel it from the outside, what will not be apparent to consciousness is how exactly its new way of looking at things is related to its previous conception, and how this new conception has come about. As we have discussed, for Hegel this sort of shift involves a revision in how consciousness thinks about the world: but, in the *Phenomenology*, although consciousness undergoes these shifts, it is not aware that this is the driving mechanism behind them, so that here 'the *origination* of the new object ... presents itself to consciousness without its understanding how this happens, which proceeds for us, as it were, behind the back of consciousness' (PS: §87, p. 56). To consciousness, it appears that its understanding of the world develops because the world has revealed itself to it in a new way; but to us, as phenomenological observers, it is clear that this has only happened because consciousness has changed its way of thinking about the world, so that these cognitive shifts do not come about 'by chance and externally', but 'through a *reversal of consciousness itself*' (PS: §87, p. 55), as it moves from one conception to another by questioning some assumptions and taking on others. Only at the end of its journey is consciousness ready to understand what has happened to it and why; it is then able to think reflectively and self-consciously about the categorial shifts that have led it forward from one problematic position to the next, to the point at which 'it gets rid of the semblance of being burdened with something alien' (PS: §89, p. 56), and can at last feel at home in the world. Before such homecoming is possible, however, we must follow Hegel as (like Dante's Virgil) he guides us through the journey of the Soul, 'so that it may purify itself for the life of the Spirit, and achieve finally, through a completed experience of itself, the awareness of what it really is in itself' (PS: §77, p. 49).

CONTENT SUMMARY

PREFACE

§§1–4 (pp. 1–3)   The inadequacy of prefaces and the difficulties of properly engaging with a philosophical work.

§§5–6 (pp. 3–4)   How philosophy is a 'science' (*Wissenschaft*) and hence systematic.

§§7–16 (pp. 4–9)   How the present time is right for the proper development of this science, which until now has not been possible, leading to an inadequate formalism (Schelling).

§§17–23 (pp. 9–13)   A preliminary exposition of some of Hegel's central doctrines, viz. that the true or absolute is not only substance, but also subject; and that it is a developing whole.

§24 (pp. 13–14)   Knowledge must therefore be systematic, to grasp this whole.

§25 (p. 14)   One way of putting these ideas is that the Absolute is Spirit.

§§26–37 (pp. 14–22)   In order to grasp these philosophical doctrines, ordinary consciousness requires a ladder to the standpoint of science; the development of this knowledge is what is outlined in this work, thereby reaching the level of conceptual thought.

§§38–47 (pp. 22–28)   This development requires the overcoming of false viewpoints on the way to the truth; but this is necessary for a proper grasp of the truth, at least in philosophy, which differs in this respect from history and mathematics.

§§48–55 (pp. 28–34)   The need to avoid schematizing formalism in the method of science.

§§56–59 (pp. 34–36)   How the method of this science needs to be speculative, in following the movement of its subject matter.

§§60–66 (pp. 36–41)   How this speculative approach views the relation between subjects and predicates, substances and attributes, in a dialectical manner.

§§67–70 (pp. 41–43)   How philosophy differs from and relates to other ways of thinking, such as common sense.

§§71–72 (pp. 44–45)   Hegel's hopes for the reception of the work.

INTRODUCTION

§§73–75 (pp. 46–48)   The instrument view of knowledge (Kant), and why this view should be resisted.

§§76–80 (pp. 48–52)   But still, it is not enough to just dog-matically proclaim a philosophical position to be true and hence science; other views must be shown to be inadequate, out of which science 'appears'.

§§81–85 (pp. 52–53)   The problem of the criterion, and how this is resolved using the method of immanent critique.

§§86–89 (pp. 55–57)   The investigation therefore involves observing the experience of consciousness, as it develops in a systematic manner.

2

THE DIALECTIC OF THE OBJECT
(*PHENOMENOLOGY*, A. CONSCIOUSNESS)

SENSE-CERTAINTY

The first chapter of the *Phenomenology*, on Consciousness, opens with a section on 'Sense-Certainty: Or the "This" and "Meaning"'. At the most general level, commentators are agreed about how Hegel intended us to conceive of sense-certainty, namely, as a form of consciousness that thinks the best way to gain knowledge of the world is to experience it directly or intuitively, without applying concepts to it: what Hegel calls 'immediate' rather than 'mediated' knowledge, which involves '*ap*prehension' rather than '*com*prehension' (PS: §90, p. 58).[1] It is clear that Hegel thinks that this is the most elementary and fundamental way we have of thinking about how the mind relates to the world, which is why he begins the *Phenomenology* here. At the same time, Hegel wishes to bring out how sense-certainty gains its attractiveness by trading on a commitment that appears plausible, but which turns out to be highly problematic, and once this is recognized our attachment to sense-certainty as a paradigm of knowledge will be lost.

What is the deceptively plausible commitment underlying sense-certainty? At this point, there is disagreement among commentators. For some interpreters, the motivation behind sense-certainty is a commitment to epistemic foundationalism, which posits direct intuitive experience as giving us the kind of unshakeable hook-up to the world on which knowledge is built; for others, it is a commitment to empiricism, according to which intuitive knowledge is prior to conceptual knowledge, because empirical concepts are learned and get their meaning by being linked to objects as they are given in experience; and for yet others, it is a commitment to realism, which holds that if the mind is not to distort or create the world, it needs to be in a position to gain access to the world in a passive manner without the mediation of conceptual activity, so the kind of direct experience envisaged by sense-certainty must be fundamental. Thus, some commentators take Hegel's principal target in this chapter to be epistemic foundationalism (cf. deVries 1988a: 305); others take it to be concept empiricism (cf. K. R. Westphal 2000: §5); and others take it to be realism (cf. Craig 1987: 205–19).

Now, Hegel certainly associates all these attitudes with sense-certainty in his preliminary characterization of it, saying that it claims to be the *'richest'* and *'truest'* form of knowledge in so far as it involves merely 'reaching out' to things, without 'omitting anything' from them (PS: §91, p. 58). However, it is arguable that although the outlook of sense-certainty is indeed foundationalist, empiricist, and realist, there is a yet deeper assumption here that is really Hegel's more fundamental concern. This is the assumption that because it does not use concepts, sense-certainty is in a position to grasp a thing as *an individual*, without any abstraction from its unique specificity or pure particularity, and that in so doing sense-certainty gives us the most important kind of knowledge, which is of things as concrete, singular entities: for this reason sense-certainty prioritizes the one-to-one relation of direct experience over the generality and abstractness of thought, and so treats apprehension as more fundamental than comprehension. (An account of sense-certainty along these lines can be found in the writings of Hegel's existentialist critics, from Ludwig Feuerbach onwards: see De Nys 1978 for discussion and further references.) This reading of the chapter on sense-certainty fits in with that offered above of the *Phenomenology* as a whole, according to which the *Phenomenology* takes us through a series of inadequate standpoints which reveal how our handling of the categories of individual and universal is one-sided. As we shall see as we proceed through the remaining chapters of Consciousness, through Perception and into Force and the Understanding, Hegel tries to show that consciousness' impoverished conception of these two categories consistently leads it into difficulties, thereby bringing out the dialectical limitations in its thinking.

Hegel emphasizes that for sense-certainty it is the individuality of the object that is taken to be ontologically fundamental; as he puts it towards the end of the section, sense-certainty holds that 'the existence of *external* objects, which can be more precisely defined as *actual*, absolutely *singular, wholly personal, individual* things, each of them absolutely unlike anything else' has 'absolute certainty and truth' (PS: §110, p. 66). The aim of this section is then to bring out how sense-certainty's aconceptual view of knowledge appears natural to it because it conceives of individuality in this way, as something an object has *apart from* universality and particularity; by showing how this conception is problematic, consciousness comes to see how this view of knowledge is mistaken, and that its epistemic paradigm is ill-founded.

Sense-certainty adopts its aconceptual view of knowledge because it thinks that it will grasp what constitutes the unique essence of the thing as an individual only if it does not use concepts in knowing that individual; for (sense-certainty holds) concepts can be applied to many different things, and so cannot tell us about the thing qua individual. This unique nature belonging to each entity is traditionally called 'haecceitas' or 'thisness'. In so far as it has this unique nature, the individual is claimed to be irreducible to any shareable qualities and so is said to be ontologically prior to any such qualities, in being what it is in a way that is wholly unlike anything else; it therefore appears to sense-certainty that it can be grasped by the subject or I directly, without any conceptual activity being required:

Consciousness, for its part, is in this certainty only as a pure 'I'; or I am in it only as a pure 'This', and the object similarly only as a pure 'This'. I, *this* particular I, am certain of *this* particular thing, not because I, *qua* consciousness, in knowing it have developed myself or thought about it in various ways; and also not because *the thing* of which I am certain, in virtue of a host of distinct qualities, would be in its own self a rich complex of connections, or related in various ways to other things. Neither of these has anything to do with the truth of sense-certainty: here neither I nor the thing has the significance of a complex process of mediation; the 'I' does not have the significance of a manifold imagining or thinking; nor does the 'thing' signify something that has a host of qualities. On the contrary, the thing *is*, and it *is*, merely because it *is*. It *is*; this is the essential point for sense-knowledge, and this pure *being*, or this simple immediacy, constitutes its *truth*. Similarly, certainty as a *connection* is an *immediate* pure connection: consciousness is 'I', nothing more, a pure 'This'; the singular consciousness knows a pure 'This', or the single item.

(PS: §91, pp. 58–59)

In so far as sense-certainty maintains that the being of the object is constituted by its unique individuality in this way, sense-certainty naturally also holds that knowledge needs to be aconceptual, and that such knowledge is the '*richest*' and '*truest*': for (it holds) if we bring in concepts, we bring in general terms that can only take us away from knowing the object in its singularity (cf. EL: §38, p. 62, 'Empiricism ... leaves thought no powers except abstraction and formal universality and identity.'). What Hegel sets out to show, however, is that 'in the event, this very *certainty* proves itself to be the most abstract and poorest *truth*' (PS: §91, p. 58).

Now, as Hegel points out, sense-certainty faces a difficulty straight away, as it is hard to see how sense-certainty can claim to be aware of nothing but the object before it as a singular individual, when it is also aware of itself as a subject having this experience of the object:

Among the countless differences cropping up here we find in every case that the crucial one is that, in sense-certainty, pure being at once splits up into what we have called the two 'Thises', one 'This' as 'I', and the other 'This' as object.

(PS: §92, p. 59)

At this stage, however, sense-certainty claims that although consciousness is aware of itself as a subject, the object is independent of it, so that the object is still a self-subsistent and singular individual that can be known immediately:

But the object *is*: it is what is true, or it is the essence. It is, regardless of whether it is known or not; and it remains, even if it is not known, whereas there is no knowledge if the object is not there.

(PS: §93, p. 59)

Having set up the basic outlook of sense-certainty, Hegel now begins to probe its coherence, by asking 'whether in sense-certainty itself the object is in fact the kind of essence that sense-certainty proclaims it to be' (PS: §94, p. 59).

Hegel's central strategy against sense-certainty is to argue that what sense-certainty grasps in experience is not unique to the individual object, so that apprehension has no advantage over conception in this regard; sense-certainty therefore cannot claim that it is justified in treating the individual as a 'this' over and above its shared properties, so that the epistemic and metaphysical priority of the individual is hereby undermined. Hegel begins his argument by asking sense-certainty what its experience of the object tells us about it: 'It is, then, sense-certainty itself that must be asked: "What is the *This?*"' (PS: §95, p. 59). Sense-certainty responds by saying that for it the object is simply present: it exists here-and-now (cf. EL: §38Z, p. 62, 'From Empiricism came the cry: "Stop roaming in empty abstractions, keep your eyes open, lay hold on man and nature as they are here before you, enjoy the present moment" … Hence, this instinct seized upon the present, the Here, the This … '). However, Hegel proceeds to argue that 'existing here-and-now' is far from unique to the object, as different times and places can come to be 'here and now', and thus so can different things; sense-certainty has therefore failed to acquire knowledge of the object in its singular individuality, but only of a property that can belong to many individuals, and hence is universal:

> in this simplicity [Now] is indifferent to what happens in it; just as little as Night and Day are its being, just as much also is it Day and Night; it is not in the least affected by this its other-being. A simple thing of this kind which *is* through negation, which is neither This nor That, a *not-This*, and is with equal indifference This as well as That – such a thing we call a *universal*. So it is in fact the universal that is the true [content] of sense-certainty ... The same will be the case with the other form of 'This', with 'Here'. 'Here' is, e.g., the tree. If I turn round, this truth has vanished and is converted into its opposite: 'No tree is here, but a house instead'. 'Here' itself does not vanish; on the contrary, it abides constant in the vanishing of the house, the tree, etc., and is indifferently house or tree. Again, therefore, the 'This' shows itself to be a *mediated simplicity*, or a *universality* ... [S]ense-certainty has demonstrated in its own self that the truth of its object is the universal.
>
> (PS: §96, §98 and §99: pp. 60–61)

Hegel therefore poses a dilemma for sense-certainty. The first option is that sense-certainty may insist that knowledge of the object requires that we grasp its unique essence; but then it must allow that such knowledge is unattainable because it turns out that nothing we can know about the object is unique to it, if we stick just to sense-certainty. The second option is that sense-certainty may deny that the object has any such unique essence, in which case there is no reason not to use concepts in seeking knowledge, and so no grounds for prioritizing sense-certainty as an epistemic position. Hegel articulates this dilemma most clearly at the end of the section, where he sums up his position against those who assert that 'the reality or being of external things taken as Thises or sense-objects has absolute truth for consciousness' (PS: §109, p. 65):

> If they actually wanted to *say* 'this' bit of paper which they mean, if they wanted to *say* it, then this is impossible, because the sensuous This that is meant *cannot be reached* by language, which belongs to

consciousness, i.e. to that which is inherently universal. In the actual attempt to say it, it would therefore crumble away; those who started to describe it would not be able to complete the description, but would be compelled to leave it to others, who would themselves finally have to admit to speaking about something which *is not*. They certainly mean, then, *this* bit of paper here which is quite different from the bit mentioned above; but they say 'actual *things*', '*external* or *sensuous objects*', '*absolutely singular entities*' and so on; i.e. they say of them only what is *universal*. Consequently, what is called the unutterable is nothing else than the untrue, the irrational, what is merely meant [but is not actually expressed].

(PS: §110, p. 66)

Before reaching this conclusion, however, Hegel allows sense-certainty to try to respond to its initial difficulty, of finding that 'Now' and 'Here' cannot constitute the unique individuating nature it is looking for, as many things can be 'Now' and 'Here'. Sense-certainty's first response is to try to make 'Now' and 'Here' a unique characteristic of *this* individual, because it is the only thing that is currently present in *my* experience qua subject. Hegel's response, however, is to point out that *other* things are present in the experience of *other* subjects, so there is nothing in this relation to a subject that individuates the object as such:

I, *this* 'I', see the tree and assert that 'Here' as a tree; but another 'I' sees the house and maintains that 'Here' is not a tree but a house instead. Both truths have the same authentication, viz. the immediacy of seeing, and the certainty and assurance that both have about their knowing; but the one truth vanishes in the other ... The 'I' is merely universal like 'Now', 'Here', or 'This' in general.

(PS: §§101–2, pp. 61–62)

In order to avoid this difficulty, sense-certainty then asserts the unique individuality of the object it is experiencing here and now by trying to ignore the existence of any other such subjects, times, and places:

I, *this* 'I', assert then the 'Here' as a tree, and do not turn round so that the Here would become for me *not* a tree; also, I take no notice of the fact that another 'I' sees the Here as *not* a tree, or that I myself at another time take the Here as not-tree, the Now as not-day. On the contrary, I am a pure [act of] intuiting.

(PS: §104, pp. 62–63)

The difficulty for sense-certainty at this point, however, is that if it does not acknowledge the existence of other places, times, subjects, and objects, it can only give an ostensive designation of what it means by 'Now', 'Here', 'I', and 'This', by pointing and saying 'Now', and so on: but this act of pointing can at best indicate a punctual present that is no longer present as soon as it is pointed out. If sense-certainty tries to get round this by trying to claim that 'Now' is a plurality of moments and hence extends long enough to be picked out, and 'Here' is a plurality of places likewise, it has been forced to abandon its solipsistic position and accept that the 'Now' can be applied to many times and the 'Here' to many places; it has then failed to avoid the admission that 'Now' and 'Here' are universal, and hence are unable to provide the kind of unique individuation it is looking for (see PS: §§107–9, pp. 64–65).

Sense-certainty therefore ends up unable to make good the kind of ontological commitment underpinning its conception of knowledge: as Marcuse has put it, 'Sense-experience has thus itself demonstrated that its real content is not the particular but the universal' (Marcuse 1955: 106). It is sometimes alleged that Hegel is here attacking the metaphysical view that there are individuals at all (cf. Löwith 1971: 140, 'Hegel's answer is abstract: what remains is only the "universal" which is indifferent to everything that exists here and now'); but this seems mistaken, as all Hegel is criticizing is the view that the individual qua individual cannot be conceived or thought about, but only apprehended, because only apprehension transcends what is universal and reaches the individual. Hegel's argument, as we have seen, is that even apprehension does not transcend the universal, for in apprehension we are just aware of the object as a 'this', which does not constitute the object's distinctive particularity, but rather its most abstract and universal character. Assuming rather than denying our capacity to grasp individuals, Hegel therefore concludes that knowledge of individuals cannot require us to go beyond universality in the way sense-certainty supposes. Adopting the method of immanent critique, Hegel has thus brought out how such metaphysical misconceptions can have philosophical consequences that are profoundly distorting; by diagnosing these misconceptions, Hegel hopes that as phenomenological observers we will no longer be tempted to adopt the one-sided epistemology of sense-certainty. As the next section on 'Perception: Or the Thing and Deception' will show, however, while consciousness itself may have learnt to reject sense-certainty, the position it now takes up instead will prove equally problematic, as consciousness responds to the difficulties faced by sense-certainty by attempting to go beyond it in an inadequate way, with a conception of individuality and universality that is still limited.

PERCEPTION

Having come to see that it cannot coherently think of individuality in terms of some sort of unique individuating essence, consciousness is now ready to conceive of individuals as being constituted by characteristics they have in common with other individuals, and so to think in terms of universality as well as individuality. Hegel therefore describes the transition from 'Sense-certainty' to the following section on 'Perception' in these terms:

> Immediate certainty does not take over the truth, for its truth is the universal, whereas certainty wants to apprehend the This. Perception, on the other hand, takes what is present to it as a universal ... Since the principle of the object, the universal, is in its simplicity a *mediated* universal, the object must express this its nature in its own self. This it does by showing itself to be *the thing with many properties*.
>
> (PS: §111, p. 67)

However, because perception is still at the level of sense-experience, the universals out of which it takes individuals to be constituted are of the simplest kind, that is, they are sensible properties, like being white, cubical, tart, and so on. As Hegel makes clear at the end of the section, this introduction of a limited conception of universality will in fact turn out to be inadequate: 'Thus the singular being of sense [at the level of sense-certainty] does indeed vanish in the dialectical movement of immediate certainty and [at the level of perception] becomes universality, but it is only a *sensuous universality*' (PS: §130, p. 77). The aim of this section is therefore to bring out that consciousness gets into difficulties if it only conceives of universals in these limited terms, difficulties that lead it to lose faith in the very ontology of things and properties on which this conception is based, and to turn to the more radical ontology of forces discussed in the following section, out of which a different conception of universality will emerge.

At first, however, the position of perception appears satisfactory and straightforward, even commonsensical: consciousness here conceives of objects as combinations of sensible properties, and so treats each individual as a bundle of universals, as an 'Also':

> This abstract universal medium, which can be called simply 'thing-hood' or 'pure essence', is nothing else than what Here and Now have proved themselves to be, viz. a *simple togetherness* of a plurality; but the many are, *in their determinateness*, simple universals them-selves. This salt is a simple Here, and at the same time manifold; it is white and *also* tart, *also* cubical in shape, of a specific weight, etc. All these many properties are in a single simple 'Here', in which, there-fore, they interpenetrate; none has a different Here from the others, but each is everywhere, in the same Here in which the others are. And, at the same time, without being separated by different Heres, they do not affect each other in this interpenetration. The whiteness does not affect the cubical shape, and neither affects the tart taste, etc.; on the contrary, since each is itself a simple relating of self to self it leaves the others alone, and is connected with them only by the indifferent Also. This Also is thus the pure universal itself, or the medium, the 'thinghood', which holds them together in this way.
>
> (PS: §113, p. 68–69; translation modified)

Perception thus treats each individual as a co-instantiation of some collection of property-instances in a single spatial region, so that (for example) this piece of salt is seen as nothing more than exemplifications of whiteness, tartness, and so on coexisting together in one place. Having introduced what is traditionally known as a 'bundle view' of the object as an 'Also', Hegel now argues that this view proves unstable, and gives rise to its opposite, which takes the object to be a 'One', that is, a unified substance or substratum over and above its properties:

> In the relationship which has thus emerged it is only the character of positive universality that is at first observed and developed; but a further side presents itself, which must also be taken into consideration. To wit, if the many determinate properties were strictly indifferent to one another, if they were simply and solely self-related, they would not be determinate; for they are only determinate in so far as they *differentiate* themselves from one another, and *relate* themselves *to others* as to their opposites. Yet; as thus opposed to one another they cannot be together in the simple unity of their medium, which is just as essential to them as negation; the differentiation of the properties, in so far as it is not an indifferent differentiation but is exclusive, each property negating the others, thus falls outside of this simple medium; and the medium, therefore, is not merely an Also, an indifferent unity, but a *One* as well, a unity which *excludes* an other. The One is the *moment of negation*; it is itself quite simply a relation of self to self and it excludes an other; and it is that by which 'thinghood' is determined as a Thing.
>
> (PS: §114, p. 69)

Unfortunately, this passage is rather obscure and hard to interpret. One interesting reading of it is given by Charles Taylor (see Taylor 1972: 168–71). He suggests that Hegel is claiming that we can only think of properties as determinate by contrasting them with other properties, but this notion of properties being contrasted with others requires us to think that nothing which has one could have another ('nothing can be red and green all over', 'nothing can be square and round', and so on); but (Taylor suggests) 'of course, without the notion of a particular or something closely resembling a particular, such a phrase would be meaningless; for it is only of particulars, of things that can bear properties, that one can say that they cannot be both red and green' (ibid.: 170). Thus, on Taylor's view, Hegel's move from the 'Also' to the 'One' is designed to show that 'there is a kind of mutual dependency here, that we couldn't logically have our property concepts if we didn't operate with particulars' (ibid.: 169).

However, the difficulty with this reading is that it mistakes the position from which the argument starts, and so fails as an interpretation. According to Taylor, the position that treats the thing as an 'Also' is said to hold that 'properties ... [exist] alongside each other in the universe but not bound together into particulars' (ibid.: 169–70). But, on my account, to conceive of the object as an 'Also' is not to deny that it is a particular, because on the bundle view we can still conceive of the object as (for example) 'this piece of salt'; it is just that the particular object is viewed as nothing over and above the instantiated universals that constitute it. I therefore think Taylor is wrong to characterize the position Hegel starts from here as one that lacks the concept of a particular altogether: it just conceives of particulars in a certain way (as bundles of instantiated universals).

So, is there another way of understanding Hegel's position here? An alternative reading can be developed by comparing the passage we are considering to the following paragraph from F. H. Bradley's *Appearance and Reality*:

We may take the familiar instance of a lump of sugar. This is a thing, and it has properties, adjectives which qualify it. It is, for example, white, and hard, and sweet. The sugar, we say, *is* all that; but what the *is* can really mean seems doubtful. A thing is not any one of its qualities, if you take that quality by itself; if 'sweet' were the same as 'simply sweet' the thing would clearly be not sweet. And, again, in so far as sugar is sweet it is not white or hard; for these properties are all distinct. Nor, again, can the thing be all its properties, if you take them each severally. Sugar is obviously not mere whiteness, mere hardness, and mere sweetness; for its reality lies somehow in its unity. But if, on the other hand, we inquire what there can be in the thing beside its several qualities, we are baffled once more. We can discover no real unity existing outside these qualities, or, again, existing within them.

(Bradley 1930: 16)

Now, Bradley does not here refer explicitly to Hegel (though his example of a lump of sugar may be supposed to recall Hegel's similar example of a piece of salt), and he is not writing as a commentator on the *Phenomenology*: nonetheless, there are interesting parallels between the two passages, and the argument of the one may help shed light on the argument of the other.

Like Hegel, Bradley here moves from a bundle view to a substratum/attribute view. He begins by taking the reductionist position of the bundle theorist, who identifies the individual thing with its properties ('It is, for example, white, and hard, and sweet'). He then asks how we can say that this is so, as this would make the single individual identical with three distinct properties. He argues that this difficulty cannot be evaded by making the thing identical with just one of these properties, because it is no more identical with this one property than the others, in so far as it also has other properties and these are distinct. Nor can the difficulty be evaded by making the thing identical with all the properties taken together as a collection: for they are many and the thing is one ('Sugar is obviously not mere whiteness, mere hardness, and mere sweetness; for its reality lies somehow in its unity', where here by 'Sugar' Bradley would appear to still mean the individual lump of sugar, rather than the stuff or kind). Faced with this puzzle, Bradley then introduces the substratum/attribute view, which holds that the unity of the thing is something over and above its many qualities: rather than identifying the individual with its properties, these are now seen as inhering in it, so that the 'is' can now be treated as an 'is' of predication rather than an 'is' of identity. However, Bradley then raises the traditional objection, that we are now left with the baffling idea of the thing as a 'bare particular', lacking in any properties (cf. Hume 1978: 16, '[N]one will assert, that substance is either a colour, or a sound, or a taste ... We have therefore no idea of substance, distinct from that of a collection of particular qualities, nor have we any other meaning when we talk or reason concerning it.').

Now, the passage from the *Phenomenology* we have been considering may be made less mysterious by interpreting it in the light of Bradley's argument. (For further helpful discussion of that argument, see Baxter 1996.) Thus, Hegel may be understood as suggesting that there is something unsatisfactory in the bundle view of the object as a co-instantiation of property instances (of the thing as an 'Also') as soon as we realize that these properties are distinct from one another, as they must be if they are to be determinate ('for they are only determinate in so far as they *differentiate* themselves from one another, and *relate* themselves *to others* as to their opposites'). For it then appears that we cannot identify *this* individual with *these* properties, for then it would be many and not one ('Yet; as thus opposed to one another they cannot be together in the simple unity of their medium, which is just as essential to them as negation'). We may then distinguish the thing as one from the properties as many, at which point we have arrived at the substratum/attribute view, of universals as predicates inhering in (rather than constituting) the individual thing. Thus, Hegel uses the one/many problem to get us from the bundle view to the substratum/attribute view, in a way that Bradley also adopted. Moreover, as we shall see shortly, Hegel like Bradley thought that the substratum/attribute view is just as problematic as the bundle view; but where Bradley went on to claim that this means we can never reach a coherent view of reality, Hegel merely took this puzzle to show that we must start with a deeper conception of universality than that adopted here by perception. (For more on the general issue of how Bradley's pessimism contrasts with Hegel's rationalistic optimism, see Stern 1993b: 200–204; Stern 2009: 333–37.)

Before we see how Hegel's discussion develops along these lines, it is interesting to ask whether the Hegel/Bradley attempt to undermine the bundle view succeeds. One standard objection to Bradley's argument (and thus to Hegel's on this Bradleyan reading) is that he fails to distinguish the 'is' of identity from the 'is' of predication (cf. Blanshard 1984: 217–18). But this objection appears misguided, as in fact the argument seems designed to take us *from* the 'is' of identity adopted by the bundle view *to* the 'is' of predication adopted by the substratum/attribute view (where this is then shown to be no more satisfactory as a way of understanding the 'is' than the bundle theorist's identity conception, because the thing of which the attribute is predicated becomes a mysterious bare particular). Another objection might be that as so far presented, the Hegel/Bradley argument overlooks an obvious response by the bundle theorist, namely, that the thing is identical with its properties *in some relation to one another*, where that relation is sufficient to make the several properties into a single individual. Now, in fact Bradley himself does consider this option, and deals with it largely by moving on to question whether relations can possibly make a many into a one in this way, or whether the many/one issue will always re-emerge (see Bradley 1930: 16–23). Hegel, however, does not consider this objection, and offers no such general argument against relations; but in fact this is not necessarily a difficulty. For, it should be remembered that at this point the universals he is considering are property-universals (whiteness, tartness, etc.), between which no relation holds, so that their diversity cannot be overcome in this way (as Hegel himself puts it: 'The whiteness does not affect the cubical shape, and neither affects the tart taste, etc.; on the contrary, since each is a simple relating of self to self it leaves the others alone, and is connected with them only by the indifferent Also' (PS: §113, pp. 68–69)).

Thus, having begun with the bundle theory of the object, Hegel uses the one/many problem to show how consciousness cannot retain the reductionist conception of the individual with which it began, so that we arrive at the substratum/attribute conception instead. Hegel now sets out to show that consciousness cannot rest content with either view, claiming that '[i]t is only a matter of developing the contradictions that are present therein' (PS: §117, p. 70). Hegel argues that consciousness oscillates between the one conception and the other, sometimes treating the object as a bundle of properties which then undermines its sense that the object is really a unified individual distinct from other individuals, and sometimes treating the object as a unity over and above its plurality of properties, which then leads to the idea of a characterless substratum and back to the 'This' of sense-certainty. Perception cannot decide which conception is the correct characterization of how things are, and which conception merely results from the delusive influence on us of how things appear to us to be:

> The object which I apprehend presents itself purely as a *One*; but I also perceive in it a property which is *universal*, and which thereby transcends the singularity [of the object]. The first being of the objective essence as a One was therefore not its true being. But since the *object* is what is true, the untruth falls in me; my apprehension was not correct. On account of the *universality* of the property, I must rather take the objective essence to be on the whole a *community*. I now further perceive the property to be *determinate*, *opposed* to another and excluding it. Thus I did not in fact apprehend the objective essence correctly when I defined it as a *community* with others, or as a continuity; on account of the *determinateness* of the property, I must break up the continuity and posit the objective essence as a One that excludes.
>
> (PS: §117, pp. 70–71)

Faced with this twofold way of viewing the object, as one and as many, perception is torn between on the one hand making the object independent of its plurality of properties, and treating them as secondary, and so as holding that 'the Thing is white only to *our eyes*, *also* tart to *our* tongue, *also* cubical to *our* touch, and so on' (PS: §119, p. 72), and on the other hand attributing these properties to the object itself, to give it a way of distinguishing it from other things and to avoid making the object's nature indeterminate, so that on this view 'it is in truth, then, the Thing itself that is white, and *also* cubical, *also* tart, and so on' (PS: §121, p. 73). Corresponding to this twofold view of the object, there is a twofold view of the role of the subject, as either breaking up the unity of the object into a plurality of properties, or as holding together that plurality into a unity; as Hegel puts it,

> If we look back on what consciousness previously took, and now takes, responsibility for, on what it previously ascribed, and now ascribes, to the Thing, we see that consciousness alternately makes

> itself, as well as the Thing, into both a pure, many-less *One*, and into an *Also* that resolves itself into independent 'matters'.
>
> (PS: §122, p. 74)

At this stage, failing to find any way to decide which way of viewing the thing is correct and which delusive, consciousness now attributes both unity and diversity to the object itself, and attempts to render this view consistent by treating the manifold properties as inessential; but because it is only these properties that distinguish it from anything else, consciousness is forced to admit that they are nonetheless necessary to the object, so the distinction between essential and inessential here collapses: 'This, however, is a distinction that is still only nominal; the unessential, which is none the less supposed to be necessary, cancels itself out' (PS: §127, p. 76).

Hegel therefore offers his diagnosis of what has gone wrong here, which, as we have already pointed out, focuses on the inadequate conception of the categories of universality and individuality being used by perception: while perception has some grasp of the category of universal, it is an extremely limited conception, which treats universals as simple sensuous property instances like 'white' and 'cubical'; this has led it to reduce the object to a plurality of unrelated attributes, with all the consequent difficulties that Hegel has analysed:

> Thus the object in its pure determinateness, or in the determinatenesses which were supposed to constitute its essential being, is overcome just as surely as it was in its sensuous being. From a sensuous being [at the level of sense-certainty] it turned into a universal [at the level of perception]; but this universal, since it *originates in the sensuous*, is essentially *conditioned* by it, and hence is not truly a self-identical universality at all, but one *afflicted with an opposition*; for this reason the universality splits into the extremes of singular individuality and universality, into the One of the properties, and the Also of the 'free matters' ... The sophistry of perception seeks to save these moments from their contradiction, and it seeks to lay hold on the truth, by distinguishing the *aspects*, by sticking to the 'Also' and to the 'in so far', and finally, by distinguishing the 'unessential'

aspect from an 'essence' which is opposed to it. But these expedients, instead of warding off deception in the process of apprehension, prove themselves on the contrary to be quite empty; and the truth which is supposed to be won by this logic of the perceptual process proves to be in one and the same respect the opposite [of itself] and thus to have as its essence a universality which is devoid of distinctions and determinations.

(PS: §§129–30, pp. 76–77)

Thus, what this section is meant to show, is that although there is some advance in moving from the irreducible individuality of sense-certainty to the instances of property-universals recognized by perception, this does not take us far enough; for, as the problems encountered by perception have revealed, '[t]he lowest conception one can have of the universal in its connexion with the individual is this external relation of it as merely a common element' (SL: 621). Faced with an irresolvable oscillation between two equally unsatisfactory accounts of 'the Thing' as 'One' and as 'Also' which has resulted from this conception of the universal, consciousness now abandons this ontology, and takes up instead the ontology of 'Force', which is the focus of the next section, as Hegel moves from Perception to Understanding.

FORCE AND THE UNDERSTANDING

In the 'Perception' section, consciousness has failed to find rational satisfaction in the ordinary world of common sense, with its ontology of things and properties, as this has led it into a dialectic of one individual and many properties which it did not have the resources to resolve. In 'Force and the Understanding', consciousness tries to get round this difficulty by setting aside common-sense ontology, and moving to a metaphysical picture that replaces the objects of ordinary sense-experience with the very different conception of the world presented to us by the natural sciences, where the 'manifest image' of things and properties is set aside in favour of the 'scientific image' of the world favoured by physics, in which this common-sense ontology is rejected (to use the terminology of Sellars 1963).

Where today we might think of this scientific image in terms of the radically revisionary metaphysics of quantum theory, in Hegel's time this scientific conception was centred on the notion of force, which appeared to open up a picture of the world very different from that presented to us by sense-experience. The concept of force came to dominate eighteenth-century physics through the work of Newton, while it plays a prominent role in the thought of Descartes, Leibniz, and Kant. In particular, Kant's dynamical view of matter was taken up by Fichte and Schelling and so became incorporated into the development of the *Naturphilosophie* (philosophy of nature) of the German idealists (for a helpful historical overview, see Lunteren 1993). In view of the centrality of this concept in making possible a new picture of reality that departed from the traditional ontology of material substances, it has been observed that

> [i]f one wanted to characterize the general scientific approach of the eighteenth-century by means of a single concept, there would be much to be said for selecting the notion of *force* ... [T]he diversity of contexts within which it was being applied [included] ... classical mechanics ... , fluid mechanics, magnetism and electricity, chemistry, biology and medicine, as well as psychology, ethics, aesthetics and physio-theology.
>
> (Neuser 1993: 383–84)

Now, in his discussion of force, Hegel's attitude is characteristically nuanced: for, while he sees how in one sense the notion of force is attractive, in that it appears to get over the aporia faced by the common-sense conception of things and properties, he also tries to show how this 'scientific image' is itself problematic, in so far as it takes us too far away from the common-sense conception, and so once again leads to a puzzle concerning individuality and universality. He thus distances himself from the contemporary philosophical enthusiasm for the notion of force, trying to show that it is not possible to solve our philosophical difficulties simply by moving from the manifest to the scientific image.

Hegel begins by bringing out how turning to the scientific image might appear to represent an advance for consciousness; we no longer have to face the dialectic of one and many that applied to things, as reality is now conceived of as an interconnected whole of internally related forces: 'In other words, the "matters" posited as independent directly pass over into their unity, and their unity directly unfolds its diversity, and this once again reduces itself to unity. But this movement is what is called *Force*' (PS: §136, p. 81). This interconnectedness is not visible to us directly in the world given to sense-experience, where it appears that reality consists of distinct entities; but this pattern is now taken by consciousness to be merely the appearance of a more holistic structure of internally connected forces:

> From this we see that the Notion of Force becomes *actual* through its duplication into two Forces, and how it comes to be so. These two Forces exist as independent essences; but their existence is a movement of each towards the other, such that their being is rather a pure *positedness* or a being that is *posited by an other*; i.e. their being has really the significance of a sheer *vanishing* ... Consequently, these moments are not divided into two independent extremes offering each other only an opposite extreme: their essence rather consists simply and solely in this, that each *is* solely through the other, and what each thus is it immediately no longer is, since it *is* the other. They have thus, in fact, no substances of their own which might support and maintain them ... Thus the truth of Force remains only the *thought* of it; the moments of its actuality, their substances and their movement, collapse unresistingly into an undifferentiated unity ... This true essence of Things has now the character of not being immediately for consciousness; on the contrary, consciousness has a mediated relation to the inner being and, as the Understanding, *looks through this mediating play of Forces into the true background of Things*.
> (PS: §141 and §143, pp. 85–86)

Thus, according to the scientific theorist, consciousness cannot find rational satisfaction if it deals with the world as presented to us by sense-experience; if, however, it treats that world as a mere appearance, and instead thinks in terms of the more holistic notion of force as underlying that appearance, then (the theorist claims) a way can be found to overcome the one/many problem that faced perception: 'Within this *inner truth* ... the *absolute universal* ... has been purged of the *antithesis* between the universal and the individual and has become the object of the *Understanding*' (PS: §144, p. 87).

However, consciousness then discovers that a price must be paid if it attempts to escape the puzzles that arise out of our ordinary conception of the world by moving to the 'two-tier' view adopted by the scientific theorist: 'The inner world is, for consciousness, still a *pure beyond*, because consciousness does not yet find itself in it. It is *empty*, for it is merely the nothingness of appearance, and positively the *simple* or *unitary* universal' (PS: §146, p. 88). The difficulty Hegel presses is a familiar one: although moving from the manifest to the scientific image may help us escape the aporia of perception, the bifurcation in our world-view this entails creates as many problems as it solves, as once we go below the level of empirical phenomena, it becomes harder to defend the claim that we have cognitive access to this underlying reality, or to know what we can say about it: it thus becomes a 'super-sensible beyond', outside the reach of our intellectual powers. Thus, it seems that the scientific theorist cannot give us grounds for taking his picture of the world seriously from an ontological point of view, unless he can give grounds for taking this picture to be true; but how can such grounds be given, when we have gone beyond the direct evidence of the senses?

At this point, the understanding attempts to render this supersensible realm less mysterious by identifying it with the laws that govern the natural phenomena, which both stand above the phenomena and are instantiated in them:

> Consequently, the *supersensible* world is an inert *realm of laws* which, though beyond the perceived world – for this exhibits law only through incessant change – is equally *present* in it and is its direct tranquil image. This realm of laws is indeed the truth for the Understanding, and that truth has its *content* in the law.
>
> (PS: §149, pp. 90–91)

Hegel sees difficulties here, however. First, he argues that on this conception of law, it is natural for the understanding to look for some way of unifying its laws into a unified theory; but, when the laws thus coincide, they lose their specific character. The law becomes more and more superficial, and as a result what is found is, in fact, not the unity of *these specific* laws, but a law which leaves out their specific character.

(PS: §150, p. 91)

In other words, in becoming unified the laws become more general, and in becoming more general they lose their applicability to the concrete world. Second, he argues that an understanding of the world in terms of laws is incomplete, because it provides no answer to the question of why these laws obtain, when it appears that the universe could have obeyed other laws: 'But in all these forms [of law], necessity has shown itself to be only an empty word' (PS: §152, p. 93). Third, he claims that while laws may help us to think about phenomena in general terms, they describe rather than properly explain:

The single occurrence of lightning, e.g., is apprehended as a universal, and this universal is enunciated as the *law* of electricity; the 'explanation' then condenses the *law* into *Force* as the essence of the law ... In this tautological movement, the Understanding, as we have seen, sticks to the inert unity of the object, and the movement falls only within the Understanding itself, not within the object. It is an explanation that not only explains nothing, but is so obvious [*klar*] that, while it pretends to say something different from what has already been said, really says nothing at all but only repeats the same thing.

(PS: §§154–55, pp. 94–95, translation modified; cf. SL: 458–59)

Here, again, it seems that the laws of the Understanding do not take us much beyond the realm of 'appearance' and so we are left with the world of forces as a mysterious 'beyond'. Thus, whereas the understanding began with a conception of forces and laws as universals underlying the particular objects as they appear to us, it now sees that without the particularity of empirical phenomena, there would be no content to our talk of general laws; its claim to have established the priority of universality over particularity in this respect has therefore proved unstable.

Then, in a final flourish, Hegel puts forward the idea of the 'inverted world', as a kind of *reductio ad absurdum* of understanding's 'two-tier' conception of reality. Hegel had first used the term in his Introduction to the *Critical Journal of Philosophy* in 1801, where he comments that in its esoteric form, 'in its relationship to commonsense the world of philosophy is in and for itself an inverted world' (CJI: 283). His discussion of the inverted world in the *Phenomenology* is linked into his previous accounts of force and law in a way that is extremely hard to follow; but the general point seems to be that once the understanding posits a super-sensible world over and above the one apparent to ordinary experience, it then becomes very difficult for consciousness to say what the world is really like 'in itself':

> Looked at superficially, this inverted world is the opposite of the first in the sense that it has the latter outside of it and repels that world from itself as an inverted *actual world*: that the one is appearance, but the other the in-itself; that the one is the world as it is for an other, whereas the other is the world as it is for itself. So that to use the previous examples, what tastes sweet is *really*, or *inwardly* in the thing, sour; or what is north pole in the actual magnet in the world of appearance, would be south pole in the *inner* or *essential being*; what presents itself as oxygen pole in the phenomenon of electricity would be hydrogen pole in unmanifested electricity.
>
> (PS: §159, pp. 97–98)

In turning from the manifest to the scientific image, conscious-ness as understanding has therefore failed to attain rational satis-faction: by conceiving of the scientific image as a simple negation of the manifest image, all that can be ascribed to the 'inner' (and 'true') world is the opposite of whatever we perceive, none of which helps us to understand or explain what we perceive.

Hegel ends this section by adopting the standpoint of the 'we' (as phenomenological observers), telling us that from this stand-point, the dualism of the Understanding can be overcome dialectically in the concept of the *infinite*:

> From the idea, then, of inversion, which constitutes the essential nature of one aspect of the supersensible world, we must eliminate

the sensuous idea of fixing the differences in a different sustaining element ... Thus the supersensible world, which is the inverted world, has at the same time overarched the other world and has it within it; it is *for itself* the inverted world, i.e. the inversion of itself; it is itself and the opposite in one unity. Only thus is it difference as *inner* difference, or difference *in its own self*, or difference as an *infinity*.

(PS: §160, pp. 98–99)

Hegel explains that from this perspective, the problems that arise for the Understanding are really pseudo-problems, as they do not apply to the infinite so conceived: 'Accordingly, we do not need to ask the question, still less to think that fretting over such a question is philosophy, or even that it is a question philosophy cannot answer, the question, viz. "*How*, from this pure essence, how does difference or otherness *issue forth* from it?" For the division into two moments has already taken place, difference is excluded from the self-identical and set apart from it. What was supposed to be the *self-identical* is thus already one of these two moments instead of being the absolute essence' (PS: §162, p. 100). Here, then, we have a dialectical structure of identity-in-difference, where the infinite is not distinct from the finite, but rather contains the finite within it (cf. EL: §94Z, pp. 137–38). As Hegel makes clear, however, consciousness as Understanding is not yet ready to grasp the concept of the infinite in this way, and so is cut off from this resolution of its difficulties:

In the contrary law, as the inversion of the first law, or in the inner difference, it is true that infinity itself becomes the *object* of the Understanding; but once again the Understanding falls short of infinity as such, since it again apportions to two worlds, or to two substantial elements, that which is a difference in itself – the self-repulsion of the selfsame and the self-attraction of the unlike.

(PS: §164, pp. 101–2)

Unable to grasp for itself this solution to its difficulties, consciousness must look for satisfaction in another way, as it no longer appears it can find intellectual harmony with the world, and so achieve what it seeks, which is 'consciousness of itself in its otherness' (PS: §164, p. 102). *We* know this is possible, once consciousness overcomes its one-sidedness; but 'it is only *for us* that this truth exists, not yet for consciousness' (PS: §164, p. 102).

Thus, in the opening chapter of the *Phenomenology*, Hegel has shown how fundamental metaphysical and epistemological problems arise for consciousness because of the ways in which it has so far conceived of the relation between universals and individuals. Hegel has tried to demonstrate that none of these ways is adequate, as each leads consciousness into certain fundamental aporias, so that some new conception of these categories must be found if consciousness is to reach a rationally satisfactory metaphysical picture of the world. Consciousness does not grasp that new conception in the *Phenomenology*, however, as this is the job of the *Logic* for which this critical discussion is supposed to prepare it: all the *Phenomenology* is meant to show is that the options exemplified by sense-certainty, perception, and the understanding have failed, so that consciousness must come to a new way of thinking if these problematic standpoints are to be avoided. Put very briefly: Hegel argues in the *Logic* that what is required is a substance-kind conception of the universal, such as 'man' or 'horse', which escapes the one/many problem by being a *single* essential property of the individual taken as a unified entity, so that the individual is neither a mere bundle of diverse property-universals, nor a bare quality-less substratum; this conception is then sufficient to secure the common-sense ontology of objects without recourse to the two-tier picture of the Understanding. (Cf. PS: §62, p. 39, 'The universal is not meant to have merely the significance of a predicate, as if the proposition asserted only that the actual is universal; on the contrary, the universal is meant to express the essence of the actual.' Cf. also SL: 36–37, '[E]ach human being though infinitely unique is so primarily because he is a *man*, and each individual animal is such an individual primarily because it is an animal: if this is true, then it would be impossible to say what such an individual could still be if this foundation were removed, no matter how richly endowed the individual might be with other predicates, if, that is, this foundation can equally be called a predicate like the others.' For further discussion of Hegel's positive position, see Stern 1990.)

THE TRANSITION TO SELF-CONSCIOUSNESS

Having come this far, Hegel is on the threshold of moving into his discussion of self-consciousness, where the focus switches from how consciousness conceives of things in the world, to how it conceives of itself qua subject. It is not entirely clear, however, how this transition from the dialectic of the object to the dialectic of the subject is supposed to come about.

On one reading (e.g. Pippin 1989: 131–42, Rockmore 1997: 56–58, Stewart 2000: 59, 99–103), this transition is to be understood in essentially Kantian terms, in that what happens after the aporia of the inverted world is that consciousness comes to accept that '[t]he essence of appearances, the origin of the unity and order of appearances, is not some beyond, or some law like generalization, but the self-conscious activity of the understanding itself' (Pippin 1989: 139). This makes the transition from object to subject easy to explain: as the object turns out to be 'constructed' by the subject, it is natural that we should now turn from the former to the latter, and so move from consciousness to self-consciousness. The difficulty, however, is that this reading aligns Hegel's outlook closely to Kant's (a fact Pippin happily acknowledges: cf. Pippin 1989: 131, where he characterizes the chapter on Force as 'the first and most significant stage in [Hegel's] phenomenological justification of idealism'). This makes this reading of the transition contentious, as this Kantian treatment of Hegel is not universally accepted (cf. Stern 1990, Wartenberg 1993, K. R. Westphal 1989 and 1993a). Moreover, even if it is right that Hegel's claim that at this point 'the Understanding experiences only *itself*' should be taken in a Kantian spirit (which on a more realist reading is highly debatable), it is hard to see that this explains the transition to self-consciousness: for, as we have seen, at this point Hegel is adopting the standpoint of the 'we' as phenomenological observer, and not of consciousness *itself*; thus, when he states that *we* see that the 'Understanding experiences only *itself*', his implication would seem to be that consciousness itself does not. If this is so, then the transition from consciousness to self-consciousness cannot be explained in Kantian terms, as a realization *by consciousness* that it somehow determines the world.

A more neutral reading is possible, however, where what underpins the transition from consciousness to self-consciousness is not a shift from realism to idealism, but from *theory* to *practice*, where in theorizing we have a 'detached' view of the world, and so abstract from our position as subjects *in* the world, whereas in practical activity we act *on* the world and so put ourselves as subjects at the centre of things. (Cf. Kojève 1969: 37–38. See also Harris 1997: I, p. 308: 'Thus, a new journey starts here – the practical journey of self-consciousness that has theoretically "set itself on one side".') Hegel frequently contrasts the theoretical and practical attitudes in these terms (cf. LA: I, pp. 112–13, EN: I, §§245–47, pp. 195–205), where in the theoretical attitude we have our focus on the object, while in the practical one we subordinate the object to the subject; if we are supposed to move between these two attitudes at this point of the *Phenomenology*, this would then explain the shift from consciousness (which, like the theoretical attitude, is object-orientated) to self-consciousness (which, like the practical attitude, is subject-orientated). It certainly seems that it is the theoretical attitude that has predominated in the 'Force and the Understanding' section, and which is apparently brought to grief with the discussion of the inverted world. Hegel's characterization of the theoretical attitude in the Introduction to the second part of the *Encyclopedia* (his *Philosophy of Nature*) parallels the dialectic of the *Phenomenology* thus far, and helps shed some light upon it:

> In the theoretical approach (a) the initial factor is our withdrawing from natural things, leaving them as they are, and adjusting to them. In doing this we start from our sense-knowledge of nature. If physics were based only on perceptions, however, and perceptions were nothing but the evidence of the senses, the activity of a natural scientist would consist only of seeing, smelling, hearing, etc., so that animals would also be physicists ... (b) In the second relation of things to us, they either acquire the determination of universality for us, or we transform them into something universal. The more thought predominates in ordinary perceptiveness, so much the more does the naturalness, individuality, and immediacy of things vanish away. As thoughts invade the limitless multiformity of nature, its

richness is impoverished, its springtimes die, and there is a fading in the play of its colours. That which in nature was noisy with life, falls silent in the quietude of thought; its warm abundance, which shaped itself into a thousand intriguing wonders, withers into arid forms and shapeless generalities, which resemble a dull northern fog. (c) Both these determinations are opposed to both practical ones, and we also find that the theoretical approach is inwardly self-contradictory, for it appears to bring about the precise opposite of what it intends. We want to know the nature that really is, not something which is not, but instead of leaving it alone and accepting it as it is in truth, instead of taking it as given, we make something completely different out of it ... The theoretical approach begins by checking appetite, it is disinterested, it leaves things to subsist in their own way, and thus immediately displays two aspects, subject and object, the separation of which is fixed on this side and that. Our aim is rather to grasp and comprehend nature however, to make it ours, so that it is not something beyond and alien to us.

(EN: I, §246Z, pp. 197–98)

Much as he does in the *Phenomenology*, Hegel here portrays the theoretical attitude as a 'stepping back' from practical engagement with the world, in a way that sets the subject to one side; as a result, the world as the subject experiences it is lost, and is replaced by the scientific image put forward by the theorist, in a search for greater 'objectivity'. The lesson of the 'inverted world', however, is that consciousness then comes to feel that the nature of reality is ungraspable, and an apparently insuperable separation occurs between the subject and the object. Faced with this breakdown, consciousness naturally recoils from the theoretical attitude, and moves over to its opposite, the practical attitude. Here the engagement of the subject with the object is much more direct, as the subject once again becomes a being *in* the world, not just a disinterested spectator *of* it, so that the world regains its 'colour' once more. Thus, the transition here is what one might expect from the *Phenomenology* as a *via negativa*: having found that the scientific theorist's position has ended in incoherence by attempting to view the world in abstraction from how it appears to us as subjects within it, consciousness now sees the world as something that the subject can engage with directly through its practical relation to it, as nothing but a vehicle for its self-expression.

Now, in the *Philosophy of Nature* Hegel makes clear that the practical attitude can also be developed one-sidedly, as consciousness now seeks to 'master' the natural world (EN: I, §245Z, pp. 195–96). Likewise, in the *Phenomenology* Hegel concludes the Consciousness chapter by warning that in dispensing with the two-tier view of reality adopted by the theoretical attitude, consciousness may find that it has moved over too quickly to a subject-centred conception, in which it attempts to arrive at '*self-consciousness*, a reflectedness-into-self, conscious of itself in its otherness' (PS: §164, p. 102):

> It is manifest that behind the so-called curtain which is supposed to conceal the inner world, there is nothing to be seen unless *we* go behind it ourselves, as much in order that we may see, as that there may be something behind there which can be seen. But at the same time it is evident that we cannot without more ado go straightaway behind appearance. For this knowledge of what is the truth of appearance as ordinarily conceived, and of its inner being, is itself only a result of a complex movement whereby the modes of consciousness 'meaning', perceiving, and the Understanding, vanish: and it will be equally evident that the cognition of *what consciousness knows in knowing itself*, requires a still more complex movement, the exposition of which is contained in what follows.
>
> (PS: §165, p. 103)

It is this 'complex movement' that Hegel now proceeds to trace out.

CONTENT SUMMARY

SENSE-CERTAINTY

§§90–91 (pp. 58–59)   Characterization of sense-certainty as immediate and purely apprehensive, which is why this is initially taken by consciousness to be the richest and truest knowledge.

§§92–94 (p. 59)   There are two elements to this knowledge: the 'I' and the 'This' which it claims to know.

§§95–99 (pp. 59–61)   Sense-certainty claims to be directly acquainted with the individual 'This', as what is present Now and Here in its experience; but it cannot differentiate between individuals in these terms.

§§100–102 (pp. 61–62)   Nor can it differentiate between itself and other 'I's.

§§103–8 (pp. 62–64)   Nor can it differentiate between its 'I–This' relation and that between other subjects and objects.

§§109–10 (pp. 64–66)   A summary of what this discussion has shown us, namely that the ontology and epistemology of sense-certainty is inadequate: reality is not made up of bare individual Thises, to which the senses alone can give us privileged access.

PERCEPTION

§§111–12 (p. 67)   Learning the lessons of sense-certainty, consciousness now moves to the standpoint of *perception*, which treats the object as an individual thing with universal properties.

§§113–16 (pp. 68–70)   But there are two ways to see the relation between the individual object and its properties: as a bundle of properties ('Also') or as a single substance underlying its properties ('One'); the former view struggles to explain what makes the properties into a unity, while the latter struggles to differentiate one propertyless substratum from another.

§§117–22 (pp. 70–74)   To find a way out of this difficulty, consciousness distinguishes between the object itself and how it appears to consciousness, first by treating the object as One but its many properties as a product of our experience (§§119–20), and then treating the object as an Also but its unity as a product of our experience (§§121–22), which again is an oscillation it cannot resolve.

§§123–28 (pp. 74–76) Consciousness now tries to see the object as unified in itself, but as a plurality in relation to other things, treating the former as essential to it and the latter as inessential; but in fact both aspects are required to make sense of the object qua individual, so these distinctions collapse.

§129 (pp. 76–77) This points the way forward to the next section on the understanding, which treats the object in terms of 'free matters' and forces.

§§130–31 (pp. 77–79) A summary of what this discussion shows us, which is that the universal/individual relation grasped by perception remains superficial, as (like sense-certainty) it only operated at the sensuous level.

FORCE AND THE UNDERSTANDING

§§132–42 (pp. 79–86) Consciousness now goes beyond the purely sensuous, and conceives of objects as constituted by the play of invisible forces, which unify and dissolve the individual.

§§143–48 (pp. 86–90) These forces are seen as an inner realm, beyond appearances.

§§149–57 (pp. 90–97) This inner realm is conceived of in terms of laws that govern these forces; but the understanding struggles to give content to such laws.

§§158–60 (pp. 97–98) These problems lead to the idea of the 'inverted world', according to which everything is the opposite to how it appears.

§§161–64 (pp. 98–102) Hegel introduces the concept of the infinite, as capable of overcoming the dialectical tensions he has gone through, but in a way that the understanding itself cannot yet grasp.

§165 (pp. 102–3) Hegel makes the transition from consciousness to *self*-consciousness, i.e. from ways of thinking about objects and the world around us, to ways of thinking about ourselves as subjects.

3

THE DIALECTIC OF THE SUBJECT
(PHENOMENOLOGY,
B. SELF-CONSCIOUSNESS)

MASTERSHIP AND SERVITUDE

With the breakdown of consciousness, and the collapse of its purely object-centred theoretical attitude, we now move to self-consciousness, which takes up the opposing stance, by placing the subject at the centre of things. As one might expect, Hegel wants to show that both attitudes are one-sided: put simply, consciousness was one-sided because it tried to displace itself from the world and take up a purely objective stance, while self-consciousness is one-sided because it tries to impose itself on the world too strongly, so the self/world distinction collapses and self-consciousness is reduced to 'the motionless tautology of: "I am I"' (PS: §167, p. 105). Hegel sets out the problem here quite clearly in the discussion of self-consciousness in the third part of the *Encyclopedia* (the *Philosophy of Spirit*):

> In consciousness, we see the tremendous *difference*, on the one side, of the 'I', this wholly *simple* existence, and on the other side, of the

infinite variety of the world. It is this opposition of the 'I' and the world which has not yet reached a genuine mediation, that constitutes the finitude of consciousness. Self-consciousness, on the other hand, has its finitude in its still quite abstract self-identity. What is present in the I = I of immediate self-consciousness is a difference that merely *ought* to be, not yet a *posited* or *actual* difference.

(ES: §425Z, p. 166)

As with his previous discussion of consciousness, Hegel attempts to bring out the one-sidedness of self-consciousness by showing that it cannot properly resolve the dialectic of universal and individual, not this time in relation to the object, but in relation to itself as *subject*, and the conception it has of its own identity.

Having introduced the turn from consciousness to self-consciousness, Hegel feels able to move from the 'arid forms and shapeless generalities' of the theoretical attitude which concluded his discussion of consciousness, to a conception of nature that is once again 'noisy with life' (EN: I, §246Z, p. 198). Thus, as self-consciousness begins by interacting with the world at the level of desire (as a *practical* rather than theoretical attitude), it finds the 'dull northern fog' has lifted to reveal a world teeming with living things:

But *for us*, or *in itself*, the object which for self-consciousness is the negative element has, on its side, returned into itself, just as on the other side consciousness has done. Through this reflection into itself the object has become Life. What self-consciousness distinguishes from itself as having *being*, also has in it, in so far as it is posited as being, not merely the character of sense-certainty and perception, but it is being that is reflected into itself, and the object of immediate desire is a *living thing*.

(PS: §168, p. 106)

Hegel goes on to suggest that self-consciousness cannot be 'certain of itself' by simply identifying itself with this world of living things, for in that world there appears to be too little room for any notion of individuality; what matters at the level of life is the *genus*, not the particular individual, so that at this level, the I, as a particular individual, does not count for much. Self-consciousness therefore conceives of itself as more than a merely animal consciousness (cf. PS: §172, pp. 108–9).

DESIRE

Once the subject has moved to the level of focusing on itself qua individual, so that it 'has itself as a pure "I" for object' (PS: §173, p. 109), Hegel now sets out to show that it is no more possible for the subject to find satisfaction in its practical relation to the world if it tries to do so 'immediately' than it was for it to find satisfaction in its theoretical relation to the world through the simplistic model of sense-certainty. At its most basic, this practical relation takes the form of *desire*, in which the subject exerts itself as a kind of pure will, where any sense of estrangement from the world is countered by the destruction of the object, and so by a negation of its otherness in a literal sense:

> Certain of the nothingness of this other, it explicitly affirms that this nothingness is *for it* the truth of the other; it destroys the independent object and thereby gives itself the certainty of itself as a *true* certainty, a certainty which has become explicit for self-consciousness itself *in an objective manner*.
>
> (PS: §174, p. 109)

Thus, with desire the subject attempts to preserve its individuality by negating the world around it. The difficulty with desire, however, is that it involves the destruction of the object, but once this object is destroyed, the subject has nothing over which to exert its control and so demonstrate its individuality. The subject must therefore find itself another object to destroy, so the process can begin again, leading to an obviously empty regress:

> Desire and the self-certainty obtained in its gratification, are conditioned by the object, for self-certainty comes from superseding this other: in order that this supersession can take place, there must be this other. Thus self-consciousness, by its negative relation to the

object, is unable to supersede it; it is really because of that relation that it produces the object again, and the desire as well.

(PS: ¶175, p. 109)

At this point, Hegel offers one of his characteristic 'previews', where he tells us how ultimately the difficulty faced by desire will be resolved. This will happen when the single self-consciousness sees the world as containing *other* self-consciousnesses; for in seeing that others are selves like it, and in thereby recognizing itself in them, the subject is no longer faced by sheer otherness, where only by negating the world can the subject find itself in it. As Hegel makes clear, when the self-conscious subject is able to 'see itself in the other', we will have arrived at a decisive turning-point in the journey of consciousness through the *Phenomenology*, after which consciousness will be capable of a much more balanced outlook than has been achieved hitherto:

A self-consciousness, in being an object, is just as much 'I' as 'object'. With this, we already have before us the Notion of *Spirit*. What still lies ahead for consciousness is the experience of what Spirit is – this absolute substance which is the unity of the different independent self-consciousnesses which, in their opposition, enjoy perfect freedom and independence: the 'I' that is 'We' and the 'We' that is 'I'. It is in self-consciousness, in the Notion of Spirit, that consciousness first finds its turning-point, where it leaves behind it the colourful show of the sensuous here-and-now [cf. sense-certainty and perception] and the nightlike void of the supersensible beyond [cf. force and the understanding] and steps out into the spiritual daylight of the present.

(PS: ¶177, pp. 110–11)

At the beginning of the section that follows this passage, entitled 'Independence and Dependence of Self-Consciousness: Mastership and Servitude',[1] Hegel continues with his 'preview', spelling out what this mutual recognition involves (PS: §§178–84, pp. 111–12). Essentially, each self-consciousness must acknowledge the other as an autonomous subject, 'as something that has an independent existence of its own, which, therefore, it cannot utilize for its own purposes, if that object does not of its own accord do what the first does to it' (PS: §182, p. 112; the Kantian echoes of treating people as ends-in-themselves rather than merely as means are unmistakable); moreover, each self-consciousness must also realize and accept that its well-being and identity as a subject is bound up with how it is seen by the other self-consciousness (which is where Hegelian recognition differs from Kantian 'respect'). If this recognition is reciprocal, Hegel argues, then neither side need fear that by acknowledging the other and feeling itself bound to it (in a relationship like love, for example) 'it has lost itself' (PS: §179, p. 111):

> Each sees the *other* do the same as it does; each does itself what it demands of the other, and therefore also does what it does only in so far as the other does the same. Action by one side only would be useless because what is to happen can only be brought about by both.
>
> (PS: ¶182, p. 112)

(For further discussion of Hegel's conception of recognition, see Honneth 1995: 3–63, Siep 1979, Williams 1992.)

THE LIFE AND DEATH STRUGGLE

Hegel makes clear, however, that with this outline account of fully developed recognition he is anticipating what is still to come, commenting that

> We have now to see how the process of this pure Notion of recognition, of the duplicating of self-consciousness in its oneness, *appears* to self-consciousness. *At first*, it will exhibit the side of the inequality of the two, or the splitting-up of the middle term into the extremes which, as extremes, are opposed to one another, one being only *recognized*, the other only *recognizing*.
>
> (PS: ¶185, pp. 112–13, my first two emphases)

Thus, at the stage we have reached, the single self-consciousness is not yet able to achieve a stable sense of its own identity in the face of the other self-consciousness: as he puts the problem elsewhere,

> In this determination lies the tremendous contradiction that, on the one hand, the 'I' is wholly universal, absolutely pervasive, and interrupted by no limit, is the universal essence common to all men, the two mutually related selves therefore constituting one identity, constituting, so to speak, one light; and yet, on the other hand, they are also two selves rigidly and unyieldingly confronting each other, each existing as a reflection-into-self, as absolutely distinct from and impenetrable by the other.
>
> (ES: §430Z, pp. 170–71)

Thus, we once again have a tension between universality (the 'wholly universal' I belonging to both self-consciousnesses) and individuality (the sense that each self-consciousness has of itself as an individual fundamentally distinct from the other self-consciousnesses). Hegel's attempt to bring out the difficulty this creates for self-consciousness in achieving a stable self-identity is one of the most well-known and influential sections of the *Phenomenology*; unfortunately, however, it is open to conflicting interpretations. For, although it is clear that the dialectic takes us from 'desire', through 'the life and death struggle', to 'mastership and servitude', it is not so obvious exactly what argument is meant to underpin the transition from 'desire' to 'the life and death struggle'.

On the simplest interpretation, the argument is as follows (cf. Shklar 1976: 28). As we have seen, the difficulty with desire is that the subject faces a continual progression, as the destruction of the object leads to the re-emergence of desire. The subject then turns from objects to other subjects in order to resolve this difficulty, for other subjects do not need to be destroyed in order to be made subservient to the will, so they can be assimilated without leading to the contradiction of desire:

> On account of the independence of the object, therefore, [self-consciousness] can achieve satisfaction only when the object itself effects the negation within itself ... Since the object is in its own self negation, and in being so is at the same time independent, it is consciousness ... [Thus] *Self-consciousness achieves its satisfaction only in another self-consciousness.*
>
> (PS: §175, pp. 109–10)

However, as I try to impose my will on you, so you will try to impose your will on me: we will then end up in conflict ('the life and death struggle'), which is only resolved when one of us concedes defeat, and succumbs to the will of the other, hence becoming a slave, while the victor becomes the master.

As an argument, this has a certain plausibility: but it seems that Hegel had something more sophisticated in mind, as it leaves out an important aspect of the text. In particular, it leaves out the significance of *recognition* as the source of the struggle, rather than *desire*: that is, it appears that it is not because I am trying to make you subject to my will that we end up fighting, but because I am seeking to secure recognition from you, where this means that I want you to see me as another subject (for which turning you into a vehicle for my desires is neither a necessary nor a sufficient condition). On this reading, recognition replaces desire as the outlook of self-consciousness, because it has realized that desire is contradictory: it hopes to find in recognition a form of practical well-being that is more realizable. Thus, when Hegel says that '[s]elf-consciousness exists in and for itself when, and by the fact that, it so exists for another; that is, it exists only in being acknowledged' (PS: §178, p. 111), he is here taken to be introducing a new step in the dialectic, where recognition rather than the imposition of will through desire has become the goal of consciousness.

Even if this reading is accepted, however, there is still room for debate over how the life and death struggle between different subjects is to be understood. On one view, the explanation is comparable to the explanation we gave above on the desire account: namely, while I want you to recognize me, I do not want to recognize you, as this seems to threaten my individuality and/ or freedom, so we are inevitably led into a battle for recognition as each tries to wrest recognition from the other while giving nothing in return; eventually, this battle is won by one subject or the other, who then serves as master to the other as slave (cf. Findlay 1958: 95). As we have seen, Hegel emphasizes this lack of mutual recognition at the outset: 'At first, [recognition] will exhibit the side of the inequality of the two, or the splitting-up of the middle term into the extremes which, as extremes, are opposed to one another, one being only *recognized*, the other only *recognizing*' (PS: §185, pp. 112–13).

However, while again this argument has a certain plausibility, on another line of interpretation it appears defective as a reading of the text, because it misses out another important aspect of Hegel's discussion, which is the significance he gives to the fact that in the life and death struggle, individuals show themselves as willing to forfeit their lives. The contrast may be put as follows: on the previous reading, risking one's life is merely a side-effect (as it were) of the lack of mutual recognition, where this leads to a struggle in which life is imperilled, while on the reading we are now considering, risking one's life is the *reason for* the struggle itself.

How can this be? On this reading, the answer is that in order to achieve recognition, I must show you that I am a subject and not a mere living thing; but although each of us knows that we are subjects, we need to convince the other that we are, for otherwise we may be seen as merely living creatures lacking in subjecthood, and so fail to be granted the recognition we require. As Sartre puts it:

> to the extent that the Other apprehends me as bound to a body and immersed in *life*, I am myself only *an Other*. In order to make myself recognized by the Other, I must risk my own life. To risk one's life, in fact, is to reveal oneself as not-bound to the objective form or to any determined existence – as not-bound to life.
>
> (Sartre 1958: 237; cf. also Kojève 1969: 40–41, Fukuyama 1992: 150–52)

Thus, on this reading, the requirement on each subject to risk its life is the reason for the life and death struggle, rather than the lack of mutual recognition, as each tries to show the other that it is not a 'mere' living creature. Now, textual support for this interpretation can be found from the following passages:

> [O]ne individual is confronted by another individual. Appearing thus immediately on the scene, they are for one another like ordinary objects, *independent* shapes, individuals submerged in the being [or

immediacy] of *Life* – for the object in its immediacy is here determined as Life. They are, *for each other*, shapes of consciousness which
have not yet accomplished the movement of absolute abstraction, of
rooting-out all immediate being, and of being merely the purely
negative being of self-identical consciousness; in other words, they
have not as yet exposed themselves to each other in the form of pure
being-for-self, or as self-consciousnesses.

(PS: §186, p. 113)

Here, Hegel appears to be claiming that the most basic way for a
subject to demonstrate its status as a subject to another, and
hence to achieve recognition for its subjecthood, is to show that it
is prepared to sacrifice its existence as an object: that is, to show
that it is prepared to give up its life:

The presentation of itself, however, as the pure abstraction of self-
consciousness consists in showing itself as the pure negation of its
objective mode, or in showing that it is not attached to any specific
existence, not to the individuality common to existence as such, that it
is not attached to life ... Thus the relation of the two self-conscious
individuals is such that they prove themselves and each other through
a life-and-death struggle. They must engage in this struggle, for they
must raise their certainty of being *for themselves* to truth, both in the
case of the other and in their own case. And it is only through staking
one's life that freedom is won; and thus it is proved that for self-
consciousness, its essential being is not [just] being, not the *immediate* form in which it appears, not its submergence in the expanse of
life, but rather that there is nothing present in it which could not be
regarded as a vanishing moment, that it is only pure *being-for-self*.

(PS: §187, pp. 113–14)

For Hegel, it appears, a creature that shows it has knowingly
and willingly risked its destruction as a living thing thereby dif-
ferentiates itself from mere animal life, and shows itself to be
human. As he puts it in the *Philosophy of Right*: 'I have these
limbs and my life only *in so far as I will it*; the animal cannot
mutilate or destroy itself, but the human being can' (PR: §47, p. 78).
(Cf. also SEL: 228, '[E]very determinacy by which [the single

being] should be gripped he can cut away from himself, and in death he can realize his absolute independence and freedom [for] himself as absolutely negative consciousness.')

However, while the reading we are now considering has an advantage over the others in doing justice to these aspects of the text, it has the disadvantage of making the argument open to an obvious objection: namely, if what is required here for recognition of my subjecthood is that I risk my life, why do I have to fight you? Why couldn't I show my lack of concern for my biological nature and ends by risking my life in front of you in a non-conflictual way (jumping off a cliff, or fighting with an animal, or enlisting in a good cause)? Even if it is right that I must risk my life at this stage, why should I do so through attempting to kill you?

Now, an obvious answer might be to say that while I am driven to try to risk my life to show myself to be a subject in your eyes, I am driven to fight you because I still want you to recognize me without giving any recognition in return. Thus, risking my life in fighting you gives me a good way of achieving both my goals at once. This, however, may seem a rather ad hoc way of bringing these two facets of the life and death struggle together. It also does not seem to fit the text very well. For Hegel seems to offer a different answer to the question of why I come to risk my life through the life and death struggle. The relevant passage is as follows:

> The individual who has not risked his life may well be recognized as a *person*, but he has not attained to the truth of this recognition as an independent self-consciousness. Similarly, just as each stakes his own life, so each must seek the other's death, for it values the other no more than itself; its essential being is present to it in the form of an 'other', it is outside of itself and must rid itself of its self-externality. The other is an *immediate* consciousness entangled in a variety of relationships, and it must regard its otherness as a pure being-for-self or as an absolute negation.
>
> (PS: §187, p. 114)

One interpretation of this passage might be this (based on the thought that the life-risker 'values the other no more than itself'):

I have no regard for myself qua natural subject, so I have no regard for you qua natural subject, and I find no reason not to kill you in so far as life is merely part of your being as a natural subject. However, while this interpretation might explain why I would be *prepared* to kill you, it does not explain why I should feel *compelled* to do so. So another interpretation might be this: I only expect recognition from you in so far as I show myself to be more than an animal subject; likewise, I will only recognize you if you show yourself to be the same; so I will not recognize you without testing you to see if you are worthy of recognition, and the way to do this is to put your life in peril and see how you behave (cf. Kainz 1976: 88, 'The ego must accordingly set itself to find proof; it must "test" the alter-ego to adjudicate the presence of freedom. And this test will involve the negation, disregard, and destruction of life.'). This then explains why subjects fight each other: each is prepared to stake its life, while each sets out to test the other, so each will attack the other, while each will respond by risking its life.

Put in schematic terms, we have identified three different accounts of the transition from 'desire' to the 'life and death struggle':

A: desire → impose will on objects → impose will on subjects → each tries to impose will on the other → life and death struggle between subjects

B: desire → impose will on objects → move from desire to one-sided recognition → life and death struggle, as one subject seeks to get recognition from other without giving anything in return

C: desire → impose will on objects → move from desire to recognition → recognition by other requires staking life, and recognition of other requires testing other for willingness to stake life → life and death struggle

As well as having different structures, these accounts also have rather different implications regarding the limitations of self-consciousness that Hegel is trying to highlight at this stage, which lead it into the life and death struggle. Under interpretation A, self-consciousness is limited because it treats subjects as it treated objects, and so tries to 'negate' them. Under interpretation B, self-consciousness is limited by the fact that it is unable to grant recognition to other subjects without feeling that its own autonomy is undermined. And under interpretation C, self-consciousness is limited because it finds it can only show itself to be a self by risking its life, because at this stage in the emergence of the self it lacks any other resources for doing so: 'In a primitive situation the only way I can demonstrate my independence from my animal being is show that it is nothing to me: I must risk my life in the eyes of the other' (Bernstein 1984: 15; cf. ES: §432Z, p. 172, where Hegel himself says that the struggle for recognition 'can only occur in the natural state, where men exist only as single, separate individuals', whereas in society proper individuals can show themselves to be 'worthy of this recognition' by showing themselves to be rational subjects by obeying the law, filling a post, following a trade, or other kinds of social activity).

If, however, we adopt interpretation C as fitting the text more completely than the other options we have considered, there is nonetheless something rather unsatisfactory about this interpretation's line on the grounds for the difficulties faced by self-consciousnesses at this stage: namely, that the social order is too limited to allow recognition to occur without the risk of life. For, up until now, the dialectic has been driven by some sort of *conceptual* one-sidedness or tension, but under interpretation C it is driven by the fact that self-consciousness is operating in a 'primitive situation', which would seem to leave no room for the kind of *categorial* diagnosis we have seen hitherto.

Now, it may be for this reason that, in a later discussion of the life and death struggle in the *Encyclopedia*, Hegel seems to revert to something more like interpretation B, where the life and death struggle is said to take place because recognition at this stage is one-sided. That one-sidedness is explained through the limited notion of *freedom* operative here, namely, that if one subject recognizes another as a subject, it takes this to undermine its freedom, and so is unwilling to grant this recognition:

It is still the case [at this point in the dialectic] that in that I recognize another as being free, I lose my freedom. At this present standpoint we have to forget completely the relationships we are used to thinking about. If we speak of right, ethicality, love, we know that in that I recognize the others, I recognize their complete personal independence. We know too that I do not suffer on this account, but have validity as a free being, that in that the others have rights I have them too, or that my right is also essentially that of the other, i.e. that I am a free person, and that this is essentially the same as the others' also being persons with rights. Benevolence or love does not involve the submergence of my personality. Here, however, there is as yet no such relationship, for one aspect of the determination is that of my still being, as a free self-consciousness, an immediate and single one. In so far as the immediate singularity of my self-consciousness and my freedom are not yet separated, I am unable to surrender anything of my particularity without surrendering my free independence ... [S]elf-consciousness at this standpoint ... must resist recognizing an other as a free being, just as, on the other hand, each must concern itself with eliciting recognition within the other's self-consciousness, being posited as an independent being ... [T]he single self [is not] able to bear the other's being independent of it, so that they necessarily drift into a struggle.

(BP: §431Z, pp. 77, 79)

Here we have something more like a conceptual limitation bringing about the life and death struggle, for each self-consciousness takes it that recognition of the freedom of the other threatens its own freedom, in so far as it assumes that to be free is to be able to ignore claims made on me by other individuals, and to act exactly as my egoistical desires ('my particularity') dictate. It is Hegel's aim to show that both these assumptions are mistaken (cf. PR: §15, pp. 48–49), in a way that self-consciousness must come to accept if it is to move beyond the impasse that leads to the life and death struggle. (Cf. also PR: §57, p. 87, where Hegel states that what 'gives rise at this stage to the *struggle for recognition* and of the relationship of *lordship* and *servitude*' is the 'as yet only immediate consciousness of freedom'.)

MASTER AND SLAVE

However the transition from 'desire' to the 'life and death struggle' is understood, the transition from here to 'mastership and
servitude' is more straightforward, as it becomes apparent that
there is something deeply unsatisfying about the life and death
struggle as a means of achieving recognition in the eyes of the
other: for either the subject succeeds in killing the other, in
which case there is no other subject to do the recognizing, or the
first subject is killed, in which case their selfhood is lost:

> This trial by death, however, does away with the truth which was
> supposed to issue from it, and so, too, with the certainty of self gen-
> erally. For just as life is the *natural* setting of consciousness, inde-
> pendence without absolute negativity, so death is the *natural* negation
> of consciousness, negation without independence, which thus
> remains without the required significance of recognition.
>
> (PS: §188, p. 114)

As soon as this occurs to self-consciousness, it gives up its struggle to appear as a subject in the eyes of the other, and hence its
struggle to 'go free', and so becomes a slave.

Once one self-consciousness realizes that 'life is as essential to it
as pure self-consciousness' (PS: §189, p. 115), and so gives up the
life and death struggle, it appears at first that the two self-
consciousnesses can now attain a kind of equilibrium, where the
one that has given up the struggle is the slave and the other is
the master. The master can now show himself to be a subject in
the eyes of the slave, not by risking his life, but by exercising
power over the slave's body, the very thing the slave was not
prepared to lose in the struggle. At the same time, the master can
overcome his estrangement from the world not simply by trying
to destroy it (which was the only possibility at the level of desire)
but by setting the slave to work on it.

However, Hegel quickly sets out to demonstrate that this
apparent stability is illusory. He begins by pointing out that
although the master has shown himself to be a subject in the eyes
of the other, it is not clear how he can view this other any

differently from an object in so far as the slave (like any object) is a mere instrument of his will, and so it is hard for him to maintain that any recognition has been achieved. So, although on the one hand '[h]ere ... is present this moment of recognition, viz. that the [slave] consciousness sets aside its own being-for-self', on the other hand because 'what the bondsman does is really the action of the lord ... [t]he outcome is a recognition that is one-sided and unequal' (PS: §191, p. 116). At the same time, Hegel argues that contrary to initial appearances, it is the slave that 'will withdraw into itself and be transformed into a truly independent consciousness' (PS: §193, p. 117). The first step, Hegel claims, comes through the experience of fear with which its servitude began: in this, the transitoriness of life was brought home to the slave in a way that the master has not come to feel, so it is the master and not the slave who has the most 'immediate' relationship to his natural existence. Likewise, through his work for the master, the slave is forced to set aside his own desires, and thus finds himself no longer driven by them. Most importantly of all, Hegel argues, 'through work ... the bondsman becomes conscious of what he truly is' (PS: §195, p. 118). This is because, in creating things not for himself but for the master, he is forced not just to consume things, but rather to labour on them while leaving them in existence. As a result he finds that he can leave his mark on the world in a way that is lasting: 'Through this rediscovery of himself by himself, the bondsman realizes that it is precisely in his work wherein he seemed to have only an alienated existence that he acquires a mind of his own' (PS: §196, pp. 118–19). Hegel is particularly insistent that all three of these elements – fear, service, and work on the world – must be present together for this realization to occur, as otherwise each will be degraded (for example, fear will remain 'inward and mute' unless the subject can find himself again through work, while work without the experience of fear will mean it once again becomes 'an empty self-centered attitude' (PS: §196, p. 119)).

The slave therefore comes to a different conception of individuality from that adopted by the master (who has not gone much beyond desire). In particular, the slave no longer sees the world as alien to it, which must therefore be negated if it is to achieve 'its unalloyed feeling of self' (PS: §195, p. 118). Rather, in his work the slave labours for someone else's satisfaction, and so learns respect for the independent existence of the objects around him, with which he finds he can work. Consciousness thus comes to a new conception of itself as an individual in the world, by now treating that world as a place to which it is attuned, not merely because it has various 'skills' that make it 'master over some things', but because it possesses 'universal formative activity', which gives it 'universal power' over 'the whole of objective being' (PS: §196, p. 119).

STOICISM, SCEPTICISM, AND THE UNHAPPY CONSCIOUSNESS

Having offered his ingeniously insightful account of the relative positions of the master and the slave, Hegel now moves on to a discussion of a position he identifies with Stoicism.

STOICISM

Broadly speaking, the transition to Stoicism seems to involve a transition from the one-sided practical attitude of desire and the master, to a new form of theoretical attitude brought about by the insights of the slave. This theoretical attitude is a kind of rationalism, for the Stoics believed that the universe was governed by *logos* or reason, and that man's rational soul is a fragment of that divine *logos*, and so we can achieve well-being by attuning ourselves to the cosmic scheme of things. (Cf. PS: §198, p. 121, '[Stoicism's] principle is that consciousness is a being that *thinks*, and that consciousness holds something to be essentially important, or true and good only in so far as it *thinks* it to be such.') In bringing in Stoicism here, and in the subsequent transitions to Scepticism and then to the Unhappy Consciousness, it is notable that Hegel is referring to actual historical episodes (as he will do later, in referring to the French Revolution, for example). Indeed, as many commentators have pointed out, in mentioning that the Stoic aims at freedom 'whether on the throne or in chains', Hegel surely meant us to think of the late or Roman Stoics Marcus

Aurelius and Epictetus, the former an Emperor, the latter a (liberated) slave. This then raises the question of how far the development of the *Phenomenology* more generally should be seen in historical terms, and how much it should be read as a form of speculative history, of the sort Hegel was later to present in his *Lectures on the Philosophy of History*. Attempts have been made to read the *Phenomenology* this way (cf. Forster 1998: 291–500), but my own view is that the two enterprises should be distinguished, and that in this text historical episodes have the place they do because they relate to particular stages in the *conceptual* development that Hegel is tracing out for consciousness. I think it would therefore be wrong to try to build up Hegel's account of this (and other) historical episodes into a historicist reading of the *Phenomenology* as a whole. (For further discussion of this issue, see Hyppolite 1974: 27–50.)

Nonetheless, it may seem tempting to treat the transition from the master/slave relation to Stoicism in primarily historical terms, given that Hegel seems to provide it with a purely socio-political rationale, by suggesting that Stoicism arises as both the master and slave seek to escape from the unsatisfactoriness of their social world, as they abstract from the reality of their situation into a world of contemplative indifference to their surroundings:

> This consciousness accordingly has a negative attitude towards the lord and bondsman relationship. As lord, it does not have its truth in the bondsman, nor as bondsman is its truth in the lord's will and in his service; on the contrary, whether on the throne or in chains, in the utter dependence of its individual existence, its aim is to be free, and to maintain that lifeless indifference which steadfastly withdraws from the bustle of existence, alike from being active as passive, into the simple essentiality of thought. Self-will is the freedom which entrenches itself in some particularity and is still in bondage, while Stoicism is the freedom which always comes directly out of bondage and returns into the pure universality of thought. As a universal form of the World-Spirit, Stoicism could only appear on the scene in a time of universal fear and bondage, but also a time of universal culture which had raised itself to the level of thought.
>
> (PS: §199, p. 121)

It may seem from this, that Hegel intends us to treat the move from the master/slave relationship to Stoicism in quasi-materialist terms, as a form of consciousness that emerges in response to its socio-political predicament, in a (doomed) attempt to come to terms with it (cf. Kojève 1969: 53, who speaks of Stoicism as an ideology of slavery).

There are signs, however, that this is not the best way to take Hegel's procedure here. Rather, it could be argued that Hegel thinks that with Stoicism, consciousness is taking a new turn, and that the insights needed to make this turn possible are only available once consciousness has been through the master/slave dialectic. In his introductory remarks to this section as a whole, Hegel signals that when consciousness moves to the rationalism of the Stoics, it has arrived at a new attitude to the world; for the Stoics saw reality as permeated by reason, so that thought is seen as giving us access to the rational structure inherent in things, which are now no longer viewed as 'other' by the subject:

> We are in the presence of self-consciousness in a new shape, a con-
> sciousness which, as the infinitude of consciousness or as its own
> pure movement, is aware of itself as essential being, a being which
> *thinks* or is a free self-consciousness. For *to think* does not mean to
> be an *abstract* 'I', but an 'I' which has at the same time the sig-
> nificance of *intrinsic* being, of having itself for object, or of relating
> itself to objective being in such a way that its significance is the *being-
> for-self* of the consciousness for which it is [an object] ... In thinking,
> I *am free*, because I am not in an *other*, but remain simply and solely
> in communion with myself, and the object, which is for me the
> *essential* being, is in undivided unity my being-for-myself; and my
> activity in conceptual thinking is a movement within myself.
>
> (PS: §197, p. 120)

The sense that '[i]n thinking, I *am free*, because I am not in an *other*' is very much what Hegel himself hopes he will give us as a result of his attempt to find rational satisfaction for the subject in the world (cf. Neuhouser 2000: 20); and to the extent that we have arrived at the idea that thought can help the subject find itself in the world, 'we are in the presence of self-consciousness in a new shape', one first represented by the rationalism of Stoicism. Consciousness was dominated by the assumption that thought contrasts to the world of concrete experience, while self-consciousness up to now has merely seen the world as an 'other' to be negated; but the Stoic adopts a rationalistic stance that offers a way out of the difficulties that these assumptions have caused, by treating thought as a vehicle through which the subject can find itself in the world, much as Hegel himself believed. (Cf. EL: §24Z, p. 37, 'The signification thus attached to thought and its characteristic forms may be illustrated by the ancient saying that "*nous* governs the world", or by our own phrase that "Reason is in the world"; which means that Reason is the soul of the world it inhabits, its immanent principle, its most proper and inward nature, its universal.')

Now if (as this suggests), Hegel saw in Stoicism not just a 'slave ideology', but the beginning of a new philosophical perspective that would ultimately culminate in something like his own outlook, the interesting question concerning this transition is: what gives it its place in the dialectic in conceptual rather than socio-historical terms? How does the position of the slave (in particular) lead consciousness into this 'new shape'? The answer, I think, can be seen by recalling Hegel's characterization of the slave's position: for the slave found through working with things in the world, that the world co-operates as he attempts to bring his ideas to realization in his products, so that nature no longer seems alien to it (and thus as something to be 'negated'), or as somehow beyond thought, thereby making the kind of shift in outlook needed to lead us into Stoicism. As Taylor has put it: 'Through work, discipline and the fear of death, the slaves have come to a recognition of the universal, of the power of conceptual thought' (Taylor 1975: 157). Thus, it is the slave's awareness of himself as achieving an insight into the workings of the world that moves the dialectic of consciousness onto a perspective that Hegel identifies as Stoicism, which holds that thought enables us to be at one with the rational universe.

However, as Hegel makes clear in his *Lectures on the History of Philosophy*, while to some extent he saw Stoicism as heir to the rationalistic world-picture of Plato and Aristotle (to which his own speculative rationalism was deeply and consciously indebted), he nonetheless saw in Stoicism a form of rationalism that was much more abstract and formulaic than it had been in 'the bright Grecian world' (LHP: II, p. 234), making its 'recognition of the universal' inadequate. Although Stoicism came after the work of Plato and Aristotle, Hegel therefore portrays it as conceptually inferior and so (in philosophical terms) as an expression of rationalism in its crudest and most primitive form:

> The selfsame consciousness that repels itself from itself becomes aware of itself as the element of *being-in-itself*; but at first it knows itself to be this element only as a universal mode of being in general, not as it exists objectively in the development and process of its manifold being.
>
> (PS: §197, p. 121)

This is rather obscure, but Hegel makes his criticism clearer later in the section, where he claims that 'the abstract thinking of Stoicism ... turns its back on individuality altogether' (PS: §216, p. 130), by adopting a rationalistic picture that is too cut off from the concrete world: 'This thinking consciousness ... is thus only the incomplete negation of otherness' (PS: §201, p. 122). By offering merely empty generalizations, the Stoics failed to relate their concept of reason to individual particulars; they could therefore only provide platitudes, not concrete advice or knowledge. As we saw in the Preface, Hegel takes rationalism that is overly abstract and formal in this way to be easily degraded, so that it can quickly become the victim of its anti-rationalist critics.

In order to show how Stoicism falls victim to these critics, Hegel briefly refers to the central cruxes that faced Stoic thought, particularly the difficulties the Stoics had in identifying any criterion for truth in their epistemology, and in giving content to their vague claims in ethics that 'living in agreement with nature' or 'in accordance with reason' constitutes the good life:

> But this self-identity of thought is again only the pure form in which nothing is determined. The True and the Good, wisdom and virtue,

the general terms beyond which Stoicism cannot get, are therefore in a general way no doubt uplifting, but since they cannot in fact produce any expansion of the content, they soon become tedious.

(PS: §200, p. 122)

(As Harris 1997, I: p. 437, n. 9 points out, his biographer Karl Rosenkranz reports that in the conclusion to his unpublished early work the *System of Ethical Life* (1802 or 1803), Hegel characterized the Roman Peace as 'the boredom of the world': see SEL: 181.) Faced with these doctrinal difficulties, Hegel argues, the Stoics came to appear merely dogmatic in their optimistic claims regarding the rationality of the world and the happiness that could come from conforming ourselves to it in some abstract sense. Such dogmatism naturally gives rise to a form of more critical (and ultimately *anti*-rationalistic) Scepticism.

SCEPTICISM

At first, the Sceptic's anti-rationalism may not be apparent, as he can claim he is merely aiming at the kind of 'freedom of thought' (PS: §202, p. 123) the Stoic was looking for, since he is prepared to question everything, even that there *is* a world in which rational satisfaction may be found; instead, the Sceptic believes we can achieve a peaceful, healthy, satisfactory life by dropping rationalistic aspirations and dispassionately following appearances:

In Scepticism, now, the wholly unessential and non-independent character of this 'other' becomes explicit *for consciousness*; the [abstract] thought becomes the concrete thinking which annihilates the being of the world in all its manifold determinateness, and the negativity of free self-consciousness comes to know itself in the many and varied forms of life as a real negativity.

(PS: §202, p. 123)

Hegel then attempts to show, however, that this 'freedom of thought' is illusory: for, once the Sceptic has accepted that everything can be doubted and thus that thought cannot take us beyond appearances, he ends up declaring that thought is in fact powerless and turns back to the senses; at the same time, by holding that everything we know is mere appearance, he implicitly retains the idea that if thought could take us beyond the sensible realm, it might achieve a higher kind of knowledge. Hegel therefore argues that the abstract rationalism of the Sceptic in fact leads into a despairing anti-rationalism, as the sceptical consciousness convinces itself that rational satisfaction is impossible for us.

In some respects, the tone of Hegel's brief analysis of scepticism here is surprising, as it is apparently more critical and dismissive of scepticism than are his discussions elsewhere, particularly in his early essay for the *Critical Journal of Philosophy*, 'The Relationship of Scepticism to Philosophy' (1802), and in his later *Lectures on the History of Philosophy* (see RSP and LHP: II, pp. 331–32). In these discussions Hegel draws an important contrast between ancient and modern scepticism, and while he is hostile to the latter, he is much more positive about the former, largely because it was more thoroughgoing, and not merely in the service of common sense *against* philosophy (as he took Humean scepticism to be, particularly as adopted by its German proponents like G. E. Schulze, whose work is reviewed in the early scepticism essay). It is this contrast that explains why, even in the *Phenomenology*, Hegel treats scepticism as a (degenerate) type of rationalism when focusing on its ancient form, while in its modern form he is more inclined to see it as an out-and-out anti-rationalism with no such 'positive' side (an anti-rationalism that therefore results in a kind of dogmatism, by seeing nothing to question in appearances).

UNHAPPY CONSCIOUSNESS

Having shown how the ancient sceptic comes to feel that thought is both all-powerful and powerless, Hegel argues that '[i]n Scepticism, consciousness truly experiences itself as internally contradictory' (PS: §206, p. 126). It is this duality that comes to be realized in what Hegel calls 'the Unhappy Consciousness':

> This new form is, therefore, one which *knows* that it is the dual consciousness of itself, as self-liberating, unchangeable, and

self-identical, and as self-bewildering and self-perverting, and it is the awareness of this self-contradictory nature of itself ... [T]he *Unhappy Consciousness* is the consciousness of self as a dual-natured, merely contradictory being.

(PS: §206, p. 126)

Thus, on the one hand, the Unhappy Consciousness believes that it is unable to transcend the world of changeable appearances, but on the other hand holds that it can only attain satisfaction by so doing: rather than hoping to achieve some measure of tranquillity or 'unperturbedness' (*ataraxia*) by 'living with appearances' (as the Sceptic did), the Unhappy Consciousness is therefore painfully aware of the gap that exists between itself as a contingent, finite individual, and a realm of eternal and universal reason, since the Stoic *logos* has now become an unknowable Beyond. So, whereas the Stoic held that the capacity for rational contemplation belonged to man, it is now seen as a capacity that belongs to 'an alien Being' (PS: §208, p. 127), to a higher form of consciousness which the Unhappy Consciousness now sets above itself.

Nonetheless, though the Unhappy Consciousness has 'projected' this capacity for rational reflection onto another being that has the kind of eternal and unchangeable nature it lacks, Hegel interprets Christianity (in a clear reference to the Trinity) as an attempt to retain something of the Stoic picture of man's rational soul as a fragment of the divine *logos*, while making the Sceptic's apparently unattainable 'unchangeable' truth something that could relate to the human. Thus, although 'the first Unchangeable [i.e. God] it knows only as the alien Being who passes judgement on the particular individual', in the Son it still sees that 'the Unchangeable is a form of individuality like itself', where 'the reconciliation of its individuality with the universal' is symbolized by the Holy Spirit (PS: §210, p. 128). Nonetheless, although traditional medieval Christianity retains something of the earlier rationalistic framework, it stresses the fragility of the link between God and man, and hence the uncertainty of any such reconciliation coming about. This fragility is symbolized in the apparent contingency of Christ's birth, on which the hope of reconciliation is founded:

> The hope of becoming one with it [the Unchangeable] must remain a hope, i.e. without fulfilment and present fruition, for between the hope and the fulfilment there stands precisely the absolute contingency or inflexible indifference which lies in the very assumption of definite form, which was the ground of hope.

> (PS: §212, p. 129)

Thus, while Christianity in this form is in some respects an advance on Stoicism and Scepticism, in that it has recognized that it is not possible for thought to simply 'turn its back on individuality' by abstracting from the contingency, finitude, and suffering of actual existence into a realm of abstract thought, it still 'has not yet risen to that thinking where consciousness as a particular individuality is reconciled with pure thought itself' (PS: §216, p. 130); the subject therefore feels that qua individual subject, he is cut off from the rational ground of existence, as 'pure thought'. Thus, while at the beginning of the chapter with 'desire', consciousness wanted to impose its individuality on the world, it has here come round to the opposite (and equally one-sided) perspective, where it now sees its 'individuality' as getting in the way of its attempts to achieve harmony with 'the Unchangeable'. As a result, Hegel argues, although the Christian consciousness in some respects has a conception of this reconciliation, it has a distorted picture of how such reconciliation might occur, in its three ideals of the Christian life, as prayer, work, and penitence. Hegel therefore criticizes each in turn.

As one might expect, Hegel is critical of prayer as placing too much emphasis on feeling at the expense of thought and rational reflection:

> [I]t is only a movement *towards* thinking, and so is devotion. Its thinking as such is no more than the chaotic jingling of bells, or a mist of warm incense, a musical thinking that does not get as far as the Notion, which would be the sole, immanent objective mode of thought.

> (PS: §217, p. 131)

The devotee seeks to find communion with God by virtue of being a 'pure heart'; but the devotee seeks to demonstrate his purity by declaring that he has not yet found God but is nonetheless still devoted to the search. Devotion is thus 'the struggle of an enterprise doomed to failure' (PS: §217, p. 132).

Hegel then considers the ideal of work, as the believer tries to serve God through labour. The Unhappy Consciousness now has a contradictory attitude to the world on which it works: on the one hand, anything worldly has no significance, as what matters is the God who stands above it; on the other hand, everything in the world is sanctified as the expression of God's nature. Likewise, the Unhappy Consciousness also sees its own capacities for labour in a twofold way: on the one hand, if it can create anything using them, it is only because God allows it to do so; on the other hand, it also sees these capacities as God-given, and so divinely ordained. Thus, though work gives the Unhappy Consciousness some sense of its union with the Unchangeable, in another sense it makes it feel more cut off from it:

> The unchangeable consciousness *renounces* and *surrenders* its embodied form, while, on the other hand, the particular individual consciousness *gives thanks* [for the gift], i.e. *denies* itself the satisfaction of being conscious of its *independence*, and assigns the essence of its action not to itself but to the beyond; through these two moments of *reciprocal self-surrender* of both parts, consciousness does, of course, gain a sense of *unity* with the Unchangeable. But this unity is at the same time affected with division, is again broken within itself, and from it there emerges once more the antithesis of the universal and the individual.
>
> (PS: §222, p. 134)

The difficulty, Hegel argues, is that Unhappy Consciousness sees that its humility here is false, for while it treats the world and its capacities as gifts from God for which it gives thanks, it also recognizes that these gifts are a source of prideful enjoyment for it: 'Consciousness feels itself therein as a particular individual, and does not let itself be deceived by its own seeming renunciation, for the truth of the matter is that it has *not* renounced itself' (PS: §222, p. 134).

From this sense of unworthiness, Hegel moves on to the third ideal of penitence, where the Unhappy Consciousness tries to overcome its hypocrisy: 'Work and enjoyment thus lose all *universal content* and *significance*, for if they had any, they would have an absolute being of their own. Both withdraw into their mere particularity, which consciousness is set upon reducing to nothingness' (PS: §225, p. 135). In its attempts to purify itself, the Unhappy Consciousness turns on its own body as a source of weakness and spiritual corruption, as standing in the way of its attempts to rise above its mere individuality; but the more it tries to overcome its physical nature, the more the body becomes an obsessive focus of attention:

> Consciousness is aware of itself as *this actual individual* in the animal functions. These are no longer performed naturally and without embarrassment, as matters trifling in themselves which cannot possess any importance or essential significance for Spirit; instead, since it is in them that the enemy reveals itself in his characteristic shape, they are rather the object of serious endeavour, and become precisely matters of the utmost importance. This enemy, however, renews himself in his defeat, and consciousness, in fixing its attention on him, far from freeing itself from him, really remains for ever in contact with him, and for ever sees itself as defiled; and, since at the same time this object of its efforts, instead of being something essential, is of the meanest character, instead of being a universal, is the merest particular, we have here only a personality confined to its own self and its own petty actions, a personality brooding over itself, as wretched as it is impoverished.
>
> (PS: §225, pp. 135–36)

In going further in this attempt at reducing its particularity 'to nothingness', the Unhappy Consciousness now gives up all freedom of action as well as all earthly goods, and puts them in the hands of a 'mediator or minister [priest]', to decide for it how it should act:

> This mediator, having a direct relationship with the unchangeable Being, ministers by giving advice on what is right. The action, since it

follows upon the decision of someone else, ceases, as regards the doing or the *willing* of it, to be its own. But there is still left to the unessential consciousness the *objective* aspect, viz. the fruit of its labour, and its enjoyment. These, therefore, it rejects as well, and just as it renounces its *will*, so it renounces the *actuality* it received in work and enjoyment ... Through these moments of surrender, first of its right to decide for itself, then of its property and enjoyment, and finally through the positive moment of practising what it does not understand, it truly and completely deprives itself of the consciousness of inner and outer freedom, of the actuality in which consciousness exists *for itself*. It has the certainty of having truly divested itself of its '*I*', and of having turned its immediate self-consciousness into a Thing, into an *objective* existence.

(PS: §§228–29, pp. 136–37)

Hegel says that here the Unhappy Consciousness comes to feel it has achieved genuine self-renunciation, in a way that was not possible through prayer and work. However, although the individual can take a step towards universality by putting himself under the sway of the priest, this is merely a *negative* loss of self, and so does not really signal the synthesis of universal and individual, as the latter is seen as negated by the former: 'The surrender of its own will, as a *particular* will, is not taken by it to be in principle the positive aspect of universal will. Similarly, its giving up of possessions and enjoyment has only the same negative meaning' (PS: §230, p. 138).

At this point, Hegel makes a transition to the next part of the *Phenomenology*, to 'Reason', where the mood suddenly changes, from gloomy religiosity to rationalistic optimism. Hegel makes this transition very quickly, in one paragraph, and it is hard to see how it is meant to work. One might understand the transition this way: once it has adopted the priest as a mediator, consciousness can now at least conceive of the possibility of blessedness, and thus can come to think that at least *in principle* its actions might be recognized as those required and ordained by God; it therefore no longer sees itself as inherently out of touch with the rational order that governs the world, even though it still sees such reconciliation as 'a *beyond*' (PS: §230, p. 138), something it is best to treat as a 'hope'. But once it takes a further step, and gives up thinking of this reconciliation as out of reach, the rationalistic self-confidence we left behind us with the Stoics can return, but this time in a new and more radical form, in which self-consciousness as an individual recognizes itself in the world of objects, and so no longer sets itself outside the rational order qua universal: 'In this movement it has also become aware of its *unity* with this universal' (PS: §231, p. 139). It is this renewed rationalism that forms the topic of the next chapter.

CONTENT SUMMARY

DESIRE

§§166–74 (pp. 104–9) Having moved from consciousness to self-consciousness, Hegel now considers how the subject first conceives of itself, which is as a pure will or desire that affirms itself in overcoming the world around it.

§§175–77 (pp. 109–11) But this is unsatisfactory, as the subject continually needs new objects to overcome; so it must find its satisfaction instead in other *subjects*, where this will eventually lead us on to Spirit, in which individuals find unity with others while preserving their independence.

MASTERSHIP AND SERVITUDE

§§178–84 (pp. 111–12) This will involve a process of mutual recognition.

§§184–88 (pp. 112–15) However, such mutual recognition has not yet been achieved; instead, each self tries to overcome the other in a life-and-death struggle.

§§189–90 (pp. 115–16) As one self realizes that with death all is lost, it gives way and becomes a slave, while the other becomes the master.

§§191–96 (pp. 116–19) However, the recognition the master achieves is inadequate, while at the same time the slave acquires an understanding of the world around it that takes him beyond desire.

STOICISM, SCEPTICISM, AND THE UNHAPPY CONSCIOUSNESS

§§197–201 (pp. 119–22)   This gives rise to the outlook of Stoicism, which seeks freedom not in practical agency but in thought.

§§202–5 (pp. 123–26)   This freedom then becomes a negation by the subject of the world around it, which occurs in Scepticism, as this world is treated as an appearance.

§§206–30 (pp. 126–38)   Finally, in the Unhappy Consciousness, an inaccessible world is set up beyond these appearances, as a divine being from which the individual is alienated; it can only seek to overcome this alienation through a move towards a more rationalistic outlook, which sees the world as a rational place in which we can be at home.

4

THE DIALECTIC OF REASON
(*PHENOMENOLOGY*, C. (AA.) REASON)

RATIONALISM AND IDEALISM

With the move from Unhappy Consciousness to Reason, the *Phenomenology* recaptures the spirit of optimism characteristic of rationalism, as consciousness once again comes to look at the world as a place where it can be 'at home': 'Now that self-consciousness is Reason, its hitherto negative relation to otherness turns round into a positive relation' (PS: §232, p. 139). Reason holds that the world is rational, and so now sets out to find *itself* in this 'otherness'. But, as we have seen, while Hegel himself was a rationalist in this sense, he was also concerned that such rationalism should take its proper form; otherwise, he believed, it could easily become distorted. In this section, we therefore find Hegel analysing the shortcomings of different kinds of rationalism, all of which turn out to be inadequate and one-sided, as an unresolved tension between the categories of individuality and universality remains.

Hegel opens the chapter with a discussion of *idealism*, which collapses the distinction between the subject and the world, and so takes thoughts and things to coincide immediately:

> Up till now [self-consciousness] has been concerned only with its independence and freedom, concerned to save and maintain itself for itself at the expense of the *world*, or of its own actuality, both of which appeared to it as the negative of its essence. But as Reason, assured of itself, it is at peace with them, and can endure them; for it is certain that it is itself reality, in that everything actual is none other than itself; its thinking is itself directly actuality, and thus its relationship to the latter is that of idealism ... [I]t discovers the world as *its* new real world, which in its permanence holds an interest for it which previously lay only in its transiency; for the *existence* of the world becomes for self-consciousness its one *truth* and *presence*; it is certain of experiencing only itself therein.
>
> (PS: §232, pp. 139–40)

Hegel is clearly sympathetic to the way in which this idealism enables consciousness to escape the urge for the transcendent, and the need to 'negate' the world:

> Apprehending itself in this way, it is as if the world had for it only now come into being; previously it did not understand the world; it desired it and worked on it, withdrew from it into itself and abolished it as an existence on its own account, and its own self qua consciousness – both as consciousness of the world as essence and as consciousness of its nothingness.
>
> (PS: §232, pp. 139–40)

Idealism therefore represents a kind of advance: in it, we have our rationalistic faith restored, our belief that the subject will find the world accessible to reason, in so far as it is created by the subject, so 'it is certain of experiencing only itself therein'.

At this point, however, Hegel exposes the weaknesses of a rationalism that takes this form, where his remarks implicitly refer to Kant, Fichte, and Schelling. His first criticism repeats the objection made against Schelling in the Preface: namely, that this idealistic rationalism does not *argue* for its position or attempt to take on board other points of view, but simply dogmatically asserts that '[Reason] is all reality' (PS: §233, p. 141). Because Schelling lacked Hegel's philosophical method, whereby other standpoints are gone through first,

> [t]he consciousness which is this truth has this path behind it and has forgotten it, and comes on the scene *immediately* as Reason; in other words, this Reason which comes immediately on the scene appears only as the *certainty* of that truth ... The idealism that does not demonstrate that path but starts off with this assertion is therefore, too, a pure *assertion* which does not comprehend its own self, nor can it make itself comprehensible to others.
>
> (PS: §§233–34, p. 141)

A second criticism is more technical, and is directed primarily at Kant, although it extends to Fichte too. This concerns Kant's metaphysical deduction in the *Critique of Pure Reason*, where Kant derives his table of categories from a table of logical judgements. Like Fichte and Schelling, Hegel argues here that this procedure is thoroughly unsatisfactory, 'an outrage on Science' (PS: §235, p. 142), because it does not really demonstrate the necessity of the categories as such; but, he claims, the attempt by Fichte to derive them from the 'absolute ego' is no more satisfactory or enlightening.

The third criticism Hegel makes is perhaps the most important, and also finds an echo in the Preface, where he claimed that 'everything turns on grasping the True, not only as *Substance*, but equally as *Subject*'. Thus, as we saw, while Hegel endorses idealism in *some* sense, it is also crucial for him to ensure that this unity 'does not again fall back into inert simplicity, and does not depict actuality itself in a non-actual manner' (PS: §17, p. 10). Hegel claims here that the Kantian idealists have violated this constraint, with the result that the emptiness of the subject requires them to reintroduce another kind of negation to give content to the experience of the subject, in the form of Fichte's *Anstoss* ('external impetus') or Kant's unknowable thing-in-itself, so that their rationalism ends up being compromised by an underlying scepticism:

[Consciousness'] first declaration is only this abstract empty phrase that everything is *its own*. For the certainty of being all reality is at first [only] the pure category. This Reason which first recognizes itself in the object finds expression in the empty idealism which grasps Reason only as it first comes on the scene; and fancies that by pointing out the pure 'mine' of consciousness in all being, and declaring all things to be sensations or ideas, it has demonstrated that 'mine' of consciousness to be complete reality. It is bound, therefore, to be at the same time absolute empiricism, for in order to give filling to the empty 'mine', i.e. to get hold of *difference* with all its developed formulations, its Reason requires extraneous impulse, in which first is to be found the *multiplicity* of sensations and ideas ... The pure Reason of this idealism, in order to reach this 'other' which is *essential* to it, and thus is the *in-itself*, but which it does not have within it, is therefore thrown back by its own self on to that knowing which is *not* a knowing of what is true; in this way, it condemns itself of its own knowledge and volition to being an untrue kind of knowing, and cannot get away from 'meaning' and 'perceiving', which for it have no truth. It is involved in a direct contradiction; it asserts essence to be a duality of opposed factors, the *unity of apperception* and equally a *Thing*; whether the Thing is called an extraneous impulse [cf. Fichte], or an empirical or sensuous entity, or the Thing-in-itself [cf. Kant], it still remains in principle the same, i.e. extraneous to that unity.

(PS: §238, pp. 144–45)

Though extremely compressed, this third criticism of Kant and his successors is highly significant for the light it sheds on how Hegel wanted his own idealistic rationalism to be understood. Although he does not use this terminology here, elsewhere he distinguishes his own idealism from that of Kant by calling the former 'absolute idealism' and the latter 'subjective idealism' (EL: §45Z, p. 73), and it is clearly subjective idealism that he is criticizing at this point in the *Phenomenology*. As Hegel sees it, Kant and his successors take the subjectivist turn because they think that reality is intelligible to consciousness only in so far as it has a form imposed upon it by the mind; at the same time, things in themselves, which do not have this form imposed upon them, stand outside the grasp of our intellects. Now, Hegel accepts that reality must have a certain form in order to be intelligible to consciousness; but he denies that it is *imposed* by the subject *on* reality, arguing instead that it is inherent in reality itself, so that this form mediates between the subject on the one hand and the world on the other. As Hegel puts it in his *Lectures on the Philosophy of History*, '[Thought] contains reconciliation in its purest essentiality, because it approaches the external [world] in the expectation that this will embody the same reason as the subject does' (PW: 208/PH: 439). For Hegel, therefore, idealism proper is the doctrine that the world has a rational structure that is accessible to thought and so can be 'brought to consciousness': that is, consciousness can make itself *aware* of this rational structure as it exists in the world. But Hegel rejects any idealism that treats such rational structures as mind-dependent or mind-imposed. In this respect, Hegel (like Plato and Aristotle) was a realist:

> But after all, objectivity of thought, in Kant's sense, is again to a certain extent subjective. Thoughts, according to Kant, although universal and necessary categories, are *only our* thoughts – separated by an impassable gulf from the thing, as it exists apart from our knowledge. But the true objectivity of thinking means that the thoughts, far from being merely ours, must be at the same time the real essence of things, and of whatever is an object to us.
>
> (EL: §41Z, pp. 67–68)

Thus, in calling himself an idealist, Hegel intended to signal his allegiance to a certain conceptual realism, rather than to any Kantian doctrine regarding the dependence of the world on a constructive mind; on this view, human consciousness reflects and makes known the fundamental conceptual order inherent in things as they are in themselves, rather than things as they are constituted by us (see Stern 2008). As this discussion in the *Phenomenology* shows, Hegel held that while subjective idealism may appear to be an option for the rationalist because in some sense it breaks down the barrier between mind and world, in fact this option is unstable, as it breaks this barrier down 'immediately', without proper respect for the mind-independence of reality, so that sceptical problems re-emerge. Hegel's argument is that while Kantian idealism may treat the phenomenal world as constituted by the mind and hence as knowable, it is forced to posit a mind-independent noumenal reality beyond it, to provide the mind with some content for its constituting activity; but this reality is then deemed unknowable, as it lies *outside* the world as the subject determines it:

> This idealism is involved in this contradiction because it asserts the *abstract Notion* of Reason to be the True; consequently, reality directly comes to be for it a reality that is just as much *not* that of Reason, while Reason is at the same time supposed to be all reality. This Reason remains a restless searching and in its very searching declares that the satisfaction of *finding* is a sheer impossibility.
>
> (PS: §239, p. 145)

Now, in claiming that '[t]his idealism therefore becomes the same kind of self-contradictory ambiguity as Scepticism' (PS: §238, p. 144), Hegel has been accused of misrepresenting Kant's position, and of misunderstanding the way in which Kant wished to distinguish between 'things as they appear to us' and 'things as they are in themselves'. For example, it is argued that Hegel mistakenly thinks that Kant is committed to a 'two worlds' account of this distinction, rather than a weaker 'two aspect' account, when it is claimed that the latter does not compromise a realist view of the world, or treat it as somehow 'second rate'. It remains an open question, however, how far Kant's position can be reconstructed in this way, and indeed whether such reconstruction is sufficient to escape Hegel's fundamental misgivings. (For references and further discussion, see Stern 1999: 255–59.)

OBSERVING REASON

Frustrated by the self-imposed limitations of idealistic rationalism, consciousness now takes up a rather different and more realist rationalistic stance, one that emerged historically as part of the scientific revolution in post-Renaissance and post-Reformation Europe. In adopting this perspective, consciousness now sees the natural world as accessible to rational inquiry using observation and experimental methods, so that consciousness can come to feel at home in the world through the successful pursuit of scientific knowledge, by which the behaviour of individuals is subsumed under categories or universal laws. Hegel calls this form of consciousness 'Observing Reason':

> Previously, its perception and *experience* of various aspects of the Thing were something that only *happened to* consciousness; but here, consciousness *makes its own* observations and experiments. 'Meaning' and 'perceiving', which previously were superseded *for us*, are now superseded by and for consciousness itself. Reason sets to work to *know* the truth, to find in the form of a Notion that which, for 'meaning' and 'perceiving', is a Thing; i.e. it seeks to possess in thinghood the consciousness only of itself. Reason now has, therefore, a universal *interest* in the world, because it is certain of its presence in the world, or that the world present to it is rational. It seeks its 'other', knowing that therein it possesses nothing but itself: it seeks only its own infinitude.
>
> (PS: §240, pp. 145–46)

As with the previous discussion of idealistic rationalism, Hegel's attitude to scientific rationalism is ambivalent: on the one hand, he is sympathetic to the rationalistic spirit that drives it, but on the other hand he thinks that this spirit here appears in a distorted form, as all the universal categories and laws that it constructs are too abstract and arbitrary. He therefore warns that a certain lack of development in consciousness' *self*-conception at this stage leads it to misunderstand what it means to see itself in the world:

> But even if Reason digs into the very entrails of things and opens every vein in them so that it may gush forth to meet itself, it will not attain this joy [of finding itself present in things]; it must have completed itself inwardly before it can experience the consummation of itself.
>
> (PS: §241, p. 146)

Hegel makes clear that one important respect in which scientific rationalism goes astray, is that in trying to overcome the subject-centred outlook of idealism (which reduced the material world to the self), it goes too far in the opposite direction (and so attempts to reduce the self to the material world), so that we have here an equally one-sided position. Hegel therefore considers how Observing Reason views the natural world (in the subsection 'Observation of Nature'), how it views itself as consciousness (in the subsection 'Observation of Self-Consciousness'), and how it views the relation between the two in the connection of mind and body (in the subsection 'Observation of the Relation of Self-Consciousness to its Immediate Actuality'). Throughout this discussion, Hegel's aim is to show that while we must respect the achievements of the natural sciences, we should not exaggerate them, for the scientific outlook still leaves the tension between universality and individuality unresolved; we therefore should not treat scientific models and explanations as if they alone can provide us with a proper way of understanding ourselves and the natural world, as this unresolved tension means that in fact Reason must remain unsatisfied by this way of viewing things.

THE OBSERVATION OF NATURE

Hegel begins his analysis of how scientific rationalism regards the natural world by suggesting that while the official allegiance of Observing Reason is to the primacy of experience and hence to empiricism, it is actually considerably more sophisticated in its outlook than the standpoints that were considered earlier in the 'Consciousness' chapter, both at the epistemological level (in allowing that there is no aconceptual 'given') and at the ontological level (in allowing that what is observed is not a bare particular):

> [Observing Reason] will ... readily admit that its concern is not wholly and solely with perception, and will not let, e.g., the perception that this penknife lies alongside this snuff-box, pass for an observation. What is perceived should at least have the significance of a *universal*, not of a *sensuous particular*.

> (PS: §244, p. 147)

Because it recognizes that things share universal properties, Observing Reason begins by attempting to describe the world in as much detail as it can, and to classify things into kinds, by distinguishing between essential and inessential properties. In doing so, it hopes to find vindication for its rationalistic picture, by showing that what is salient to us is also salient for nature itself, in a way that suggests that our classifications reflect structures inherent in things: '*Differentiae* are supposed, not merely to have an essential connection with cognition, but also to accord with the essential characteristics of things, and our artificial system is supposed to accord with Nature's own system and to express only this' (PS: §246, p. 149). Observing Reason finds support for this 'objectivity' in its classifications in some areas, as when in zoology we find that the claws and teeth with which certain animals set themselves apart from one another are also the features we use to mark off these animals into kinds. However, this argument for the rational transparency of nature does not take Observing Reason very far, as at other levels (particularly in botany and the inorganic sciences) it finds it hard to adopt any sort of stable and non-arbitrary classificatory scheme:

> Observation, which kept them [i.e. its biological categories] properly apart and believed that in them it had something firm and settled, sees principles overlapping one another, transitions and confusions developing; what it at first took to be absolutely separate, it sees combined with something else, and what it reckoned to be in combination, it sees apart and separate. So it is that observation which clings to passive, unbroken selfsameness of being, inevitably sees itself tormented just in its most general determinations – e.g. of what are the *differentiae* of an animal or a plant – by instances which rob it of every determination, invalidate the universality to which it has risen, and reduce it to an observation and description which is devoid of thought.
>
> (PS: §247, p. 150)

Hegel suggests that though the scientist wishes to vindicate a rationalistic outlook, he cannot do so, because he is torn between on the one hand adopting an empirical approach, which attempts to group creatures together using their merely observed similarities (claws, teeth, etc.), and on the other hand trying to base a system of natural kinds on these similarities; the scientist tries to treat these characteristics as fixed and essential, when the changeability and heterogeneity of creatures at this level makes this impossible. This scientific outlook therefore faces a fundamental tension between the 'universality' of its classificatory scheme and the 'particularity' of the individuals it tries but fails to subsume under the scheme.

Finding itself frustrated by the apparent vagueness and arbitrariness of its attempts to 'carve nature at the joints' using a conception of natural kinds, Observing Reason now attempts to rise above mere observation and description and to satisfy thought by attempting to uncover the laws that govern phenomena. The difficulty for Observing Reason, however, is to know how to reconcile a conception of laws as universal and necessary with its residual empiricism. Hegel speaks here of an 'instinct of Reason', by which he means that while such empiricism should lead it to feel a Humean scepticism about such universality and necessity, nonetheless consciousness finds it hard to doubt that laws represent how it is that things must be, given their underlying natures: 'That a stone falls, is true for consciousness because in its heaviness the stone has in and for itself that essential relation to the earth which is expressed in falling' (PS: §250, p. 152).

Observing Reason thus finds itself constructing laws that are increasingly general and removed from the concreteness of the experimental situation, while its conception of a property becomes more abstract, culminating in the notion of 'matters' (such as positive and negative electricity, or heat), which are not observable particulars but are theoretical entities which have a status similar to universals. This allows Observing Reason to frame laws in a more and more abstract and 'pure' way:

> We find, as the truth of this experimenting consciousness, *pure law*, which is freed from sensuous being; we see it as a *Notion* which, while present in sensuous being, operates there independently and unrestrained, and, while immersed in it, is free of it, and a *simple* Notion.
>
> (PS: §253, p. 154)

In finding itself drawn away from empiricism and nominalism, Observing Reason gains an important insight into how the world incorporates structures that can only be uncovered by thought (cf. EL: §21Z, pp. 33–34).

However, although this is an important lesson for Observing Reason to learn, and one which allows it to fit inorganic nature into an increasingly complex and satisfying theoretical framework, it finds itself frustrated as it attempts to treat another part of the natural world in law-like terms: namely, living organisms. Here, Observing Reason attempts to find laws that will explain the nature of organisms in terms of their environment, which it hopes will enable it to classify organisms in ecological terms (e.g. pike are fish because they live best in water). However, Observing Reason finds that these laws are mere correlations, which appear to have no underlying necessity or rational force, for example in the sort of general theory of environmental influence proposed by the biologist G. E. Treviranus, according to which 'animals belonging to the air have the nature of birds, those belonging to water have the nature of fish, animals in northern latitudes have thick hairy pelts, and so on'. Hegel comments:

> [S]uch laws are seen at a glance to display a poverty which does not do justice to the manifold variety of organic Nature. Besides the fact that organic Nature in its freedom can divest its forms of these characteristics, and of necessity everywhere presents exceptions to such laws, or rules as we might call them, the characterization of the creatures to which they do apply is so superficial that even the necessity of the laws cannot be other than superficial, and amounts to no more than the *great influence* of environment; and this does not tell us what does and what does not strictly belong to this influence. Such relations of organisms to the elements [they live in] cannot therefore in fact be called *laws*. For, firstly, the *content* of such a relation, as we saw, does not exhaust the range of organisms concerned, and secondly, the sides of the relation are mutually indifferent and express no necessity.
>
> (PS: §255, p. 155)

Now, once Observing Reason recognizes that there is no necessary relation between the nature of the organism and its environment (e.g. there are birds which cannot fly), it then looks for a different way of explaining the nature of the organism, which it now does in *teleological* terms. Such explanations assume that the organism has a purpose, and account for its various properties by showing how they help the organism to achieve that purpose. Hegel argues, however, that Observing Reason has an *intentional* model of teleology, according to which for an organism to have an end, it must either have that end intentionally, as a conscious goal, or it must have that end bestowed on it by some external designer who has adapted it for his or her purposes. The difficulty is that Observing Reason cannot make either view fit with natural organisms, for they can scarcely be said to have chosen their ends, while if we say that they are as they are because they have been adapted as such by an external designer, we cannot use this idea to provide us with an explanation of the organism's nature. Thus, while Observing Reason acknowledges that 'the organism shows itself to be a being that *preserves* itself, that *returns* and *has returned* into itself' (PS: §259, p. 158), it thinks that this is not really teleological behaviour because it is not the *intention* of the organism to preserve itself, so

> this observing consciousness does not recognize in this being [i.e. in the fact that the organism acts to preserve itself] the Notion of End, or that the Notion of End exists just here and in the form of a Thing, and not elsewhere in some other intelligence. It makes a distinction between the Notion of End, and being-for-self and self-preservation, a distinction which is none.

> (PS: §259, p. 158)

Because Observing Reason does not really recognize the self-preservation of the organism as a purpose intrinsic to the thing itself (internal teleology), it only explains the nature of the organism by appealing to how that organism is adapted to serve purposes *outside* itself (external teleology), which then results in an unsatisfying explanatory account of why the organism is as it is. As Hegel puts it elsewhere:

> The notion of purpose is not merely external to nature, as it is when I say that sheep bear wool only in order that I may clothe myself. Silly

> remarks of this kind are often made, as for example in the *Xenia*, when the wisdom of God is admired because He causes cork trees to grow that we might have bottle-stoppers, herbs that we might cure disordered stomachs, and cinnabar that we might make ourselves up.
>
> (EN: I, §245Z, p. 196)

(The *Xenia* were a series of epigrams written by Goethe and Schiller and published in 1796–97, in which they lampooned the views of their contemporaries. For a helpful general discussion of Hegel's views on teleology, see deVries 1991.)

An obvious question to raise at this point is *why* Hegel thinks that Observing Reason operates only with this intentional model of teleology, such that it does not think that self-preservation really counts as a goal of the organism, and hence believes that teleological explanations cannot be internal (e.g. the function or purpose of bark on a tree is to stop it dehydrating) but must be external (e.g. the purpose of bark on trees is so we can put stops in our bottles). One answer can of course be historical: that is, many scientists and philosophers associated with the scientific revolution actually did have such an intentional model of teleology, so that Hegel would seem justified in attributing to this view with Observing Reason. But another answer relates more directly to my overall interpretation of the *Phenomenology*: namely, that Observing Reason lacks a properly Aristotelian understanding of universals as natural kinds, and so does not see that each organic thing, as an organism of a particular type, is striving to realize its nature as a thing of that type (cf. deVries 1988b: 9).

Failing properly to understand the organism in teleological terms, Observing Reason goes back to looking for laws governing the central processes and capacities of living animals. In Hegel's time these were identified as the capacity for sensibility (meaning the capacity to transfer information about stimuli from one part of the body to another), irritability (meaning the capacity to respond to stimuli), and reproduction (meaning the capacity of the organism to grow and reproduce its tissue). These capacities were said to be located in the nervous system, the muscular system, and the viscera respectively. Observing Reason therefore sets about finding laws that relate these capacities to one another, and to the parts of the body said to possess these capacities. Hegel then proceeds to show how difficult it is for Observing Reason to find any real law-like correlations in this area, partly because sensibility, irritability, and reproduction are interrelated functions, partly because Observing Reason cannot meaningfully apply quantitative determinations in trying to relate these capacities, and partly because the organism cannot really be divided into separate anatomical systems: 'In this way the idea of a *law* in the case of organic being is altogether lost' (PS: §278, p. 167). Hegel therefore concludes that in its study of nature, Observing Reason cannot find the kind of rational satisfaction it seeks:

> [H]ere observation cannot do more than to make clever remarks, indicate interesting connections, and make a friendly approach to the Notion. But clever *remarks* are not a knowledge of necessity, *interesting* connections go no further than being 'of interest', while the interest is still nothing more than a mere subjective opinion about Reason; and the *friendliness* with which the individual alludes to the Notion is a childlike friendliness which is childish if it wants to be, or is supposed to be, valid in and for itself.
>
> (PS: §297, pp. 179–80)

We have therefore seen the dialectic of universal and individual operating at several levels through this section, as Observing Reason has tried to bring the individual under some intelligible scheme of universal laws, but where these laws have turned out to be too ad hoc and empty, to be no more than mere regularities and correlations. Consciousness' conception of the natural world thus remains one in which universality and individuality stand opposed as categories, and so it is still unable to find in nature the rational structures that will enable it to feel 'at home'.

THE OBSERVATION OF SELF-CONSCIOUSNESS

Having failed to find any satisfactory role for laws at the level of inorganic and organic nature, consciousness now turns upon itself, and moves from the observation of nature to the 'Observation of

Self-Consciousness', in an effort to find laws governing the human mind. Hegel begins by discussing the attempt to treat laws of logic as laws of human thought, governing the way in which we reason. Hegel argues that although such laws are meant to be necessary and universal, 'the way in which this form or content *presents itself to observation* qua observation gives it the character of something *found*, something that is *given*, i.e. a content that merely *is*' (PS: §300, p. 181), so all that can be established is how as a matter of fact we *do* think, not why we *must* think that way, or why we *should* so think.

Observing Reason then turns from trying to find laws governing the subject's thoughts, to trying to find laws governing its actions, and so arrives at observational psychology. As before, it begins by trying to describe and classify people into different types, but it quickly finds that this is unsatisfying, 'much less interesting even than enumerating the species of insects, mosses, etc.' (PS: §304, p. 183). Observing Reason therefore begins to frame psychological laws instead: 'it … seems now to have a rational aim and to be engaged in a necessary activity' (PS: §304, p. 183). Observing Reason then looks for links between how the individual behaves and its social environment, to determine how the latter affects the former. However, there is always an element that distorts this effect, namely how the individual himself chooses to respond to his environment. This freedom possessed by the individual makes a nonsense of attempts by psychology to establish law-like correlations between the way in which individuals behave and their social circumstances:

> [T]he individual either *allows* free play to the stream of the actual world flowing in upon it, or else breaks it off and transforms it. The result of this, however, is that 'psychological necessity' becomes an empty phrase, so empty that there exists the absolute possibility that what is supposed to have had this influence could just as well not have had it.
>
> (PS: §307, pp. 184–85)

Hegel emphasizes that this freedom means it is not possible to see the individual as determined by its social environment, although he is happy to allow that '[i]f these circumstances, ways of thinking, customs, in general the state of the world, had not been, then of course the individual would not have become what he is' (PS: §306, p. 184). The reason is that while the individual may choose to conform to that environment, he may also choose to rebel against it, so while this environment will have a role to play in understanding him or her, what role that is will ultimately depend on the choices made by the individual, and these choices lie beyond the kinds of explanation offered by the social psychologist. For Hegel, therefore, Observing Reason is here once again operating with a simplistic model of the relation between the individual and the universal qua 'habits, customs, and way of thinking already to hand':

> On the one hand, Spirit receives these modes into itself ... ; and, on the other hand, Spirit knows itself as spontaneously active in face of them, and in singling out from them something for itself, it follows its own inclinations and desires, making the object conform to *it*: in the first case it behaves negatively towards itself as an individuality; in the second case, negatively towards itself as a universal being.
>
> (PS: §302, p. 182)

Observing Reason does not properly grasp this complex interrelation.

As Observing Reason can find no laws governing its thought or actions *per se*, or its thought and actions as they relate to the world outside the subject, it now looks to find some sort of correlation between its thoughts or actions as mental phenomena with the body in which the mind belongs; it therefore moves to the 'observation of the relation of self-consciousness to its immediate actuality', in the third subsection on Observing Reason. In this subsection, Hegel turns to the pseudo-sciences of physiognomy (which attempted to draw conclusions about a person's character from anatomical features) and phrenology (which attempted to do the same using the shape of the skull), where both of these approaches had considerable popularity at the time Hegel was writing (due to the work of J. C. Lavater and Joseph Gall respectively). Beginning with physiognomy, Hegel accepts that we ordinarily use a person's expression as a way of gauging their thoughts or emotions, treating the former as signs of the latter; but where physiognomy claims to go beyond this and become a proper science, is in making *predictions* about how people will behave on the basis of their anatomical features, and in being prepared to use such features to tell a person about their character in a way that overrules the evidence of their actions and their own self-knowledge. As a result, this science is forced to treat character traits as hidden dispositions, a desperate manoeuvre that has no methodological credibility. In this context, Hegel approvingly quotes Georg Christoph Lichtenberg, who had written a pamphlet criticizing Lavater:

> If anyone said, 'You certainly act like an honest man, but I see from your face that you are forcing yourself to do so and are a rogue at heart'; without a doubt, every honest fellow to the end of time, when thus addressed, will retort with a box on the ear.
>
> (see PS: §322, p. 193)

Hegel then moves on to a discussion of phrenology, which sees the outer as an immediate expression of the inner, where the obvious place for such expression to occur is the skull. Hegel first points out that it is difficult for the phrenologist to say whether it is the skull that determines the nature of the brain or the brain that determines the shape of the skull; but even if there is some sort of 'pre-established harmony' between the two, it is harder still to do anything more than find mere statistical correlations between the shape and size of a person's head and their character and behaviour, where these correlations are no more significant than the correlations that might exist between rain and a house-wife's washday. The phrenologist cannot use these correlations to make meaningful predictions; instead he reverts again to the notion of 'unrealized dispositions', which allow him to avoid making such predictions in a way that is nonetheless scientifically spurious (as spurious as the housewife in Hegel's example who claims that today there is a tendency to rain, because today is a washday, although this tendency does not imply that it actually *will* rain). Hegel is confident that Reason will come to see through this sort of absurdity, and in doing so will recognize that scientific rationalism cannot do justice to our capacity for self-determination:

> The crude instinct of self-conscious Reason will reject out of hand such a 'science' of phrenology – this other observational instinct of self-conscious Reason which, having attained a glimpse of the cognitive process, has grasped it unintelligently in a way that takes the outer to be an expression of the inner ... [T]he antithesis we are here concerned with has for its sides the individuality that is conscious of itself, and the abstraction of externality that has become wholly a *Thing* – that inner being of Spirit grasped as a fixed non-spiritual being, opposed to such a being. But Reason, in its role of observer, having reached thus far, seems also to have reached its peak, at which point it must abandon itself and do a right-about turn; for only what is wholly bad is implicitly charged with the immediate necessity of changing round into its opposite.
>
> (PS: §340, pp. 205–6)

The 'right-about turn' that Reason now takes is one we have seen before within the dialectic, namely a move from theory to practice, as consciousness goes from observing the world, to seeing itself as an agent within it; the limitations of scientific rationalism seem to show that the essence of the subject lies in its capacity for free self-determination, so that consciousness now sets itself apart from the world of causally determined objects:

> The given object is ... determined as a negative object; consciousness, however, is determined as *self*-consciousness over against it; in other words, the category which, in the course of observation, has run through the form of *being* is now posited in the form of being-for-self: consciousness no longer aims to *find* itself *immediately*, but to produce itself by its own activity. It is *itself* the End at which its action aims, whereas in its role of observer it was concerned only with things.
>
> (PS: §344, p. 209)

Hegel thus moves from Observing Reason, which has found the satisfaction promised by theoretical science to be illusory, to 'active Reason' (PS: §348, p. 211), which holds instead that consciousness can come to feel 'at home in the world' once it sees how its purposes can be fulfilled within it. Hegel makes clear, therefore, that just as Observing Reason repeats at a higher level the object-centred outlook of Consciousness, so Active Reason repeats at a higher level the subject-centred outlook of Self-Consciousness:

> Just as Reason, in the role of observer, repeated, in the element of the category, the movement of *consciousness*, viz. sense-certainty, perception, and the Understanding, so will Reason again run through the double movement of self-consciousness, and pass over from independence into its freedom.
>
> (PS: §348, p. 211)

Looking back on this section, some may feel that Hegel's stance with respect to Observing Reason must be modified, either on historical grounds (Hegel's criticisms here apply only to the scientific ideas and theories of his period, and rest on an impoverished picture of what sciences such as psychology can achieve), or on philosophical ones (Hegel here betrays aspects of his Romantic distrust of science, a distrust that seems outdated in the modern world). This may be so; but it could equally be argued (cf. MacIntyre 1972a) that Hegel's criticisms apply no less fundamentally to current developments within broadly physicalist approaches to human behaviour and mentality, and that Hegel's position is not Romantic in any narrow sense, but is merely concerned to highlight the difficulties of attempting to apply physicalistic explanations across the board. This is a position which many today (although not of course all) would see as perfectly reasonable, and they may well take our capacity for free action to show why it is inappropriate to apply the physicalistic model to the human realm, in a way that is also emphasized by Hegel. Of course, the debate has moved on in terms of its depth and sophistication since Hegel's day, and developments in science of which Hegel knew nothing have played their part in this; but these issues remain current, and Hegel's general position remains a live option within this discussion.

ACTIVE REASON

Hegel continues his analysis of how Reason tries to make itself 'at home in the world' in this section and the next (entitled 'The Actualization of Rational Self-Consciousness Through Its Own Activity' and 'Individuality Which Takes Itself To Be Real In And For Itself'). In considering these sections, it is important to take into account the introductory preamble to the first of them (PS: §§348–59, pp. 211–17). Hegel makes clear here that the strategies he considers in the rest of this chapter are all ones that take as their starting point 'modern' assumptions about the individual and his place in the social world, and so should be contrasted with the less individualist outlook of premodern (specifically Greek) accounts of what it means to be 'at home in the world'. Only once these 'modern' standpoints have been shown to be inadequate will consciousness 'turn back' to see how this premodern outlook came to be lost (in the chapter on Spirit). Hegel's characterization of the fundamental differences between the ancient and modern conceptions of the individual here is therefore vital to the rest of his discussion.

ANCIENTS AND MODERNS

For the Greeks, in Hegel's view, it was accepted as axiomatic that the only way in which an individual can come to find practical satisfaction within the world is inside the state or *polis*, so the question of satisfaction for the individual is immediately taken to be a social question: only if the individual lives within a properly constituted social framework can he ever find himself 'at home'. According to Hegel, the Greeks therefore held that reconciliation between the individual and the world could only be achieved by an individual who lived in accordance with the customs and traditions of a properly constituted community. Hegel outlines this view as follows:

> In a free nation, therefore, Reason is in truth realized. It is a present living Spirit in which the individual not only finds his essential character, i.e. his universal and particular nature, expressed, and present

> to him in the form of thinghood, but is himself this essence, and also has realized that essential character. The wisest men of antiquity have therefore declared that wisdom and virtue consist in living in accordance with the customs of one's nation.
>
> (PS: §352, p. 214)

In adopting this position, the 'wisest men of antiquity' showed themselves to be thinking at a time before the individual had learnt to distinguish himself from his social role, and to regard himself as an independent source of moral assessment, and when the divisions between self and society had not been felt. Hegel presents a sketch of this premodern social life in the preceding paragraphs (one that he elaborates elsewhere: cf. ETW: 154–55, PH: 250–77):

> This ethical *Substance*, taken in its abstract universality, is only law in the form of *thought*; but it is no less immediately actual *self-consciousness*, or it is *custom*. The single individual consciousness, conversely, is only this existent unit in so far as it is aware of the universal consciousness in its individuality as its *own* being, since what it does and is, is the universal custom ... They are conscious of being these separate independent beings through the sacrifice of their particularity, and by having this universal Substance as their soul and essence, just as this universal again is their own doing as particular individuals, or is the work they have produced ... The *labour* of the individual for his own needs is just as much a satisfaction of the needs of others as of his own, and the satisfaction of his own needs he obtains through the labour of others. As the individual in his *individual* work already *unconsciously* performs a *universal* work, so again he also performs the universal work as his *conscious* object; the whole becomes, as *a* whole, his own work, for which he sacrifices himself and precisely in so doing receives back from it his own self ... This unity of being-for-another or making oneself a Thing, and of being-for-self, this universal Substance, speaks its *universal language* in the customs and laws of its nation. But this existent unchangeable essence is the expression of the very individuality which seems opposed to it; the laws proclaim what each individual is and does; the individual knows them not only as his universal objective thinghood,

but equally knows himself in them, or knows them as *particularized* in his own individuality, and in each of his fellow citizens. In the universal Spirit, therefore, each has only the certainty of himself, of finding in the actual world nothing but himself; he is as certain of the others as he is of himself. I perceive in all of them the fact that they know themselves to be only these independent beings, just as I am. I perceive in them the free unity with others in such wise that, just as this unity exists through me, so it exists through the others too – I regard them as myself and myself as them.

(PS: §§349–51, pp. 212–14)

As the conclusion here indicates, Hegel in many ways took it that the Greek social world was one in which the individual could find himself 'at home', where 'each has only the certainty of himself, of finding in the actual world nothing but himself'. There is here no division of the individual from the customs of his society, of self-interest from the general interest, of individual moral convictions from the laws laid down by the *polis*: in this sense, Hegel (like many of his contemporaries) saw the life of the citizen in fifth-century BC Athens as a model for the sort of harmony and reconciliation he thought a proper understanding of the self and the world might provide. (Cf. Schiller 1967: 33, 'I do not underrate the advantages which the human race today, considered as a whole and weighed in the balance of intellect, can boast in the face of what is best in the ancient world. But it has to take up the challenge in serried ranks, and let whole measure itself against whole. What individual Modern could sally forth and engage, man against man, with an individual Athenian for the prize of humanity?' For helpful background to Hegel's discussion here, see Forster 1998: 17–125.)

However, Hegel makes clear at this point that Reason does not and cannot any longer take this Greek conception seriously in its way of making itself 'at home'; for Reason begins with a conception of the free individual that is not recognized by the Greeks, a conception that then leads to divisions not apparent in their social world, between the individual and the customs of society, between the individual and the general good, and between the individual and the laws of the state. Thus, from this modern perspective, custom and tradition appear as morally arbitrary; the individual no longer identifies himself with the interests of the group; and the laws enacted by the state clash with the moral authority of the individual. Consciousness can thus no longer find itself 'at home in the world' in a way that was available to the Greeks, but which is lost to Reason:

> Reason *must* withdraw from this happy state; for the life of a free people is only in principle or immediately the *reality* of an ethical order. In other words, the ethical order exists merely as something *given* ... [T]he single, individual consciousness as it exists immediately in the real ethical order, or in the nation, is a solid unshaken trust in which Spirit has not, for the individual, resolved itself into its *abstract* moments, and therefore he is not aware of himself as being a pure individuality on his own account. But once he has arrived at this idea, as he must, then this *immediate* unity with Spirit, the [mere] *being* of himself in Spirit, his trust, is lost. Isolated and on his own, it is he who is now the essence, no longer universal Spirit ... In thus establishing himself ... the individual has thereby placed himself in opposition to the laws and customs. These are regarded as mere ideas having no absolute essentiality, an abstract theory without any reality, while he as this particular 'I' is his own living truth.
>
> (PS: §§354–55, pp. 214–15)

It is vital to recognize, therefore, that the strategies taken up by Reason in the next two sections, to show that practical consciousness can find satisfaction in the world, are ones adopted by consciousness *after* this modern notion of individuality has emerged; they are not strategies the Greeks would have understood, as they dealt with such issues against the background of a social conception that Reason has overturned.

Now, as we shall see, Hegel sets out to show that such individualist strategies are doomed to failure, and that some part of the Greek picture must be recovered if we are to find the kind of harmony between self and world that Reason takes to be possible. Nonetheless, here as elsewhere Hegel is at pains to stress that the individualistic turn taken by Reason is inevitable and progressive. For though the Greek citizen was 'at home in the world', this harmony remains unthinking and unreflective, based on an unquestioning acceptance of the social order and of the individual's place within it, until a proper conception of individuality has emerged (cf. PR: §124). Hegel therefore hopes to show how we can learn from the social conception of the Greeks and how the failed individualistic strategies of Reason can be improved upon, without *merely* 'going back to the Greeks', something which modern individualism has made impossible. Thus, although the Greeks were able to be 'at home in the world' in a way that was satisfactory for their own time, it is not an answer that can be satisfactory in *our* own time, when a greater degree of individualism has emerged. On the other hand, Hegel sets out to show that modern answers to this question have not been able to succeed, because they have all been based on the division between self and society that this individualist turn has set in place; he thereby sets the context for his own attempt to resolve this question in a way that draws on *both* these traditions, a middle way that will become clearer once the one-sidedness of individualistic Reason has been exposed.[1]

PLEASURE AND NECESSITY

Hegel begins his discussion of Active Reason with a subsection entitled 'Pleasure and Necessity', where consciousness holds that the best way to make itself feel 'at home in the world' is not by obeying custom and tradition (as 'the wisest men of antiquity' held), or by acquiring a theoretical understanding of nature (as Observing Reason held), but by turning to the world as a vehicle for pleasure and enjoyment: 'the individual is sent out into the world by his own spirit to seek his happiness' (PS: §356, p. 215). It is therefore the first expression of the individualistic outlook adopted by Reason:

> In so far as it has lifted itself out of the ethical Substance and the tranquil being of thought to its being-*for-self*, it has left behind the law of custom and existence, the knowledge acquired through observation, and theory, as a grey shadow which is in the act of passing out of sight. For the latter is rather a knowledge of something whose

> being-for-self and actuality are other than those of this self-consciousness. Instead of the heavenly-seeming Spirit of the universality of knowledge and action in which the feeling and enjoyment of individuality are stilled, there has entered into it the Spirit of the earth, for which true actuality is merely that being which is the actuality of the *individual* consciousness ... It plunges therefore into life and indulges to the full the pure individuality in which it appears.
>
> (PS: §§360–61, pp. 217–18)

Hegel contrasts this outlook with the position of Observing Reason that preceded it by making reference to Goethe's Faust, alluding to the *Faust Fragment* (1790), where he echoes Mephisto's words in making fun of knowledge and theory. Although, as we have seen, Hegel draws a parallel between the opening of this section and the opening of the 'Self-Consciousness' section, and talks here of 'an immediate will or *natural impulse* which obtains its satisfaction, which is itself the content of a fresh impulse' (PS: §357, p. 215), Hegel nonetheless distinguishes Faust's pursuit of pleasure from mere desire: for in his sexual relation with Gretchen, there is a greater degree of recognition, 'the vision of the unity of the two independent self-consciousnesses' (PS: §362, p. 218). However, Hegel suggests that while Faust feels a kind of hedonistic attachment to Gretchen, she still remains for him a vehicle for pleasure, in the sense that 'the object which individuality experiences as its *essence*, has no content' (PS: §363, p. 219), so while he may want to enter into a more ethical relation with her, he finds his commitment to seeking pleasure means he cannot do so; he remains bound by the consequences of his pact with Mephisto. Rather than constituting the essence of the individual, pleasure-seeking now appears as an alien constraint on his happiness, a kind of external necessity or fate which seems set to destroy him. Consciousness thus moves from seeing pleasure as 'individual' to seeing it as 'universal', something which stands over against the individual and leads to his downfall: 'The *abstract necessity* therefore has the character of the merely negative, uncomprehended power of universality, on which individuality is smashed to pieces' (PS: §365, pp. 220–21).

THE LAW OF THE HEART

In the next subsection, entitled 'The Law of the Heart and the Frenzy of Self-Conceit', Hegel considers a form of consciousness that thinks it has an explanation for the pain and suffering that previously appeared to be an 'abstract necessity' and attempts to do away with it, thereby turning away from its *own* pleasure-seeking to a more high-minded interest in the pleasure of others and in 'promoting the welfare of mankind' (PS: §370, p. 222). This form of consciousness holds that every individual *ought* to be able to find happiness, but cannot do so because the sovereign authority of the individual and his sensibility have not been recognized: the individual has not been allowed to follow 'the law of the heart', and instead has been subjected to the power of the church and state, 'that authoritative divine and human ordinance [which] is separated from the heart' (PS: §371, p. 222). This form of consciousness (which commentators have generally associated with Rousseau's Savoyard Vicar: see Rousseau 1991) therefore maintains that the world is a rational place, because it thinks it can bring about a society in which all individuals will find the happiness they are looking for, once they are allowed to listen to what their hearts tell them.

According to Hegel, however, this form of consciousness faces several difficulties. First, this social reformer will become increasingly alienated in the process of constructing his social programme, as it takes on a universalizing and generalizing aspect at odds with the particularity of 'the law of the heart': 'For in its realization it received the form of an [affirmative] *being*, and is now a *universal* power for which this particular heart is a matter of indifference, so that the individual, by setting up his own ordinance, no longer finds it to be his own' (PS: §372, p. 223). Second, this consciousness comes to see that others may not identify themselves with its social programme, just as it did not identify with the social programme that already existed, leading it to adopt a contradictory dismissiveness to the 'hearts' of others:

[O]thers do not find in this content the fulfilment of the law of *their* hearts, but rather that of someone else; and, precisely in accordance with the universal law that each shall find in what is law *his* own heart, they turn against the reality *he* has set up, just as he turned against theirs. Thus, just as the individual at first finds only the rigid law, now he finds the hearts of men themselves, opposed to his excellent intentions and detestable.

(PS: §373, p. 224)

Third, it also comes to find that others may oppose it in the name of the existing order, so it can no longer reject that order as alien to the will of individuals:

It took this divine and human ordinance which it found as an accepted authority to be a dead authority in which not only its own self – to which it clings as this particular independent heart opposed to the universal – but also those subject to that ordinance would have no consciousness of themselves; but it finds that this ordinance is really annihilated by the consciousness of all, that it is the law of every heart.

(PS: §374, pp. 224–25)

Faced with these contradictions 'the law of the heart' becomes 'the frenzy of self-conceit' (where Hegel's most obvious model is Karl Moor from Schiller's play *The Robbers*). This form of consciousness is a crazed conspiracy-theorist, blaming the corrupting influence of evil social forces for the refusal of others to join it in its battle against the establishment:

The heart-throb for the welfare of humanity therefore passes into the ravings of an insane self-conceit, into the fury of consciousness to preserve itself from destruction ... It therefore speaks of the universal order as a perversion of the law of the heart and its happiness, a perversion invented by fanatical priests, gluttonous despots and their minions, who compensate themselves for their own degradation by degrading and oppressing others, a perversion which has led to the nameless misery of deluded mankind.

(PS: §377, p. 226)

Abandoning the stance of an idealistic social reformer, consciousness now comes to view others in more cynical terms, as it sees that in their hearts the behaviour of others is ruled by self-interest, and that this is the 'way of the world':

> What seems to be public *order*, then, is this universal state of war, in which each wrests what he can for himself, executes justice on the individuality of others and establishes his own, which is equally nullified through the action of others. It is the 'way of the world', the show of an unchanging course that is only *meant* to be a universality, and whose content is rather the essenceless play of establishing and nullifying individualities.
>
> (PS: §379, pp. 227–28)

Thus, although the individual here in some sense sets the universal over himself, he does so in a simplistic manner, assuming that all must share his conception of what is right, leaving him to see nothing but the worst motives in those who do not.

VIRTUE AND THE WAY OF THE WORLD

Hegel now moves to a discussion of 'Virtue and the Way of the World', where Virtue tries to show how this egoism cannot lead consciousness to feel 'at home'. Given Hegel's earlier positive invocation of the Greeks, it might be expected that he would have some sympathy with the standpoint adopted by Virtue; but it becomes clear that it is a *modern* version of this position (represented perhaps by the Earl of Shaftesbury) that is his focus here, which sees the pursuit of virtue as an *individual* project, something that can be achieved even in a corrupt society. In this way, on the modern conception of virtue the individual can achieve true happiness and can come to feel 'at home' even in a world that is spiritually and ethically rotten (something that Aristotle, for example, would not have accepted, as he took it for granted that the ethical outlook of the individual was shaped by that of his society). Hegel argues that as a result, while modern 'knights of virtue' pretend to be concerned to reform those corrupted by the 'way of the world', their battle for the good is really a sham. In fact, it is hard for Virtue to say what this corruption is supposed to consist in, and it ends up as no more than empty rhetoric, for it cannot really explain what is wrong when (as Bernard Mandeville claimed in his *Fable of the Bees*, and as Adam Smith had argued that the capitalist economy showed) it appears that self-interest can lead to the common good:

> Virtue in the ancient world had its own definite sure meaning, for it had in the *spiritual substance* of the nation a foundation full of meaning, and for its purpose an actual good already in existence. Consequently, too, it was not directed against the actual world as against something *generally perverted*, and against a 'way of the world'. But the virtue we are considering has its being outside of the spiritual substance, it is an unreal virtue, a virtue in imagination and name only, which lacks that substantial content ... In its conflict [consciousness] has learnt by experience that the 'way of the world' is not as bad as it looked; for its reality is the reality of the universal. With this lesson in mind, the idea of bringing the good into existence by means of the sacrifice of individuality is abandoned; for individuality is precisely the actualizing of what exists only in principle, and the perversion ceases to be regarded as a perversion of the good, for it is in fact really the conversion of the good, as a mere End, into an actual existence: the movement of individuality is the reality of the universal.
>
> (PS: §§390–91, pp. 234–35)

Thus, while Virtue works with a clear antithesis between the individual as virtuous and the individual as self-interested, because it sets the good of the community against the good of the individual, Hegel believes that this rests on a failure to acknowledge the dialectical interrelation between the two, whereby the universal good can be satisfied through the pursuit of individual interests. (Cf. PR: §199, p. 233, 'In this dependence and reciprocity of work and the satisfaction of needs, *subjective selfishness* turns into a *contribution towards the satisfaction of the needs of everyone else*. By a dialectical movement, the particular is mediated by the universal so that each individual, in earning, producing, and enjoying on his own account [*für sich*], thereby earns and produces for the enjoyment of others.')

In examining this section, we have therefore seen how Hegel presents three standpoints that contradict the Greek view that 'wisdom and virtue consist in living in accordance with the customs of one's nation', and instead try to show how consciousness can be 'at home' in a more individualistic manner, by seeking pleasure, or following 'the law of the heart', or by exercising 'unreal' virtue, where each standpoint sets the perspective of the individual at odds with the existing social order, in a way that ultimately undermines them. As we have seen, Hegel believed that with the rise of modern individualism it was inevitable that views of this kind would emerge as consciousness tried to find a way to make itself 'at home' when the customs and traditions that made up Greek ethical life had lost their authority; but it is clear that for Hegel consciousness must find some way to give a role to a different kind of social framework, if the balance lost by this turn to individualism is to be restored.

PRACTICAL REASON

In the section we have been considering, consciousness has discovered that its individualistic turn has not enabled it to find 'wisdom and virtue'; on the contrary, the pursuit of pleasure has merely led to unhappiness, the law of the heart has become self-conceit, and virtue has been revealed as high-minded hypocrisy. In the section we will now discuss, entitled 'Individuality Which Takes Itself To Be Real In And For Itself', Hegel examines other ways in which modern individualism makes it hard to avoid moral failures of this kind.

THE SPIRITUAL ANIMAL KINGDOM

In the next subsection (enigmatically entitled 'The Spiritual Animal Kingdom and Deceit, or the "Matter In Hand" Itself') Hegel considers an important aspect of this individualistic turn, which is that the subject evaluates himself in terms of his 'works' (i.e. his deeds and products), which he views as an expression of himself, coming to know what he is through what he can do:

> Consciousness must act merely in order that what it is *in itself* may become explicit *for it*; in other words, action is simply the coming-to-be

> of Spirit as *consciousness* ... Accordingly, an individual cannot know what he [really] is until he has made himself a reality through action.
>
> (PS: §401, p. 240)

In this way, it might appear that the individual would allow himself to be judged on the basis of his actions; but in fact all acts of self-expression are viewed as unique, and equally valuable:

> It would only be put down as a bad work by a comparing reflection, which, however, is an idle affair, since it goes beyond the essential nature of the work, which is to be a self-expression of the individuality, and in it looks for and demands something else, no one knows what.
>
> (PS: §403, p. 241)

This form of consciousness thus adopts a non-judgemental attitude (which Forster 1998: 331–35 claims is modelled on Herder's historicism), as a result of which Reason takes up an attitude of joyous self-affirmation:

> Therefore, feelings of exaltation, or lamentation, or repentance are altogether out of place. For all that sort of thing stems from a mind which imagines a *content* and an *in-itself* which are different from the original nature of the individual and the actual carrying-out of it in the real world. Whatever it is that the individual does, and whatever happens to him, that he has done himself, and he *is* that himself. He can have only the consciousness of the simple transference *of himself* from the night of possibility into the daylight of the present ... The individual, therefore, knowing that in his actual world he can find nothing else but its unity with himself, or only the certainty of himself in the truth of that world, *can experience only joy in himself.*
>
> (PS: §404, p. 242)

On the one hand, the individual's scheme of values is so relativistic, and on the other his sense of himself is so vacuous, that he feels that nothing he does can possibly be held against him, so that he can shake off all the spiritual alienation he has so far experienced, and see himself as 'an absolute interfusion of individuality and being' (PS: §405, p. 242).

Hegel argues, however, that things are not as satisfactory as they appear. The difficulty is that consciousness finds that its works are an unstable form of self-expression because they persist while it changes, whilst the significance of the work is open to the interpretation of others, so that its work now seems to stand against it:

> [C]onsciousness is thus made aware in its work of the *antithesis* of willing and achieving, between end and means, and, again, between this inner nature in its entirety and reality itself, an antithesis which in general includes within it the contingency of its action.
>
> (PS: §408, p. 245)

Faced with this antithesis, consciousness now tries to guarantee that it will be well thought of by others by making sure it can be associated with whatever is the current 'big thing' or 'matter in hand', as then it knows it will be thought of as 'honest'. This 'honesty' is, however, a great humbug, as the individual will try to say he is part of this worthwhile project even if he has done nothing, by asserting that at least he has stimulated others, or was not in a position to do anything (even though he wanted to), or by claiming credit for things he has not done. This humbug quickly becomes apparent to others, who see that the individual has associated himself with their project merely to look good in their eyes; all individuals thus come to seem hypocritical to one another, as it comes to seem that all action is self-promotion:

> It is, then, equally a deception of oneself and of others if it is pretended that what one is concerned with is the *'matter in hand' alone*. A consciousness that opens up a subject-matter soon learns that others hurry along like flies to freshly poured-out milk, and want to busy themselves with it; and they learn about that individual that he, too, is concerned with the subject-matter, not as an *object*, but as his *own* affair.
>
> (PS: §418, p. 251)

Joyous self-affirmation thus becomes transformed into poisonous cynicism.

Consciousness then comes to accept that others will participate in the 'matter in hand', and that it cannot expect to keep this to itself. In so doing, it comes to see that the 'matter in hand' is something universal:

> [The matter in hand's] nature [is] such that its *being* is the *action* of the *single* individual and of all individuals whose action is immediately *for others*, or is a 'matter in hand' and is such only as the action of *each* and *everyone*: the essence which is the essence of all beings, viz. *spiritual essence* ... [I]t is the universal which has being only as this action of all and each, and a *reality* in the fact that *this particular* consciousness knows it to be its own individual reality and the reality of all.
>
> (PS: §418, pp. 251–52)

As consciousness comes to recognize that its projects form part of a wider enterprise, it no longer succumbs to the self-regarding jealousies of the Spiritual Animal Kingdom, and instead comes to see in its actions a moral purpose, rather than the mere expression of self that comes from creative activity:

> Thus what is object for consciousness has the significance of being the True; *it is* and it is *authoritative*, in the sense that it exists and is authoritative in and for itself. It is the *absolute* 'matter in hand', which no longer suffers from the antithesis of certainty and its truth, between universal and individual, between purpose and its reality, but whose existence is the *reality* and *action* of self-consciousness. This 'matter in hand' is therefore the *ethical substance*; and consciousness of it is the *ethical* consciousness.
>
> (PS: §420, pp. 252–53)

REASON AND MORALITY

In this way, Hegel makes the transition from action seen as self-expression, to moral action, undertaken to fulfil ethical purposes. At first, consciousness sees no great difficulty in setting out to act morally, for it makes the assumption that each individual can see for himself what is right, and behave accordingly:

> [I]t expresses the existence of the law within itself as follows: sound Reason knows immediately what is right and good. Just as it knows the law immediately, so too the law is valid for it immediately, as it says directly: 'this is right and good' – and, moreover, this particular law. The laws are *determinate*; the law is the 'matter in hand' itself filled with significant content.

(PS: §422, p. 253)

Hegel then suggests that consciousness has this confidence because it thinks it can decide how to act in a particular situation by simply consulting certain self-evident and universally valid moral rules which will tell it immediately how to behave, rules like 'Everyone ought to tell the truth', or 'Love thy neighbour as thyself', where it appears that these imperatives in themselves provide guidance for action. Hegel argues that this is not the case, however, because whether I should act in a certain way in a certain situation is not something I can determine immediately by consulting rules of this sort: for in fact they require further qualification if they are to provide us with proper guidance, and this qualification makes determining the right action harder than Reason first thought, so that in particular cases these rules may not help us at all. For example, with regard to the rule 'Everyone ought to tell the truth', Hegel argues that this cannot mean 'Everyone ought to say whatever they believe', because people may believe things that are false; but if we modify the rule to 'Everyone ought to tell the truth if what they say is true', then as my beliefs are clearly fallible, I cannot be sure in a particular situation whether I should say anything or not. And, with regard to the rule 'Love thy neighbour as thyself', Hegel argues that this only leads to a good action if I love my neighbour 'intelligently', that is, do things for him that are in his real interests, not just in his interests as I happen to see them, because then my action is not much more than a self-indulgence on my part. But then, as before, the problem is that in a particular case my neighbour's real interests will in fact be hard to determine, so that the rule when properly developed does not really provide me with much guidance, and looks rather empty. Thus, as these cases show, the idea that determining how to act rightly just requires nothing more than grasping a few self-evident moral rules has turned out to be problematic.

Consciousness continues to believe that the individualistic stance of Reason can be made to work, however, not because various moral rules make the right action easy to determine, but because the individual does not have to rely on these rules, but can instead apply a procedural 'test' to his actions to make sure his actions are ethically justified; that test is the Kantian test of universalizability, where the subject asks himself if the maxim of his action can be conceived of or willed as a universal law on which everyone acted (cf. Kant, GMM, 4: p. 421). In the subsection on 'Reason as Testing Laws', Hegel critically discusses this attempt by Reason to provide the individual with a way of determining the content of morality, and so offers a critique of this part of Kantian ethics. However, while Hegel's well-known attack on the 'formalism' and 'emptiness' of the Kantian position has convinced some, it has left others cold; moreover, the exact nature of the attack is not easy to pin down, particularly when the discussion in the *Phenomenology* is set alongside other treatments of the issue in the 'Natural Law' essay and the *Philosophy of Right* (see NL: 79–85 and PR: §135, pp. 162–63).

The most straightforward way of taking Hegel's critique is to see him as claiming that the universalizability test itself is empty, in the sense that every maxim can pass the test. Thus, for example, while Kant argued that making lying promises or obtaining property by stealing from others cannot be universalized (because the practice of promise-keeping relies on participants keeping their word, and the institution of property depends on participants respecting the rules of ownership), on this view Hegel is arguing that the maxim of these actions *can* be universalized without difficulty. However, Hegel never actually discusses the issue in this way: that is, he never argues that (for example) promising could continue to function in a situation where everyone lied, or that property could continue to exist in a world where everyone stole from everyone else, so that it seems that this way of taking Hegel's critique is too simplistic.

Nonetheless, even if Hegel is interpreted as allowing that some maxims cannot be universalized, and thus as accepting that in this sense the test is not empty, he can also be interpreted as saying that this in itself is insufficient in helping us determine how we should behave: for we *also* need to be told why it would be wrong to act in such a way as to undermine the institution in question in this manner, and no *formal* test (of contradiction) can tell us *that*. Thus (to use a Kantian example: cf. Kant, CPrR, 5: p. 27), while Hegel does not consider whether or not the keeping of deposits would undermine the institution of property, he does consider whether Kant can give any reason to show that a world without property would fail any sort of formal test, which perhaps suggests that he thought this further issue required some sort of answer. (Cf. Solomon 1983: 532, '[A]ll that Kant's criterion shows, at most, is that a certain institution, which a given maxim presupposes, could not be sustained, given a certain generalized principle. But surely the question of stealing depends on our evaluation of the institution of private property ... ').

It is indeed the case that Hegel's discussion of property in the *Phenomenology* and elsewhere seems focused primarily on the difficulty of using a formal test of non-contradiction to tell us whether the *institution* of property is to be preferred to that of non-property, rather than on whether a *maxim* like deposit-keeping can be universalized. Hegel claims that if the test of non-contradiction we apply is to see whether there is some sort of dialectical tension in the position, then both property and non-property are contradictory: for, a system of common ownership involves a system of distribution according to need (in which case some get more than others) and distribution according to equality (in which case all get the same), while a system of private property involves a tension between a thing belonging to an individual (in which case it doesn't matter how their possession of it affects others) and that individual feeling they are just one amongst many individuals (in which case it does). On the other hand, Hegel says, there is nothing *logically* contradictory in either system; so this kind of testing is inconclusive when asked to deliver a verdict on either institution:

> Consequently, property is just as much an all-round contradiction as non-property; each contains within it these two opposed, self-contradictory moments of individuality and universality. But each of these determinatenesses when thought of as *simple*, as property or non-property, without explicating them further, is as *simple* as the other, i.e. is not self-contradictory. The criterion of law which Reason possesses within itself fits every case equally well, and is thus in fact no criterion at all.
>
> (PS: §431, p. 259)

Now, although Hegel may be right that a test of non-contradiction is inconclusive when it comes to institutions, it is not clear that the switch from testing maxims of actions to testing institutions is one the Kantian need feel obliged to make. Commentators on Hegel have suggested that this switch *is* required, because otherwise it is not clear why the contradiction test applied to maxims reveals anything of ethical significance: for, even if making lying promises undermines the institution of promise-keeping (for example), unless promising is shown to be a morally sound institution, then this would not show lying to be wrong. (Cf. Walsh 1969: 23, 'We may agree that in these circumstances the whole institution of giving and accepting promises would collapse without possibility of revival. But it does not follow that a world without promises would be morally inferior to the existing world ... Hegel is quite correct in arguing that it is a presupposition of Kant's argument that it is right to keep promises: the very conclusion his appeal to the universalization test is supposed to justify.' Cf. also K. R. Westphal 1995: 40, '[T]o show that a maxim contradicts an institution it presupposes shows nothing about the moral standing of the maxim until we know something, by some other means, about the moral standing of the institution.') However, the Kantian may respond to this argument, by claiming that it underestimates and misidentifies the moral force of the universalizability test as applied to maxims: for this test shows that if the agent acts as he is planning to do (by making a false promise or whatever) he would be free-riding, by acting in a way that can only succeed if others do not do the same, and it is *this* that shows his action to be wrong, in a way that is independent of our ethical evaluation of the institution on which his action relies. (Cf. Korsgaard 1996: 92, 'What the test shows to be forbidden are just those actions whose efficacy in achieving their purposes depends upon their being exceptional.' Cf. also Kant, GMM 4: p. 424.) Or, on another interpretation, the test shows that my action can only succeed if I use the fact that others participate in the institution in order to control their behaviour. (For a clear account of the difference between these readings, and their respective merits, see Herman 1993: 132–43.) Either way, both readings show why failing the universalizability test in itself has moral significance, so it is not clear why the moral standing of the institution relevant to the maxim (property, promise-keeping, or whatever) needs to be brought in to settle this. It appears therefore that these objections to the formalism of 'Reason as testing laws' do not carry much weight.

Nonetheless, Hegel's discussion does raise an important question mark over what exactly the Kantian moralist can expect to achieve. For, on the one hand, if the test of non-contradiction is purely formal, it is not clear that failing the test reveals anything of moral relevance: why, if a maxim fails the test, does this show that acting on the maxim would be wrong? If, on the other hand, the test is seen as a way in which the agent can discover whether or not by acting in a certain manner she would be free-riding, then it is not clear that the test 'compares a content only with itself' (PS: §429, p. 257), as it then presupposes some moral content as part of the test (namely, the wrongness of free-riding, or of manipulating others), rather than determining what is right and wrong through the test, and so is no longer purely formal in this sense.

The way Hegel concludes this section, and makes the transition from Kantian morality to Greek ethical life, suggests that he sees the Kantian as facing a dilemma: either the Kantian treats the universalizability test as purely formal (but then why should passing this test matter from a moral perspective?), or he accepts that the test has some moral content (in which case he has not shown that reason can distinguish between right and wrong actions on a purely formal basis). The Kantian can thus either threaten the authority of morality itself by trying to determine what is moral by using a purely formal (morally empty) test, or he can accept that the test is not purely formal but itself part of morality, in which case we have not in fact got beyond a kind of moral foundationalism, which just takes certain moral principles (concerning the wrongness of free-riding, for example) as given.

From this, Hegel therefore makes a transition from the Kantian standpoint, back to the ethical life of the Greeks:[2] for, according to Hegel, they were simply prepared to accept the foundational nature of moral principles in precisely this manner, without any attempt to 'ground' or 'derive' them in some extra-moral test. (As ever, of course, the Kantian can reply that this was never Kant's intention in proposing the Formula of the Universal Law; but then the Hegelian response might be that in that case, the Kantian cannot claim to have added much to the way in which we ordinarily determine the rightness or wrongness of our actions, by assessing them in terms of substantive moral principles.) Hegel therefore ends the section by returning to the standpoint of the Greeks, who would have seen this whole idea of testing actions using certain formal (non-moral) criteria as an anathema. In contrast to the position of 'Reason as testing laws', Hegel characterizes the Greek position as follows:

> The *relationship* of self-consciousness to them [the laws] is equally simple and clear. They *are*, and nothing more; this is what constitutes the awareness of its [self-consciousness'] relationship to them. Thus, Sophocles' *Antigone* acknowledges them as the unwritten and infallible law of the gods.
>
> They are not of yesterday or today, but everlasting,
> Though where they came from, none of us can tell.
>
> They *are*. If I inquire after their origin and confine them to the point whence they arose, then I have transcended them; for now it is I who am the universal, and *they* are the conditioned and limited. If they are supposed to be validated by *my* insight, then I have already denied their unshakeable, intrinsic being, and regard them as something which, for me, is perhaps true, and also is perhaps not true. Ethical disposition consists just in sticking steadfastly to what is right, and abstaining from all attempts to move or shake it, or derive it. Suppose something has been entrusted to me; it *is* the property of

someone else and I acknowledge this *because* it *is so*, and I keep myself unfalteringly in this relationship ... It is not, therefore, because I find something is not self-contradictory that it is right; on the contrary, it is right because it is what is right. That something *is* the property of another, this is fundamental; I have not to argue about it, or hunt around for or entertain thoughts, connections, aspects, of various kinds; I have to think neither of making laws nor of testing them.

(PS: §437, pp. 261–62)

Hegel thus uses the failure of the Kantian standpoint (as he conceives it) to take consciousness back to the ethical life of the Greeks, where consciousness did not see itself qua individual as having the capacity to 'step back' from the moral world and ground it in some way: rather, it was simply immersed in that world, living unreflectively within its teachings and precepts. At this point, therefore, consciousness finds itself ready to 'put its merely individual aspect behind it' (PS: §436, p. 261), and so move from Reason to Spirit. Here consciousness is prepared to recognize that perhaps something fundamental was lost as well as gained in the transition from the outlook of the ancient to the outlook of the modern world, and that this has resulted in the one-sidedness of Reason. Consciousness therefore turns from a consideration of Kantian morality to an investigation of Greek ethical life.

CONTENT SUMMARY

RATIONALISM AND IDEALISM

§§231–39 (pp. 139–45)   Discussion of the relation between rationalism and idealism, which is criticized in its Kantian and Fichtean forms.

OBSERVING REASON

§§240–43 (pp. 145–47)   Observing Reason turns to the more realist outlook of scientific rationalism, which seeks to find rational order in the world using the methods of the natural sciences.

§§244–47 (pp. 147–50)   Observing Reason begins by considering the natural world, which it first sees as embodying a
system of natural kinds; but hard to make this classificatory
system satisfactory.

§§248–53 (pp. 150–54)   Therefore it tries to find natural laws,
which it applies to the non-living, inorganic world.

§§254–55 (pp. 154–56)   But it is hard to find such laws
governing living beings.

§§256–61 (pp. 156–59)   So Observing Reason introduces
teleological explanations; but finds such explanations
problematic.

§§262–97 (pp. 159–80)   So it turns to looking for laws governing biological processes; but again finds it hard to identify
such laws.

§§298–308 (pp. 180–85)   So it now moves from laws governing
the natural world to laws governing the mind, in both logic
and psychology; but in both areas it is hard to find proper
laws, as logic tells us how we *should* think but not how we
do, while psychological laws can always be broken by the
free individual.

§§309–46 (pp. 185–210)   Hegel now considers laws that relate
the mind to the body qua facial features (physiognomy) or
shape of the skull (phrenology), but where both are rejected
as pseudo-sciences.

ACTIVE REASON

§§347–48 (pp. 211–12)   Consciousness turns now to reason as it
guides action, qua practical reason.

§§349–59 (pp. 212–17)   Characterization of the premodern
view of the agent, as forming a unity with the *polis*, but
where that view has now been lost within modernity.

§§360–66 (pp. 217–21)   The first modern outlook Hegel discusses seeks for pleasure and happiness for itself as an individual
(cf. Faust), but where this leads to unhappiness.

§§367–80 (pp. 221–28) The second outlook tries to find satisfaction in following the 'law of the heart' and not the rules

of society; but degenerates into 'the frenzy of self-conceit' as it sets itself above all social norms.

§§381–93 (pp. 228–35) The third outlook turns to private virtue, which it contrasts with public vice; but again becomes corrupted and individualistic.

PRACTICAL REASON

§§394–96 (pp. 236–37) Consciousness now focuses on action, and how this is expressive of the individual.

§§397–418 (pp. 237–52) This expression occurs in the works that the individual produces, but which it cannot prevent being judged by others; to escape this judgement, it tries to follow the crowd and lose some of its individuality in a common project.

§§419–28 (pp. 252–56) This gives rise to a more ethical outlook, where the individual now relies on reason to give it certain basic moral principles and so tell it how to act; but in fact, the complexity of ethical situations cannot be reduced to such laws.

§§429–36 (pp. 256–61) The individual thus tries to use reason instead as a test for what is right and wrong, by seeing if the maxim of its actions can be universalized (Kant); but these tests prove empty.

§437 (pp. 261–62) Having investigated the problems with these modern approaches, Hegel thus takes us back to the outlook of the Greeks which was put aside earlier (§§349–59); by understanding how modernity emerged out of the collapse of that outlook, we may learn what it needs to put it right.

5

THE DIALECTIC OF SPIRIT
(*PHENOMENOLOGY*, C. (BB.) SPIRIT)

TRUE SPIRIT: ETHICAL LIFE

'Reason *must* withdraw from this happy state' (PS: §354, p. 214): so Hegel had declared when presenting us with his sketch of how the premodern individual felt 'at home in the world' at the start of the 'Active Reason' section (PS: §§347–59, pp. 211–17). There, this 'withdrawal' had not seemed particularly significant, as Reason was confident that it could find itself 'at home' in a distinctively *modern* way, one that left the Greek world entirely behind. It was then not inclined to lament the passing of this world, or concerned to understand why it '*must*' withdraw from it. However, Reason has found that its modern way of seeking to be 'at home in the world' has so far failed, so it now turns to inquire into the force of this '*must*': to see why the 'happy state' of Greek ethical life collapsed, and why it was compelled to seek a new way of being 'at home in the world'. Hegel called consciousness in this 'happy state' 'a present living Spirit', because in this state the subject felt no alienation from the world; as he puts it now,

'Reason is Spirit when its certainty of being all reality has been raised to truth, and it is conscious of itself as its own world, and of the world as itself' (PS: 263). The question to be considered by consciousness, therefore, is why Greek ethical life was not stable, despite the fact that here consciousness felt itself 'at home' in a way that constituted a realization of (what Hegel calls) Spirit:

> Spirit is the *ethical life* of a nation in so far as it is the *immediate truth* – the individual that is a world. It must advance to the consciousness of what it is immediately, must leave behind it the beauty of ethical life, and by passing through a series of shapes attain to a knowledge of itself. These shapes, however, are distinguished from the previous ones by the fact that they are real Spirits, actualities in the strict meaning of the word, and instead of being shapes merely of consciousness, are shapes of a world.
>
> (PS: §441, p. 265)

The task of this section on 'The Ethical Order', therefore, is to explore what makes it necessary for consciousness to look for a new way of being 'at home in the world', or (to put it in the terminology used here) to see why Spirit was not fully realized in 'the beauty of ethical life'; by understanding why this 'beauty' must be 'left behind', we may then be able to see what form the final realization of Spirit is required to take.

THE GREEK WORLD

Hegel presents his positive discussion of Greek ethical life in the subsection entitled 'The Ethical World. Human and Divine Law: Man and Woman', in which he portrays Greek society as a complex balance of individuality and universality, where 'these determinations [of individuality and universality] express only the superficial antithesis of the two sides' (PS: §446, p. 267). Thus, though we find here a social structure marked by important divisions – between the human law and the divine law, between the *polis* and the family, and between man and woman – Hegel argues that it was possible to harmonize these divisions, since each side complemented the other.

So, according to Hegel, the divine law regulated the private realm of the family in which women were confined, while the human law regulated the *polis*, which was the domain of men, and as such each could coexist alongside the other. (Cf. PH: 239, 'The divine receives its honour through the respect paid to the human, and the human in virtue of the honour paid to the divine.') It was crucial here for the man to be able to make the transition from the family as private individual to the state as citizen: but this he could do because the family had an ethical character, in which the individual did not merely find gratification for his desires, but also an education in the virtues, in a way that made him fit for public life. Then, on his death, when the individual no longer counted as a citizen, he could be 'returned' to his family for burial. In this the family served an important role that could not be served by the state (for which 'it is an accident that his death was directly connected with his "work" for the universal and was the result of it' (PS: §452, p. 270)), since this gives meaning to the individual's life in the face of this natural process. The family was associated not with the law of the state, but with the divine law standing over and above nature.

Hegel emphasizes two respects in which this structure was harmonious. First, although the death of the individual was given meaning within the sphere of the family and divine law, nonetheless at times of war this served a social function and reinforced social bonds within the sphere of the *polis*, so bringing these spheres together: 'The community therefore possesses the truth and the confirmation of its power in the essence of the Divine Law and in the realm of the nether world' (PS: §455, p. 273). Second, these spheres were brought into harmony in the brother–sister relationship (which Hegel portrays as being more stable than the husband–wife or parent–child relationship, which are based around the contingencies of desire and love). Hegel argues that the brother and sister fully recognize each other and what they stand for as equal (in a way that husband and wife do not), where the sister represents the family and the divine law, and the brother represents the *polis* and the human law, each seeing itself as the complement of the other:

[The brother] passes from the divine law, within whose sphere he lived, over to human law. But the sister becomes, or the wife remains, the head of the household and the guardian of the divine law. In this way, the two sexes overcome their [merely] natural being and appear in their ethical significance, as diverse beings who share between them the two distinctions belonging to the ethical substance.

(PS: §459, p. 275)

Hegel thus argues that the harmony of Greek ethical life rested on a kind of division of labour between the sexes, one that was acknowledged by both sides, and on which the stability of the Greek social world depended:

The difference of the sexes and their ethical content remains ... in the unity of the substance, and its movement is just the constant becoming of that substance. The husband is sent out by the Spirit of the Family into the community in which he finds his self-conscious being. Just as the Family in this way possesses in the community its substance and enduring being, so, conversely, the community possesses in the Family the formal element of its actual existence, and in the divine law its power and authentication. Neither of the two is by itself absolutely valid; human law proceeds in its living process from the divine, the law valid on earth from that of the nether world, the conscious from the unconscious, mediation from immediacy – and equally returns whence it came. The power of the nether world, on the other hand, has its actual existence on earth; through consciousness, it becomes existence and actuality ... The whole is a stable equilibrium of all the parts, and each part is a Spirit at home in this whole, a Spirit which does not seek satisfaction outside of itself but finds it within itself, because it is itself in this equilibrium with the whole.

(PS: §460 and §462, pp. 276–77)

Hegel therefore provides a highly suggestive (although not of course uncontentious) picture of the structure of the 'happy state' in which Spirit was realized in the Greek world, one in which divisions existed in a balanced equilibrium, each side finding its own domain in harmony with its opposite, so that 'their antithesis is rather the authentication of one through the other' (PS: §463, p. 278).

'ANTIGONE'

Having presented this positive picture, Hegel now proceeds in the next subsection to examine why a balance of this kind could not be sustained, in order to show why 'Spirit ... must leave behind it the beauty of ethical life' (PS: §441, p. 265). He attempts to bring this out by focusing on the story of Antigone, as told by Sophocles in one of his Theban plays. Hegel expressed his admiration for this drama in many places; for example, in his *Lectures on Aesthetics* he called it 'one of the most sublime and in every respect most excellent works of art of all time' (LA: I, p. 464), and it formed an important part of his theory of tragedy; his influential treatment of the play remains a matter of interpretative controversy (see Donougho 1989). In the *Phenomenology*, however, his concern is not so much aesthetic as cultural–historical: he uses the play as a key to diagnose the failure of Greek ethical life, where the ground has been prepared in the themes already emphasized (the brother–sister relationship, the role of the family in burial, the role of the divine law, and the significance of war), all of which are central to Sophocles' drama, as Hegel's plot-summary from the *Lectures on Aesthetics* makes clear:

> Everything in this tragedy is logical; the public law of the state is set in conflict over against inner family love and duty to a brother; the woman, Antigone, has the family interest as her 'pathos', Creon, the man, has the welfare of the community as his. Polynices [Antigone's brother], at war with his native city, had fallen before the gates of Thebes, and Creon, the ruler, in a publicly proclaimed law threatened with death anyone who gave this enemy of the city the honour of burial. But this command, which concerned only the public weal, Antigone could not accept; as sister, in the piety of her love for her brother, she fulfils the holy duty of burial. In doing so she appeals to the law of the gods; but the gods whom she worships are the underworld gods of

Hades ... , the inner gods of feeling, love, and kinship, not the daylight gods of free self-conscious national and political life.

(LA: I, p. 464)

Hegel thus introduces the story of Antigone at this point in the *Phenomenology*, because he believes it tells us much about why Greek ethical life was unsustainable.

However, while this much is clear, it is less clear exactly how Hegel wants us to understand the play, and thus exactly what lesson he wants us to draw from it. Some have argued that on Hegel's reading of the play, we are meant to side with Antigone over Creon, in so far as she represents the emerging modern sense of individuality that will ultimately undermine the kind of authoritarian Greek state represented by Creon. Thus, on this account, we are told that '[a]ccording to Hegelian hermeneutics, Antigone represents the eternal conflict between the individual and the State' (Pietercil 1978: 304), where it is Antigone as such an individual who brings down the harmony of Greek ethical life (cf. Fleischmann 1971: 228, '[Hegel] shows, primarily with the example of Greece (here Antigone, elsewhere Socrates), that the questioning by individuals of established injustice is the end of an epoch and the beginning of another, more just, age.'). Now, it is certainly true that Hegel was impressed by Antigone as a tragic figure, and in this sense viewed her sympathetically, famously calling her 'the heavenly Antigone, that noblest of figures that ever appeared on earth' (LHP: I, p. 441). However, it seems wrong to infer from this that Hegel therefore thought Antigone was 'right', and in particular that she was 'right' because she acted as a modern individualistic consciousness, out of personal conviction and conscience in opposition to the tyranny of the state. In fact, Hegel simply took Antigone to be representing her social sphere, and in that sense as no more 'modern' than Creon, who represented his. As Hegel makes clear, he thinks that it was Creon's tragic *mistake* to take Antigone to be acting out of merely self-righteous indignation, when in fact she was acting out of respect for traditional values:

Since it sees right only on one side and wrong on the other, that consciousness which belongs to the divine law [Antigone] sees in the other side only the violence of human caprice, while that which holds to the human law [Creon] sees in the other only the self-will and disobedience of the individual who insists on being his own authority.

(PS: §466, p. 280)

Taken in this way, Hegel's position is also arguably closer to a proper understanding of the play itself, which is only anachronistically treated as a study of 'the individual' against the state, many contemporary productions notwithstanding.

However, once his position is no longer understood in these terms, it may seem that Hegel took the play to show that Greek ethical life was unsustainable because it could not accommodate the kind of secular, rational state represented by Creon, and thus it may seem that Creon is the hero in his eyes (cf. Solomon 1983: 548, 'Antigone represents the losing battle against the breakdown of the most elementary and "natural" *Sittlichkeit* and the hegemony of "civil society".'). Now, Hegel is certainly less obviously critical of Creon than many commentators on the play, who take it as unquestionable that (in Richard Jebb's words) Sophocles means 'us to feel that, in this controversy, the right is wholly with [Antigone], and the wrong wholly with her judge [Creon]' (Jebb 1902: §4, p. xix). Those hostile towards Hegel expect him to respond to the play in this idiosyncratic way: for (to these critics) it is clear that Hegel would prefer the authoritarianism of Creon to the individualism represented by Antigone, so that 'it is easy to see how Hegel, with his semi-mystical worship of the state, could take Creon as representing "genuine ethical pathos"' (Vickers 1973: 535).

I think this second account is as mistaken as the first, however. First, it ignores the way in which Hegel presents Antigone in a positive light (as we have seen). Second, while Hegel may not favour Antigone over Creon in the way that many commentators on the play suppose we should, it does not follow that he believed Creon's position to be right, or superior to Antigone's. And third, those who take Hegel to be an admirer of Creon because his own political philosophy was authoritarian are misguided, as no proper reading of Hegel can support the claim that he went in for a 'semi-mystical worship of the state', and no proper reading of the play can treat Creon as a mere tyrant. (For a helpful discussion of Hegel's political outlook, see Houlgate 1991: 77–125.)

In fact, it seems to me, the mistake both these accounts make is to look for evidence that Hegel wanted to 'take sides', and to show that either Antigone or Creon were representative of the 'forces of modernity', which the Greek world could not accommodate, and which therefore brought it down. A better account is that Hegel used the play to argue that the tragedy shows how in the Greek world each side (Antigone and Creon) had fixed allegiances to one sphere or the other, so that when these spheres came into conflict (through the figure of Polynices, who was significantly *both* a male political figure and thus part of the *polis*, *and* a dead brother and thus part of the family), this conflict could not be resolved in any way. As I understand it, in Hegel's view the central reason why this opposition was inevitable was the fact that in Greek ethical life, each individual (man or woman, brother or sister) had their 'station', and saw their duties defined for them in these terms. Hegel refers to this aspect of Greek ethical life when he declares that:

> in this ethical realm ... self-consciousness has not yet received its due as a particular individuality. There it has the value, on the one hand, merely of the universal will [Creon, as a man], and on the other, of consanguinity [Antigone, as a woman]. *This* particular individual counts only as a shadowy unreality.
>
> (PS: §464, p. 279)

There is, then, a sense in which the Greek ethical world collapsed because it had insufficient space for 'the individual': it is not because Antigone represented this individualistic rebellion against the state, but because neither Antigone or Creon were able to rise above their social spheres and see value in the position of the other. As a result of this socially defined self-conception, Antigone felt that she had no choice but to bury her brother when called upon to do so, since this was her role within the scheme of things; likewise, as head of state, Creon felt equally obliged to forbid the burial and so to punish Antigone for her disobedience. It is because each individual identifies him- or herself wholly with one overriding ethical imperative that Hegel characterizes the clash between Antigone and Creon as tragic. Neither is able to step back from the obligations that go with their naturally determined place in the ethical order:

> In [this ethical consciousness] there is no caprice and equally no struggle, no indecision, since the making and testing of law has been given up; on the contrary, the essence of ethical life for this consciousness is immediate, unwavering, without contradiction. Consequently, we are not faced with the sorry spectacle of a collision between passion and duty, nor with the comic spectacle of a collision between duty and duty ... The ethical consciousness ... knows what it has to do, and has already decided whether to belong to the divine or the human law. This immediate firmness of decision is something implicit, and therefore has at the same time the significance of a natural being as we have seen. Nature, not the accident of circumstances or choice, assigns one sex to one law, the other to the other law; or conversely, the two ethical powers themselves give themselves an individual existence and actualize themselves in the two sexes.
>
> (PS: §465, pp. 279–80)

Thus, as soon as an issue arises in which the duties of the man and the duties of the woman pull in opposite directions, the individuals concerned could only find themselves in conflict, as neither could see how any other course of action was open to them: Antigone *must* bury her brother, Creon *must* uphold the law of the state. Neither can therefore feel any real guilt for what they have done, as each believes they have done what was required of them, even if the result of so acting has been disastrous; neither do they feel any fear or any personal animosity towards their opponent:

> [I]t is not *this* particular individual who acts and is guilty; for as *this* self he is only the unreal shadow, or he exists merely as a universal self, and individuality is purely the *formal* moment of the act as such, the content being the laws and the customs which, for the individual, are those of his class and station ... Self-consciousness within the

nation descends from the universal only as far down as mere particularity, and not down to the single individuality which posits an
exclusive self, an actual existence which in its action is negative
towards itself. On the contrary, its action rests on secure confidence
in the whole, unmixed with any alien element, neither with fear nor
hostility.

(PS: §468, pp. 282–83)

On this picture, therefore, individuals simply act in the way they
feel obliged to by their social responsibilities; in finding their
action leads to suffering, they realize that what they were called
upon to do was ethically inferior to what others were called upon
to do, whilst still feeling that this was due to fate, rather than an
ethical misjudgement that they could have foreseen.

This then explains why on the question of 'Antigone or
Creon?', Hegel most often adopts a balanced view. (Cf. Kaufmann
1971: 202, 'Hegel's understanding of Greek tragedy far surpassed
that of most of his detractors. He realized that at the centre of the
greatest tragedies of Aeschylus and Sophocles we find not a tragic
hero but a tragic collision, and that the conflict is not between
good and evil but between one-sided positions, each of which
embodies some good.' For a similar view, see Shklar 1976: 82–83.)
So, rather than taking either to represent any sort of progressive
modern standpoint (either individual conscience in the case of
Antigone, or the secular state in the case of Creon), he sees them
both as typical of their Greek world, a world that has no method
for overcoming its underlying dualisms. He thus does not con-
demn either of them, but rather sees each as a victim of their
limited social and moral conception, where it is the limitedness of
that conception that brings about the collapse of the Greek
ethical world:

> The collision between the two highest moral powers is set forth in a
> plastic fashion in that supreme and absolute example of tragedy,
> *Antigone*. In this case, family love, what is holy, what belongs to the
> inner life and to inner feeling, and which because of this is also called
> the law of the nether gods, comes into collision with the law of the
> State. Creon is not a tyrant, but really a moral power; Creon is not in

the wrong; he maintains that the law of the State, the authority of government, is to be held in respect, and that punishment follows the infraction of the law. Each of these two sides realizes only one of the moral powers, and has only one of these as its content; this is the element of one-sidedness here, and the meaning of eternal justice is shown in this, that both end in injustice just because they are one-sided, though at the same time both obtain justice too. Both are recognized as having a value of their own in the untroubled course of morality. Here they both have their own validity, but a validity which is equalized. It is only the one-sidedness in their claims which justice comes forward to oppose.

(LPR: II, pp. 264–65)

Thus, as one commentator has observed, 'For Hegel, it is not an unfortunate contingent fact that humans must leave the harmonious Garden of Eden in which they are at home in the world; instead, it is conceptually necessary that this moment of immediacy be overcome' (Stewart 2000: 309).

Now, characteristically, Hegel does not really tell us in the *Phenomenology* how it might be possible for *us* to go beyond this 'one-sidedness' in a way the Greeks could not: this positive task is largely left to the *Philosophy of Right*, where tensions between family and state, and the human and divine law, are treated at length, and supposedly resolved. So, to take one example, while for the man in the Greek world there existed a sharp division between family and state, in Hegel's view of the modern state, there is no such sharp division, in so far as man is both part of the family and part of the state, where, for example, he represents the family *in* the state as head of the household. It is an interesting question, but one we cannot consider further here, how far Hegel succeeds in overcoming the further dualisms he has diagnosed in his discussion of Greek ethical life; it is also an interesting question, which we cannot dwell on either, how far such overcoming is even desirable (cf. Nussbaum 1986: 68).

Following his discussion of *Antigone* in the *Phenomenology*, Hegel then looks again at the Greek social world, showing how the latent tensions between the spheres of men and women, state and family, became explicit once their ethical differences brought these spheres into conflict. On the one side, the state tried to undermine the 'separatism' of women and their particularistic allegiance to the family, while on the other side 'womankind – the everlasting irony [in the life] of the community' (PS: §475, p. 288) – became a source of intrigue and corruption in the life of the state, encouraging the young to challenge the authority of their elders, who could then only reassert their position by sending the young to war. In this constant battling of city states, all satisfaction for consciousness in Greek ethical life has been lost; individuals are shaken free of their social identities, as the 'living unity' of the *polis* 'shattered into a multitude of separate atoms' (PS: §476, p. 289).

THE ROMAN WORLD

In the next subsection, entitled 'Legal Status', Hegel argues that the social world built up by the Roman empire was shaped by this 'shattering' of the *polis*, and as a result individuals now came to conceive of themselves as *persons*, rather than citizens (cf. 'The Positivity of the Christian Religion', in ETW: 156–57). For Hegel, 'person' is a quintessentially modern social category, whereby individuals see themselves as occupying private spheres with their own interests, legally protected from the interference of others. In contrast to the 'thick' self-conception of Greek ethical life, in which the individual is seen as part of the universal ethical substance, the individual qua 'person' views himself in abstract terms, rather than identifying himself with any particular character or social station (hence, Hegel claims, the attraction of the kind of self-renunciation preached by Stoics in this period). Because personhood involves merely 'that One qua self-consciousness in general' (PS: §479, p. 291), the action persons undertake is to secure *property* for themselves, for while private ownership forces other individuals to recognize the legal status of the property-owner, no individual is *defined by* their property (in the way that Antigone and Creon were defined by their social roles), since this can always be transferred or legally 'alienated'. The person is thus never really engaged with the world as such, and hence Hegel associates this outlook with Scepticism.

Now, in his *Philosophy of Right*, Hegel begins his account of the rational state with this notion of personhood, and makes clear that he intends to incorporate this notion into his final picture, in a way that the Greeks were unable to do (cf. PR: §185). However, Hegel makes equally clear that the rational state cannot be constructed around this social category *alone*, but that personhood must be balanced with a less abstract, less legalistic self-conception, which leaves room for some of the sense of political community felt by consciousness in the 'happy state' of Greek ethical life. In his discussion in the *Phenomenology* Hegel also attempts to bring out the one-sidedness of the social structure represented by imperial Rome. The difficulty Hegel identifies seems to be this: on the one hand, the only way the legal persons that made up the Roman state could feel any social unity with each other was through the figure of the emperor, who embodied the sovereignty of that state; on the other hand, such was the dissolution of the political community into a collection of self-interested individuals that the emperor could only stand up for the state by opposing those individuals and becoming a tyrant, so undermining any possibility of social cohesion. Once he is subjected to the arbitrary power of the emperor, the Roman citizen quickly comes to see how empty his appeals to legal right are, and hence feels himself to be alone in a morally arbitrary universe, in which 'might is right'. Much as Unhappy Consciousness had done before, consciousness now struggles to make itself feel 'at home' in a world from which it feels fundamentally alienated and estranged.

SELF-ALIENATED SPIRIT: CULTURE

In the previous section, Hegel has presented a portrait of 'the happy state' of Greek ethical life, with an account of how it came to break down. In this section, he explores the consequences of that breakdown for the modern world, in which we face a series of oppositions that were not experienced as such prior to modernity, between state and individual, divine and human, duty and individual conscience. Hegel characterizes this shift as a transition from 'True Spirit' to 'Self-Alienated Spirit':

[T]his [Self-Alienated] Spirit constructs for itself not merely *a* world, but a world that is double, divided and self-opposed. The world of the ethical Spirit [i.e. True Spirit] is its own *present* world; and therefore each of its powers exists in this unity, and in so far as they are distinct from one another they are in equilibrium with the whole ... Here [i.e. for Self-Alienated Spirit], however ... [n]othing has a Spirit that is grounded within itself and indwells it, but each has its being in something outside of and alien to it. The equilibrium of the whole is not the unity which remains with itself, nor the contentment that comes from having returned to itself, but rests on the alienation of opposites. The whole, therefore, like each single moment, is a self-alienated actuality.

(PS: §486, pp. 295–96)

In this section, therefore, Hegel tries to show how modern consciousness has adopted a series of fundamental dichotomies in its conception of the world, and how this has made it impossible for consciousness in this modern form to feel 'at home'.

CULTURE

Hegel opens his discussion by focusing on 'Culture and its Realm of Actuality'. 'Culture' here is a translation of the German term *'Bildung'*, which has connotations of education as well as of cultivated society and mores. Hegel associates several important dichotomies with this form of consciousness, the first being the way it distinguishes between the 'natural' self and the 'civilized' or cultured one. Whereas in the Greek and Roman world, nature played a fundamental role in determining the social identity of the individual (as 'man' and 'woman', for example), here the individual sees society as requiring the transformation of his or her purely natural being: 'Although here the self knows itself as *this* self, yet its actuality consists solely in the setting-aside of its natural self' (PS: §489, p. 298). This is the kind of opposition between society and nature of which Rousseau complained, where man sets about trying to transform himself *against* nature.

As well as seeing an opposition between nature and culture, modern consciousness also distinguishes its ends as an individual from those of the state, and so sets up an opposition between self-interest and the general interest, where it takes the former to be 'bad' and the latter to be 'good'. It then divides the social realm into 'wealth', which it views as 'bad' because it involves the pursuit of particular interests, and 'state power', which it views as 'good' because it is the realm of universal concerns. It then comes to see, however, that as an individual it is alienated from these concerns, and so comes to find the state alien and oppressive: 'It follows, then, that the consciousness that is in and for itself does find in the state power its simple essence and subsistence in general, but not its individuality as such; it does find there its *intrinsic* being, but not what it explicitly is *for itself*. Rather, it finds that the state power disowns action qua individual action and subdues it into obedience' (PS: §497, p. 303). At the same time, the individual sees wealth as addressing his interests as an individual, his particular needs, while also benefiting other individuals in the same way: he therefore comes to see 'wealth' as good and state power as 'bad'. But consciousness may also reverse this evaluation once again, and see service of the state as ethically higher than mere individual self-enjoyment.

Faced with this contradiction, consciousness now tries to resolve it by carving things up slightly differently, and either treating state power and wealth as *both* 'good', or treating them as *both* 'bad'. Hegel labels this as a contrast between *noble* and *ignoble* (or base) consciousness respectively, where the former is happy to serve the state and has a positive evaluation of its prosperity, and the latter resents its subordination to the ruler and despises the wealth that it nonetheless seeks. Hegel argues that just as consciousness could not uphold a simple dichotomy between state power as 'good' and wealth as 'bad', so too it cannot uphold this dichotomy between the noble and the ignoble, as the noble consciousness finds it impossible to put itself genuinely in the service of the state, and so shows itself to be no better than the ignoble consciousness. Hegel's discussion proceeds as follows.

First, the noble consciousness identifies itself with the state in a spirit of self-renunciation, as 'the heroism of *service*, the *virtue* which sacrifices the single individual to the universal, thereby bringing this into existence – the *person*, one who voluntarily renounces possessions and enjoyment and acts and is effective in the interests of the ruling power' (PS: §503, p. 306). However, as the noble consciousness is aware that the state depends on its self-sacrifice, and as it does not really believe that the state is in a position to command its obedience, it is no more than 'the *haughty* vassal' (PS: §505, p. 307), who when it comes to the point is not really prepared to forgo his life or particular interests:

> It means that he has in fact reserved his own opinion and his own particular will in the face of the power of the state. His conduct, therefore, conflicts with the interests of the state and is characteristic of the ignoble consciousness which is always on the point of revolt.
>
> (PS: §506, p. 307)

In order to preserve the noble/ignoble distinction, consciousness must achieve a more meaningful self-sacrifice than it has managed hitherto: we therefore move from 'the heroism of service' to 'the heroism of flattery', where the power of the state is established in the form of an individual monarch, another will set above that of his subjects, who swear allegiance to his power (cf. PS: §511, pp. 310–11). However, the ruler now becomes divorced from the universal interest, and himself becomes a self-serving despot. As a result, the noble consciousness finds itself despising the sovereign, much like the ignoble consciousness did. Consequently, while initially the noble consciousness saw the monarch's role as a dispenser of wealth in a positive light, and was grateful to him for his largesse, once the monarch becomes a despot, the noble consciousness now views his need for royal patronage as humiliating, and so wealth becomes nothing more than a badge of enslavement:

> [I]t finds that it is outside of itself and belongs to another, finds its *personality* as such dependent on the contingent personality of another, on the accident of a moment, on a caprice, or some other utterly unimportant circumstance ... The spirit of gratitude is, therefore, the feeling of the most profound dejection as well as of extreme rebellion.
>
> (PS: §517, pp. 313–14)

Once again, the outlook of the noble consciousness has become that of the base consciousness. At the same time, the monarch becomes corrupted yet further, as the power that comes with wealth leads him to despise those whom he rules:

> In this arrogance which fancies it has, by the gift of a meal, acquired the self of another's 'I' and thereby gained for itself the submission of another's inmost being, it overlooks the inner rebellion of the other; it overlooks the fact that all restraints have been cast off, overlooks this state of sheer inner disruption in which, the *self-identity* of being-for-self having become divided against itself, all identity, all existence, is disrupted, and in which the sentiment and view-point of the benefactor suffer most distortion.
>
> (PS: §519, p. 315)

In this socially alienated world (based on the court culture of Louis XIV), where consciousness has found it impossible to overcome the division between society and the individual, nothing has retained the value it appeared to have, as each has become transmuted into its opposite:

> It is this absolute and universal inversion and alienation of the actual world and of thought; it is *pure culture*. What is learnt in this world is that neither the *actuality* of power and wealth, nor their specific *Notions*, 'good' and 'bad', nor the consciousness of 'good' and 'bad' (the noble and the ignoble consciousness), possess truth; on the contrary, all these moments become inverted, one changing into the other, and each is the opposite of itself ... What we have here, then, is that all the moments execute a universal justice on one another, each just as much alienates its own self, as it forms itself into its opposite and in this way inverts it.
>
> (PS: §521, pp. 316–17)

In becoming aware of this interchange between its categories, what Hegel calls 'the disrupted consciousness' begins to have a more dialectical understanding of such concepts, in contrast to the rigid thinking of what Hegel calls 'the honest individual':

> The honest individual takes each moment to be an abiding essenti-ality, and is the uneducated thoughtlessness of not knowing that it is

equally doing the reverse. The disrupted consciousness, however, is consciousness of the perversion, and, moreover, of the absolute perversion. What prevails in it is the Notion, which brings together in a unity the thoughts which, in the honest individual, lie far apart, and its language is therefore clever and witty.

(PS: §521, p. 317)

Using as his model here Diderot's *Rameau's Nephew* (which was published posthumously, in Goethe's translation, in 1805), Hegel contrasts this nihilistic wit of the nephew's 'disrupted consciousness' with the inarticulacy of the 'honest' narrator, who tries to calm the former's attempt to overturn all values. In the face of the nephew's deep self-knowledge and profound social criticism, the 'honest individual' is made to look naive and foolish, particularly in his suggestion that the individual remove himself from the world of perversion and return to nature. In fact, however, Hegel suggests that while the 'honest individual' is powerless to change the cynical nephew, this 'disrupted consciousness' will transform itself, for in its wit there is already a higher seriousness, as its sense of the hollowness of the cultural world leads this consciousness beyond it.

FAITH AND ENLIGHTENMENT

For Hegel, this move beyond the alienated world of culture can take two directions, either as 'faith' or as 'pure insight', where the former seeks reconciliation in a 'beyond' outside the individual subject, while the latter seeks reconciliation by turning inward, to the self that can remain unsullied by the vanity of the social world:

[T]he essence of faith ... becomes a supersensible world which is essentially an '*other*' in relation to self-consciousness. In pure insight, on the other hand, the transition of pure thought into consciousness has the opposite determination; objectivity has the significance of a merely negative content, a content which is reduced to a moment and returns into the self; that is to say, only the self is really the object of the self, or the object only has truth so far as it has the form of the self.

(PS: §529, p. 324)

Hegel goes on to contrast faith and pure insight according to how they respond to cultural consciousness. On the one hand, faith accepts the claim of Rameau's nephew, that 'the real world is a soulless existence' (PS: §534, p. 326); but it gets beyond the nephew's despair by setting up another world in which true satisfaction can be found. On the other hand, pure insight acknowledges the nephew's cynical claims that genius and talent have no real meaning or significance, but learns from this a kind of liberal egalitarianism, where all are seen as equally capable of using their reason, and hence as equally valuable: '[Individuality] counts merely as something universally acknowledged, viz. as an educated individuality' (PS: §536, p. 327). With this turn towards a rationalistic humanism, Hegel takes us on to the next part of the section, where his discussion of the Enlightenment tries to bring out how 'faith' and 'pure insight' come to be opposed to one another, and thus how neither can bring satisfaction to consciousness.

This discussion has attracted much interest, as it is a matter of controversy whether Hegel should be interpreted as a counter-Enlightenment figure, or whether (on the contrary) he represents perhaps the highest expression of the ideals and ambitions of the *Aufklärer*. In my view, Croce was closest to the truth, when he remarked that '[Hegel] did not simply reject the Enlightenment from which he too originated, but resolved it into a more profound and complex rationalism' (Croce 1941: 71; translation modified); that is, Hegel's ambivalence towards the Enlightenment as such is explained by his conviction that it failed to achieve what it promised, and it must therefore all be 'done again' in a more satisfactory way. In his earlier work, *Faith and Knowledge*, Hegel had made clear how this was particularly true of the relation between reason and faith: far from setting reason above faith in a proper manner, the Enlightenment had only succeeded in reintroducing a new form of irrationalism, because of the simplistic way in which it conceived of the issues religious thought raises: 'Philosophy has made itself the handmaid of faith once more' (FK: 56), because the Enlightenment's superficial critique left faith untouched, so that it is to faith rather than to the Enlightenment that philosophy has returned. It is in order to avoid this return to an anti-rationalism that sets 'the Absolute ... beyond Reason' (FK: 56) that the Enlightenment's earlier attack on faith must be revisited, and 'resolved' into something more satisfactory. Thus, though Hegel takes faith in a sense more *seriously* than many of the thinkers of the Enlightenment, by seeing it as a fundamental aspect of consciousness that runs deep, he does so because he thinks that otherwise rationalism will itself become trivialized and one-sided, leaving it vulnerable to faith once more.

Hegel characterizes the Enlightenment's superficial and purely negative view of faith at the outset of his discussion in the *Phenomenology*:

> [Pure insight] knows that faith is opposed to pure insight, opposed to Reason and truth ... [I]t sees faith in general to be a tissue of super-stitions, prejudices, and errors ... The masses are the victims of the deception of a *priesthood* which, in its envious conceit, holds itself to be the sole possessor of insight and pursues its other selfish ends as well ... From the stupidity and confusion of the people brought about by the trickery of priestcraft, despotism, which despises both, draws for itself the advantage of undisputed domination and the fulfilment of its desires and caprices, but is itself at the same time this same dullness of insight, the same superstition and error.
>
> (PS: §542, pp. 329–30)

Faced with this 'tissue of superstition', the Enlightenment sets out to liberate the 'general mass' of the people, whose 'naive consciousness' has become corrupted but who can be brought over to 'pure insight': it therefore finds it surprisingly easy to topple the idols of faith, which confirms for it how insubstantial and empty religious consciousness is: 'the new serpent of wisdom raised on high for adoration has in this way painlessly cast merely a withered skin' (PS: §545, p. 332). At the same time, the Enlightenment sees itself as bringing about a kind of 'new dawn' for mankind, and thus must come on the scene with all the fan-fare of an intellectual revolution, 'as a sheer uproar and a violent struggle with its antithesis' (PS: §546, p. 332).

In *Faith and Knowledge*, Hegel memorably calls the Enlightenment 'a hubbub of vanity without a firm core' (FK: 56); he now explores the emptiness of this vanity in the *Phenomenology*, arguing that it loses all substance and integrity by failing to see the real significance of the outlook that it attacks so contemptuously:

> We have therefore to see how *pure insight* and *intention* behaves in its *negative* attitude to that 'other' which it finds confronting it. Pure insight and intention which takes up a negative attitude can only be – since its Notion is all essentiality and there is nothing outside it – the negative of itself. As insight, therefore, it becomes the negative of pure insight, becomes untruth and unreason, and, as intention, it becomes the negative of pure intention, becomes a lie and insincerity of purpose.

(PS: ¶547, p. 332)

Hegel argues that the shallowness of the Enlightenment can be seen in the way in which its supposedly devastating critique of religious consciousness reveals itself as superficial in the eyes of faith.

Thus, against the claim that the object of faith does not exist outside the believer's own consciousness, the believer can respond that far from being 'new wisdom', this is what it has always held, in viewing the deity and itself as one (PS: §549, p. 334). Second, this first charge is in tension with the claim that religious belief is a deception brought about by priests and despots: for if the object of faith is something *it* has created, how can it be 'alien' to it? 'How are delusion and deception to take place where consciousness in its truth has directly the *certainty of itself*, when in its object it possesses *its own self*, since it just as much finds as produces itself in it?' (PS: §550, pp. 335–36). In fact, Hegel claims, the Enlightenment's conspiracy-theory view of religion is simply incredible to the believer: 'the idea of delusion is quite out of the question' (PS: §550, p. 336). Third, the Enlightenment condemns faith for worshipping mere objects like pieces of stone, blocks of wood or wafers made of bread; but of course faith does not revere any such merely physical things. Fourth, the Enlightenment attacks the Bible as a historical document; but faith has no such reliance on external evidence, and only a religious consciousness that has been corrupted by the Enlightenment could think otherwise (see PS: §554, p. 338). Finally, the Enlightenment accuses faith of a foolish asceticism and self-denying disregard for material property. But faith easily shows the worldliness of pure insight to be empty of real value, in holding 'a meal or the possession of things ... to be an End in itself' (PS: §556, p. 339), while also being hypocritical:

> [Pure insight] affirms as a pure intention the necessity of rising above natural existence, above acquisitiveness about the means of existence; only it finds it foolish and wrong that this elevation should be demonstrated *by deeds*; in other words, this pure insight is in truth a deception, which feigns and demands an *inner* elevation, but declares that it is superfluous, foolish, and even wrong to be *in earnest* about it, to put this elevation into *actual practice* and *demonstrate its truth* ... It is thus that Enlightenment lets itself be understood by faith.
>
> (PS: §§556–57, pp. 339–40)

Hegel then turns from an examination of the Enlightenment's critical position, to its positive position, again as viewed through the eyes of faith: 'If all prejudice and superstition have been banished, the question arises, *What next? What is the truth Enlightenment has propagated in their stead?*' (PS: §557, p. 340). Here once more Hegel suggests that faith can rightly feel unimpressed. For first, in so far as the Enlightenment has a place for God at all, it will be as the empty God of deism, a mere *'vacuum* to which no determinations, no predicates, can be attributed' (PS: §557, p. 340). Second, the Enlightenment returns us to the simplistic empiricism of Observing Reason. Third, the Enlightenment adopts the value-system of utility, and an instrumental view of the world and others: 'Just as everything is useful to man, so man is useful too, and his vocation is to make himself a member of the group, of use to the common good and serviceable to all' (PS: §560, p. 342). To all this, Hegel claims, faith will respond with disgust.

Despite this, Hegel argues, the Enlightenment serves an important role in forcing faith to deepen its self-understanding, and in preventing it from becoming dogmatic irrationalism: thus, while to a consciousness with faith the Enlightenment merely appears to be hostile, in fact it helps bring out the way in which faith tries to mediate and relate God and man, revelation and reason, inner and outer, and so stops faith from becoming one-sided: 'Consequently, [the Enlightenment] is neither alien to faith, nor can faith disavow it' (PS: §564, p. 344). At the same time, the Enlightenment is insufficiently dialectical about its *own* position vis-à-vis faith, in failing to see how much common ground they share. Thus, for example, while the Enlightenment helps to remind faith that God cannot be alien to the believer, by talking of God as a 'product of consciousness', the Enlightenment insists on taking this in a merely negative way, as if it were thereby *overturning* faith, without seeing that this is something that faith can incorporate. Likewise, the Enlightenment saves faith from the worship of mere finite things (stone, wood, bread); but it does so while itself thinking of things in a purely materialistic manner. Also, the Enlightenment helps remind faith of the insignificance of historical evidence to religious understanding, while at the same time thinking that such evidence is the only grounds for belief there can be. Finally, the Enlightenment saves faith from the hypocrisy of its asceticism, which involves the token sacrifice of goods in a way that is essentially meaningless; but again, the Enlightenment moves too quickly from this valid criticism, to thinking that *no* attempt to control the desire for pleasure has any significance.

Nonetheless, while the Enlightenment can help faith to develop into a more sophisticated religious standpoint (hence its effectiveness), this will not be immediately apparent to faith itself, since it will initially seem to the faithful that the Enlightenment has simply destroyed all the old certainties:

> Enlightenment, then, holds an irresistible authority over faith because, in the believer's own consciousness, are found the very moments which Enlightenment has established as valid. Examining the effects of this authority more closely, its behaviour towards faith seems to rend asunder the *beautiful* unity of *trust* and immediate *certainty*, to pollute its *spiritual* consciousness with mean thoughts of *sensuous*

reality, to destroy the soul which is *composed* and *secure* in its submission, by the vanity of the Understanding and of self-will and self-fulfilment. But as a matter of fact, the result of the Enlightenment is rather to do away with the *thoughtless*, or rather *non-notional*, separation which is present in faith.

(PS: §572, p. 348)

To the religious believer, therefore, it initially appears that while the enlightened consciousness may claim to have found satisfaction, it has left faith behind. However, Hegel observes, faith may be wrong about this, for it may prove harder than the enlightened consciousness thinks to achieve satisfaction if it leaves faith estranged in this way, and sticks merely to a this-worldly philosophy of materialism and utilitarianism: 'we shall see whether Enlightenment can remain satisfied; that yearning of the troubled Spirit which mourns over the loss of its spiritual world lurks in the background' (PS: §573, p. 349).

The Enlightenment, Hegel claims, is essentially split between two camps, of deism on the one hand and materialism on the other, where in fact for both camps the central categories of God and matter are equally abstract and empty. Underlying both, however, is an essential humanism, and a commitment to the happiness of mankind as the fundamental value – that is, a commitment to utility: 'The Useful is the object in so far as self-consciousness penetrates it and has in it the *certainty* of its *individual self*, its enjoyment (its *being-for-self*) … The two worlds are reconciled and heaven is transplanted to earth below' (PS: §581, p. 355). Hegel has warned us, however, that such optimism is premature: the shadow is cast in the following part of this section, entitled 'Absolute Freedom and Terror', where Hegel offers his famous analysis of the French Revolution.

THE FRENCH REVOLUTION

As most commonly and simply understood, Hegel's treatment of the French Revolution is structured around a critique of Rousseau, and of his conception of freedom; this seems clear, given the numerous indirect and occasional direct references to Rousseau in

Hegel's discussion of the French Revolution elsewhere (cf. PR: §258, p. 277, PH: 442–52/PW: 210–19). However, in the case of Hegel's analysis of the Revolution in the *Phenomenology*, it is in fact not a simple matter to identify what exactly it is about Rousseau's position that Hegel is criticizing here, and thus to show that it is Rousseau's notion of freedom that is central in this text.

On some accounts, Hegel's argument is supposed to rest on a critique of Rousseau's contractarianism, where freedom in society is preserved through the social contract, as freedom to do as one likes is exchanged for freedom to live by laws of one's own making (cf. Suter 1971: 55, Wokler 1998: 46, Franco 1999: 111–14). Textual support for this reading comes mainly from the *Philosophy of Right*, where Hegel's criticism of Rousseau appears to be that individuals here remain committed merely to their own interests, so that the result is a factional war of all against all (see PR: §29, p. 58; §258, p. 277). However, defenders of Rousseau have pointed out that this criticism is misguided: for it seems to overlook his crucial distinction between 'the will of all' and 'the general will', where the latter is taken to be the more fundamental to a free society, and to consist in more than just a collection of individual interests. (See Rousseau 1994: Bk II, Chap. 3, p. 66. Cf. Wokler 1998: 46, 'Hegel, following Fichte before him, never noticed that Rousseau's account of the general will pertained specifically to a collective will, resembling [Hegel's] own notion of the *allgemeine Wille*, rather than to a compound of particulars which, as Rousseau described it, would have been merely the will of all.' Cf. also Franco 1999: 9–10, Riley 1995: 21–22, and Taylor 1975: 372.) Thus, even if Hegel is right to see the Revolution and the Terror as arising out of a kind of individualistic frenzy, it seems wrong-headed to trace the roots of this individualism back to Rousseau, when his conception of the 'general will' is self-consciously and fundamentally collectivist (as Hegel himself acknowledges: see EL: §163Z, p. 228).

Moreover, even if Hegel can be defended on this point, there is also an interpretative issue here, for in the *Phenomenology* at least, Hegel's critique of Rousseau does not appear to focus on his supposed individualist contractarianism (although Hegel's remark concerning 'a general will, the will of all *individuals* as such' (PS: §584, p. 357) may perhaps be taken as a reference to it). Rather, if any implicit criticism of Rousseau is being voiced (he is not mentioned by name), it is the opposite one: namely that it is Rousseau's conception of the *general will* that is problematic (the term *'allgemeine Wille'* is used several times, though sometimes Miller translates it as 'general will', and sometimes as 'universal will': see PS: §584, p. 357 and §591, p. 360). On this reading, Hegel's objection is that because according to Rousseau every autonomous individual can transcend the distortions of desire, self-interest, and social position, he is then given the right to speak for all, as it appears that nothing now stands in the way of his claim to discern the general good: '[E]ach, undivided from the whole, always does everything, and what appears as done by the whole is the direct and conscious deed of each' (PS: §584, p. 357). Taking this to be Hegel's objection, Judith Shklar puts Hegel's diagnosis of the problem raised by the Revolution as follows:

> Each individual not only decides for himself what is useful for him but also what is generally useful. Each will regards itself as a perfect expression of the general will, which alone is valid, but which cannot be found except in the perfect union of all wills. That precludes compromise and submission. Indeed, the two seem identical now. For each one speaks for all, not only for himself. To accept the decision of another person is, thus, to betray the general will, of which one's own is an inseparable and surely perfect part. Unless all agree, there is no general will; for each one regards his own will as the correct general will. Since agreement is impossible, given the multiplicity of actual wills, only anarchy is conceivable. Anything else is a limitation upon one's will.

> (Shklar 1976: 175–76)

On Shklar's reading, Hegel appears to be arguing that Rousseau's doctrine of freedom encouraged individuals to believe that they could each speak for the general will and thus act on behalf of all, with the disastrous result that when difference and disagreement emerged, no compromise was possible, because no one was prepared to accept that they might be mistaken: 'What remains is an anarchy of wills, which Hegel imputed to Rousseau's teachings' (Shklar 1976: 175, cf. also Nusser 1998: 296).

However, once again, if Hegel is read in this way, it leaves his treatment of the Revolution unpersuasive as a critique of Rousseau. For it seems clear that Rousseau never thought that each individual could claim direct and unproblematic access to the general will. Indeed, in Book II, Chapter 3 of the *Social Contract*, Rousseau goes out of his way to emphasize that each of us as individuals must accept our fallibility in discerning the general will, so that we can only know what it is when the distortions created by our particular interests are 'cancelled out' through agreements arrived at between us. Likewise, in Book IV, Chapter 2, he famously claims that where a citizen finds himself in a minority, this shows that he was mistaken about the general will, and that as such he should accept the democratic decision. Thus, Rousseau himself seems to warn against taking seriously the idea that we could ever be able to say that as individuals, we know what is in the public interest prior to any sort of political process: 'If there were no differing interests, we would scarcely be aware of the common interest, which would never meet any obstacle; everything would run by itself, and there would no longer be any skill in politics' (Rousseau 1994: Bk II, Chap 3, p. 66 n.). It would therefore seem misguided to claim that Rousseau's doctrine of the general will means that individuals should see themselves as capable of ruling on behalf of all, and thus to associate Rousseau directly with the 'anarchy of wills' that such a doctrine might bring about.

A third option is to argue that Hegel objected to Rousseau's doctrine of the general will, not because it made it too *easy* for individuals to claim to speak on its behalf and thus set themselves up as sovereign, but because it made it too *difficult*, so no individual or set of individuals could claim legitimacy for their political authority or actions. For the problem now is how such individuals can claim to speak for the general will, when others may see them as representing merely particular interests and not the 'universal will':

> On the one hand, [the government] excludes all other individuals from its act, and on the other hand, it thereby constitutes itself a

government that is a specific will, and so stands opposed to the universal will; consequently, it is absolutely impossible for it to exhibit itself as anything else but a *faction*.

(PS: §591, p. 360)

Thus, on this reading, Hegel's critique of Rousseau is that he does not show how, from the point of view of the individual, an authority within the state can claim to represent the general will and thus operate legitimate political power, as the individual can always say that that authority is acting on a merely individualistic basis, and so can resist and seek to overthrow it. (Cf. Hinchman 1984: 147, 'Thus for Hegel the problem of how the general will can take on a determinate form is tantamount to asking whether legitimate authority can be exercised at all. How can the general will direct the actions of the state if it is always real, flesh-and-blood individuals who must act and decide matters of common interest?') Again, however, it is arguable that this criticism is unfair to Rousseau: for he tries hard to overcome this problem, by explaining, for example, how it is that particular kinds of democratic procedure can and should be taken by citizens as determining the general will, so that the general will has a content that must be accepted by all and can legitimately be acted upon. Hegel does not engage with these suggestions, so as a critique this looks uncharitable and ill-founded.

A fourth option is to argue that Hegel blamed Rousseau for the Terror because of the kind of constitutional arrangements Rousseau supported, in particular his hostility to the idea of political representation, most famously and forcefully expressed in Book III of *The Social Contract*:

Sovereignty cannot be represented, for the same reason that it cannot be transferred; it consists essentially in the general will, and the will cannot be represented; it is itself or it is something else; there is no other possibility. The people's deputies are not its representatives, therefore, nor can they be, but are only its agents; they cannot make definitive decisions. Any law that the people in person has not ratified is void; it is not a law.

(Rousseau 1994: Bk III, Chap. 15, p. 127)

Now, in the *Phenomenology* Hegel makes a number of references to this Rousseauian idea that the general will cannot be represented, stating that for the Revolutionaries 'a real general will' 'is not the empty thought of a will which consists in silent assent, or assent by a representative' (PS: §584, p. 357), and that 'self-consciousness [does not] let itself be cheated out of reality' 'by being *represented* in law-making and universal action' (PS: §588, p. 359). Moreover, in the *Philosophy of Right*, Hegel goes out of his way to defend the legitimacy of representation within the state and to reject direct democracy (see PR: §§308–11, pp. 346–50).

Nonetheless, while Hegel may here be justified in taking Rousseau to be hostile to the principle of representation, and while he may have thought that opposition to representative structures played a central role in the Revolution and its collapse into the Terror, Hegel in fact traces this opposition back to a conception of freedom that appears to have little to do with Rousseau, so that once again Rousseau is arguably less significant here than is traditionally supposed. To see what this conception of freedom is, it is necessary first to look at what Hegel says about the Revolution in the Introduction to his *Philosophy of Right*, where Rousseau is not mentioned (cf. also PH: 442–43/PW: 210–12).

Hegel's reference to the Revolution occurs here as part of his general discussion of the will, during which he tries to resolve a tension in our conception of the willing subject. On the one hand, he argues, we see the subject as 'finite' and 'particularized': that is, in acting the subject does one thing rather than another (chooses red paint over green paint, chooses to become a philosopher rather than a statesman), and hence is 'determinate' and differentiated from other subjects through its actions and lifechoices. On the other hand, he argues, we also see the subject as 'infinite' and 'universal', in so far as nothing prevents the subject from acting differently, from picking another course of action (I *could* have chosen green paint, and I *could* have chosen to be a statesman). Now, the tension arises, because it may appear to the subject that if in fact it does choose to do A rather than B, then this will compromise its 'universality', because this choice will rule out various options for it (once I have decided to become a philosopher, becoming a statesman will be extremely difficult if not impossible for me). As a result, Hegel claims, the subject may be tempted to think it would be better to refrain from making any choices at all, and to act in such a way as to 'keep all options open'; but, he points out, this will also exclude certain options. Rather, Hegel argues, the way to overcome this tension is for the subject to identify itself with its choices, so that even though option A rules out option B, this does not appear to the subject as any sort of limitation, because in A it sees a reflection of its own essential nature, which it does not see in B. As Hegel puts it in his preferred terminology: 'Freedom is to will something determinate, yet to be with oneself [*bei sich*] in this determinacy and to return once more to the universal' (PR: §7Z, p. 42). He puts the same point less formally but at greater length as follows:

> A will that resolves on nothing is not an actual will; the characterless man can never resolve on anything. The reason [*Grund*] for such indecision may also lie in an over-refined sensibility which knows that, in determining something, it enters the realm of finitude, imposing a limit on itself and relinquishing infinity; yet it does not wish to renounce the totality which it intends. Such a disposition [*Gemüt*] is dead, even if its aspiration is to be beautiful. 'Whoever aspires to great things', says Goethe, 'must be able to limit himself'. Only by making resolutions can the human being enter actuality, however painful the process may be; for inertia would rather not emerge from that inward brooding in which it reserves a universal possibility for itself. But possibility is not yet actuality. The will which is sure of itself does not therefore lose itself in what it determines.
>
> (PR: §13Z, p. 47)

As his references to 'inward brooding' and the 'aspiration ... to be beautiful' indicate, Hegel was here in part engaging with a Romantic longing for the 'whole man', who has not become 'limited' by the increased specialization of modern existence. But for Hegel (as his later discussion of the 'beautiful soul' in the *Phenomenology* will show), this longing was misplaced, as he believed that only with some limitation does the individual take on a meaningful life. As he puts this point in the *Logic*: 'Man, if he wishes to be actual, must be-there-and-then, and to this end he must set a limit to himself. People who are too fastidious towards the finite never reach actuality, but linger lost in abstraction, and their light dies away' (EL: §92Z, p. 136). (For further discussion, see Stern 1989.)

Now, Hegel's comments about the French Revolution come before he has reached this resolution of the tension between 'universality' and 'particularity'; rather, he treats the French Revolution as paradigmatic of just the kind of 'over-refined' sensibility that sees anything 'particular' or 'determinate' as a limitation on its freedom, and as something from which it should 'step back':

> Only *one aspect* of the will is defined here – namely this *absolute possibility* of *abstracting* from every determination in which I find myself or which I have posited in myself, the flight from every content as a limitation. If the will determines itself in this way ... this is *negative* freedom or the freedom of the understanding. – This is the freedom of the void, which is raised to the status of an actual shape and passion. If it remains purely theoretical, it becomes in the religious realm the Hindu fanaticism of pure contemplation; but if it turns to actuality, it becomes in the realm of both politics and religion the fanaticism of destruction, demolishing the whole existing social order, eliminating all individuals regarded as suspect by a given order, and annihilating any organization which attempts to rise up anew. Only in destroying something does this negative will have a feeling of its own existence [*Dasein*]. It may well believe that it wills some positive condition, for instance the condition of universal equality or of universal religious life, but it does not in fact will the positive actuality of this condition, for this at once gives rise to some kind of order, a particularization both of institutions and of individuals; but it is precisely through the annihilation of particularity and of objective determination that the self-consciousness of this negative freedom arises. Thus, whatever such freedom believes [*meint*] that it wills can in itself [*für sich*] be no more than an abstract representation [*Vorstellung*], and its actualization can only be the fury of destruction ... [During] the Reign of Terror in the French Revolution ... all differences of talents and authority were supposed to be cancelled out [*aufgehoben*]. This was a time of trembling and quaking and of intolerance towards everything

particular. For fanaticism wills only what is abstract, not what is articulated, so that whenever differences emerge, it finds them incompatible with its own indeterminacy and cancels them [*hebt sie auf*]. This is why the people, during the French Revolution, destroyed once more the institutions they had themselves created, because all institutions are incompatible with the abstract self-consciousness of equality.

(PR: §5 and §5Z, pp. 38–39)

This brief discussion in the *Philosophy of Right* is helpful, because it shows what for Hegel underlies the mistaken outlook of consciousness at the time of French Revolution, in a way that involves no reference to Rousseau: namely, that this standpoint holds that the subject is free only if it is in a state in which all 'particularity' (such as social roles, classes, and constitutional functions) is abolished, whereas for Hegel the proper conception of freedom allows that the subject can live within these structures without being 'limited' or diminished. According to Hegel, a subject may find that its place within society is very different from those of other subjects, without thereby feeling that it is rendered 'unfree', in so far as the subject can be '*bei sich* in this determinacy' (cf. also PR: §207, pp. 238–39). Thus, while Rousseau opposed the idea of political representation at the legislative level because he saw it as involving an unacceptable transfer of sovereignty from the people to their representatives, on Hegel's account this opposition has a very different source. For Hegel, it comes from the unwillingness of individuals to tolerate any 'particularization' and hence any identification with the kind of concrete social structures and differentiation that representative government involves.

As we shall now see in more detail by looking at the *Phenomenology*, Hegel wants to trace back the 'fanaticism' of the Terror to just this conception of 'universality', which treats 'particularity' as something the subject must escape or overcome. First of all, Hegel argues, consciousness moves from seeing itself as a desiring subject, to seeing itself as a willing subject, as it abandons the ideology of utility in favour of a doctrine of freedom based on the will; thus, rather than wishing to satisfy its particular desires, the individual now sets them aside and sees itself as 'the universal Subject' (PS: §583, p. 356):

> The object and the [moment of] *difference* have here lost the meaning of *utility*, which was the predicate of all real being; consciousness does not begin its movement in the object as if this were something *alien* from which it first has to return into itself; on the contrary, the object is for it consciousness itself. The antithesis consists, therefore, solely in the difference between the *individual* and the *universal* consciousness; but the individual consciousness itself is directly in its own eyes that which had only the *semblance* of an antithesis; it is universal consciousness and will.
>
> (PS: §586, pp. 357–58)

Once it thinks of itself as 'universal' in this way, Hegel argues, the individual will no longer accept that society is properly structured around different social groups, for it rejects any kind of 'particularization' of this sort, which treats the subject as defined or fixed by its place in the social order; rather, it thinks the subject is able to 'rise above' this kind of determination, and adopt a purely universal standpoint:

> each individual consciousness raises itself out of its allotted sphere, no longer finds its essence and its work in this particular sphere, but grasps itself as the *Notion* of will, grasps all spheres as the essence of this will, and therefore can only realize itself in a work which is the work of the whole. In this absolute freedom, therefore, all social groups or classes which are the spiritual spheres into which the whole is articulated are abolished; the individual consciousness that belonged to any such sphere, and willed and fulfilled itself in it, has put aside its limitation; its purpose is the general purpose, its language universal law, its work the universal work.
>
> (PS: §585, p. 357)

Now, Hegel argues here, just as he does later in the *Philosophy of Right*, that this conception of the 'universal subject' is problematic, because it seems to have no room for 'particularization': for it finds that qua subject, it is unwilling to tolerate any determinate action, or constitution, or role within the state, as this seems to limit its freedom:

> [W]hen placed in the element of *being*, personality would have the significance of a specific personality; it would cease to be in truth universal self-consciousness ... Universal freedom, therefore, can produce neither a positive work nor a deed; there is left for it only *negative* action; it is merely the *fury* of destruction.
>
> (PS: ¶¶588–89, p. 359)

At the same time, the subject loses all respect for the 'mere' individuality of others, as particular selves with their own meaningless lives, and so slides into the Terror:

> The sole work and deed of universal freedom is therefore *death*, a death too which has no inner significance or filling, for what is negated [i.e. the individual] is the empty point of the absolutely free self. It is thus the coldest and meanest of all deaths, with no more significance than cutting off a head of cabbage or swallowing a mouthful of water.
>
> (PS: ¶590, p. 360)

However, those in power quickly find that the citizens see them as limiting their freedom by attempting to impose some sort of social structure upon them: 'The government, which wills and executes its will from a single point, at the same time wills and executes a specific order [*Anordnung*] and action' (PS: §591, p. 360): these rulers therefore appear to represent merely factional interests and so are deposed, while the rulers themselves suspect everyone of plotting against them. Out of the fear of death that the Terror brings, individuals eventually come to terms with a less one-sided self-conception, in which they now accept that the state may require them to occupy specific roles with it: 'These individuals who have felt the fear of death, of their absolute master, again submit to negation and distinctness, arrange themselves in the various spheres, and return to an apportioned and limited task, but thereby to their substantial reality' (PS: §593, p. 361). However, Hegel insists that this restoration of the social order is no mere return to what went before: for now the consciousness of freedom that underpinned the French Revolution takes a new form, in 'the *moral* Spirit' (PS: §595, p. 363).

Thus, as Hyppolite puts it, 'Hegel interprets the Terror in the language of his dialectical philosophy' (Hyppolite 1974: 458). For Hegel, the Terror poses a deep and highly significant problem, which is that once the modern individual has discovered that he has 'this power to give himself universality, that is, to extinguish all particularity, all determinacy' (PR: §5Z, p. 38), how can this be prevented from making the individual feel alienated from all the structures that make up the state and society (its social roles, its constitutional institutions, its representative mechanisms, its decision-making procedures)? As Hegel's discussion of the French Revolution shows, he thinks that once this alienation has occurred, then anarchy follows, including the anarchy of direct democracy, which in Hegel's presentation seems to have its source not in Rousseauian qualms about the transfer of sovereignty, but in the unwillingness of modern individuals to identify themselves with any particular constituency, which is required if representational structures are to have their proper constitutional significance. On the other hand, he sees that previous ways of reconciling the individual to their social position are no longer applicable, once the self has recognized its capacity for reflective separation between the self qua particular and the self qua universal. Hegel needs to show how the reflective modern subject can be reconciled to 'particularity', by showing how in the modern world, these roles and institutions need not compromise the subject's strong sense of universality and equality. Hegel sets out to realize this project in the *Philosophy of Right*, to which this discussion in the *Phenomenology* is designed to lead us, via Hegel's further analysis of the categories of universal, particular, and individual in the *Logic*. He aims to show that customs, laws, and social institutions are not simply constraints, but are enabling conditions for human freedom, because they both provide necessary resources for human development, and enable us to identify and obtain various ends and goals we can set ourselves. (For further discussion of how this project is meant to work in the *Philosophy of Right*, see Hardimon 1994: 144–73 and K. R. Westphal 1993b.)

SPIRIT THAT IS CERTAIN OF ITSELF: MORALITY

At the heart of Hegel's analysis of the French Revolution, as we have seen, is a critique of the one-sidedness of the conception of freedom it embodied, which required the subject to 'extinguish all particularity' (all determinate desires, traits, and social roles) in order to achieve 'universality'; this 'universal freedom', Hegel argued, 'can produce neither a positive work nor a deed' (PS: §589, p. 359). Hegel now tries to show how a similar one-sidedness lies behind the ethical systems of Kant and Fichte, where on their account of freedom, the autonomous moral subject who acts out of duty is set apart from the natural subject who acts out of desires and inclinations; he argues once again that this sets up an antithesis between the individual and concrete actions, such that the subject is left feeling that it might be best from a moral perspective if he gave up trying to do anything, as there is nothing he can do to actualize pure duty. (Hegel famously saw a close relation here between philosophy in Germany and political events in France, observing of the idea of the pure will that 'With the Germans, [it] remained tranquil theory; but the French wished to put it into practice' (PH: 443/PW: 212).) Hegel aims to show how this conception of freedom and moral goodness commits the Kantian to a dualistic picture, which distinguishes sharply between the natural and the moral order, inclination and duty, and happiness and morality, in a way that ultimately leads to incoherence.

THE POSTULATES OF KANTIAN MORALITY

In order to bring out this incoherence, Hegel focuses on the series of *postulates* to be found in the Kantian conception of practical reason, where Kant tried to show that the moral agent must have certain hopes about the efficacy of his endeavours, and that to make these hopes rational, he must commit himself to the following propositions:

> There is a God, there is in the nature of the world an original although incomprehensible disposition for agreement with moral

> purposiveness, and there is finally in the human soul a disposition that makes it capable of a never-ending progress to this moral purposiveness.
> (Kant RP, 20: 300)

Kant sees a need for these postulates because without them we would have no grounds for thinking that our moral actions will succeed, as nothing in the natural world taken on its own gives us any reason to think that virtuous behaviour will bring about happiness, while the achievement of moral goodness seems impossible in this life, but becomes conceivable if the soul is thought of as immortal. Kant treats these postulates as theoretically unprovable, but as propositions that we must endorse if our moral undertakings are to make any practical sense. (For further discussion, see Wood 1970.)

Now, Kant's doctrine of the postulates has drawn fire from many quarters. In general, critics have seen the postulates as inconsistent with the rest of the Kantian framework, and thus as compromising the integrity of his fundamental position. To some, the main inconsistency is with what they see as the anti-metaphysical position of the First *Critique*, claiming that Kant now tries to give some kind of rational support for belief in the existence of God and the soul, where he had previously succeeded in showing such beliefs to be unsupportable (cf. Heine 1986: 119, 'As the result of this argument, Kant distinguishes between the *theoretical reason* and the *practical reason*, and by means of the latter, as with a magician's wand, he revivifies deism, which theoretical reason had killed'; cf. also Nietzsche 1974: §335, p. 264). To others, the inconsistency introduced by the postulates is with Kant's ethical theory, and in particular with his anti-eudaemonism: for, having sharply distinguished virtue from happiness, Kant is nonetheless said to compromise his position with the idea of the Highest Good, where virtuous actions bring about happiness in a way that will only seem attainable (according to Kant) if we introduce the postulate of a supreme and benevolent God who can govern nature to bring this about (cf. Schopenhauer 1965: §3, p. 49, 'Kant had the great merit of having purged ethics of all *eudaemonism* ... [But] Of course, strictly speaking, even Kant has banished eudaemonism from ethics more in appearance than in reality, for he still leaves a mysterious connection between virtue and supreme happiness in his doctrine of the highest good, where they come together in an abstruse and obscure chapter; whereas virtue is obviously quite foreign to happiness.').

Though they have a certain rhetorical force, these criticisms of Kant's position can be met by the Kantian. Given Kant's distinction between theoretical and practical reason, it is not clear that there is any inconsistency in rejecting theoretical arguments for God and the soul, but defending practical arguments; and there is no reason to accuse Kant of bad faith on this score. And it also seems incorrect to hold that the doctrine of the Highest Good is in tension with Kant's anti-eudaemonism: for although Kant here makes happiness a goal of the moral agent, it is not *his* happiness that motivates him, so Kant does not in any way treat happiness as the agent's *reward* for virtue (cf. Guyer 2000: 343–45).

Now, although Hegel's critique of the postulates is often assimilated with these standard objections, when looked at more closely this critique is of a rather different kind: put simply, his objection is that the fundamental dualism of Kant's position means that Kant can do no more than postulate the coincidence of nature and morality, inclination and duty, and happiness and morality, but making the connection in this very weak way leaves the dualism unresolved, so that the subject is left feeling that any action it performs is worthless from a moral point of view. According to Hegel, therefore, the difficulty with the Kantian framework is that it is obliged to see the Highest Good and moral perfection as something that we can do no more than *hope* for, as something that *ought* to be, because the divisions Kant sets up between the natural sphere and the moral sphere force him to posit this realization in the 'beyond'. Hegel's objection to the postulates therefore takes the form of a so-called *Sollenkritik*: that is, he rejects them because they rely on a fundamental distinction between how things are and how things ought to be, in which this 'ought' (*Sollen*) is introduced to overcome a dualism that is presupposed at the outset, and so cannot be set aside. Hegel summarizes this objection quite clearly in the *Lectures on the History of Philosophy*:

> [For Kant] Will has the whole world, the whole of the sensuous, in opposition to it, and yet Reason insists on the unity of Nature or the

moral law, as the Idea of the Good, which is the ultimate end of the world. Since, however, it is formal, and therefore has no content on its own account, it stands opposed to the impulses and inclinations of a subjective and an external independent Nature. Kant reconciles the contradiction of the two ... in the thought of the highest Good, in which Nature is conformed to rational will, and happiness to virtue ... [But] The unification spoken of itself therefore remains only a Beyond, a thought, which is not actually in existence, but only ought to be ... [The postulate of God], like that of the immortality of the soul, allows the contradiction to remain as it is all the time, and expresses only in the abstract that the reconciliation ought to come about. The postulate itself is always there, because the Good is a Beyond with respect to Nature; the law of necessity and the law of liberty are different from one another, and are placed in this dualism. Nature would remain Nature no longer, if it were to become conformed to the Notion of the Good; and thus there remains an utter opposition between the two sides, because they cannot unite. It is likewise necessary to establish the unity of the two; but this is never actual, for their separation is exactly what is pre-supposed.

(LHP: III, pp. 462–63)

Hegel thus has two aims in criticizing Kant's postulates: first, he tries to show that Kant's dualistic picture means he can do no more than treat the Highest Good and moral perfection as goals we can strive for, and second he tries to show that there is something incoherent in this position with respect to moral action, so that the Kantian should abandon the dualism that has led him to it.

In the *Phenomenology*, Hegel sets out Kant's postulates in the subsection entitled 'The Moral View of the World'. Hegel first discusses the postulate that 'there is in the nature of the world an original though incomprehensible disposition for agreement with moral purposiveness': that is, the assumption that good deeds will succeed, while bad ones will fail. The need for this postulate arises, because the moralist divides nature off from the moral consciousness, by taking the natural order to be governed by causal necessity, while the moral order is governed by the imperatives of duty: 'The object has thus become ... a *Nature* whose laws like its actions belong to itself as a being which is indifferent to moral self-consciousness, just as the latter is indifferent to it' (PS: §599, p. 365). On the other hand, the moral agent must take his duties as something he can actually *perform* in the world, and so must see nature as hospitable to human happiness as a goal. This need to overcome the initial dualism is what gives rise to the postulate:

> The harmony of morality and Nature – or, since Nature comes into account only in so far as consciousness experiences its unity with it – the harmony of morality and happiness, is *thought of* as something that necessarily *is*, i.e. it is *postulated*.
>
> (PS: §602, p. 367)

The moral world-view therefore divorces morality from nature at one level, but tries to moralize it at another.

A related dualism underlies the second postulate, of immortality. Here, the problem is that on the one hand the Kantian sees moral subjects as possessing a 'pure will' which directs them to follow the moral law, though on the other hand they are nonetheless also natural beings who are 'affected by wants and sensuous motives' (Kant CPrR, 5: p. 32), which qua natural beings they cannot overcome; they therefore fall short of the 'pure thought of duty' (PS: §603, p. 368) that has no such affliction. Thus, while the moral world-view requires that as moral agents we should act on this pure will and 'set aside' our natural being, on the other hand as natural subjects it accepts we cannot do so, thereby apparently making moral goodness unachievable. It therefore attempts to overcome this tension by introducing the postulate of immortality, which allows for the possibility of an endless process of self-improvement, so at no point need we accept that we cannot achieve such goodness. So, for the Kantian, '[t]his unity is likewise a *postulated being*, it is not actually *there*; for what *is* there is consciousness, or the antithesis of sensuousness and pure consciousness' (PS: §603, p. 368).

Finally, Hegel considers the third postulate, of God. Here Hegel's discussion is more remote from Kant's own derivation of the postulate, and is closer to a 'rational reconstruction' than an interpretation. Central to Hegel's account is a distinction he draws between 'pure duty' and 'specific duty'. He does not explain this terminology very clearly, but one way of understanding it is as follows. As a moral consciousness, the individual finds that he must act in particular circumstances, where what is right for him to do is determined by his specific duties (for example, his obligations to his family dependants, or his friends, or his countrymen). However, though the moral consciousness may accept that these specific duties make a certain course of action right for him in his particular situation, he may feel that this course of action is still not his 'pure duty', where 'pure duty' is understood as what it would be right for him to do if he were free of his specific duties (for example, his specific duties make it right that he should provide for his family, while his pure duty is to give a greater proportion of his income to charity). The moral consciousness may therefore come to feel it has a clash: it may feel that it is 'held back' from doing what is its pure duty by the particularity of its situation, and it may therefore question the validity of the specific duties which apply to it by virtue of being in that situation. At the same time, the moral consciousness sees that that situation is one to which it belongs, and so accepts that it is not free to do its 'pure duty' alone. As Hegel puts it:

> The moral consciousness as the *simple knowing* and *willing* of pure duty is, in the doing of it, brought into relation with the object which stands in contrast to its simplicity, into relation with the actuality of the complex case, and thereby has a complex moral *relationship* with it. Here arise, in relation to content, the *many* laws generally, and in relation to form, the contradictory powers of the knowing consciousness and of the non-conscious.
>
> In the first place, as regards the *many* duties, the moral consciousness in general heeds only the *pure duty* in them; the many duties *qua* manifold are *specific* and therefore as such have nothing sacred about them for the moral consciousness. At the same time, however, being *necessary*, since the Notion of 'doing' implies a complex actuality and therefore a complex moral relation to it, these many duties must be regarded as possessing an intrinsic being of their own.

(PS: §605, pp. 369–70)

Now, this is obviously an uncomfortable situation for the moral agent to be in: on the one hand, as a particular individual, he sees that he has specific duties (e.g. to his dependants and friends), but on the other hand, from a more universal standpoint, he sees that it would be better if he were free to do his pure duty (e.g. give more money to charity). The problem here is this: how can the moral world-view ground the obligatoriness of specific duties, when they appear to go against the competing demands of pure duty? Here, Hegel claims, the moralist introduces God, who 'sanctifies' these specific duties, by so arranging the world that they are just as effective at bringing about the good as pure duties are:

> Thus it is postulated that it is *another* consciousness which makes them [i.e. the specific duties] sacred, or which knows and wills them as duties. The first holds to pure duty, indifferent to all *specific* content, and duty is only this indifference towards such content. The other, however, contains the equally essential relation to 'doing', and to the necessity of the *specific* content: since for this other, duties mean *specific* duties, the content as such is equally essential as the form which makes the content a duty. This consciousness is consequently one in which universal and particular are simply one, and its Notion is, therefore, the same as the Notion of the harmony of morality and happiness ... This is then henceforth a master and ruler of the world, who brings about the harmony of morality and happiness, and at the same time sanctifies duties in their multiplicity.
>
> (PS: §606, p. 370)

Once it has postulated God in this way, the moral consciousness can feel liberated from the demands of 'pure duty', as its role can be confined to the observance of specific duties: 'Duty in general thus falls outside of it into another being, which is consciousness and the sacred lawgiver of pure duty' (PS: §607, p. 371). This then leads the Kantian to have an equivocal position on the issue of the relation between happiness and virtue: on the one hand, the moral consciousness knows it has not performed its pure duty, and so feels unworthy and undeserving of happiness; on the other hand, it believes that God will see that this failure is not its fault, as it has done what is right in the circumstances, and so may expect forgiveness and hence some measure of well-being (PS: §§608–9, p. 371).

Thus, without following Kant's own discussion, Hegel has brought out the three central features of Kant's moral argument for God, namely that the moral consciousness treats the moral law as commanded by God (God sanctifies the specific duties); that it sees God as helping us to bring about the existence of a good world (God so arranges things that our specific duties lead to the realization of the Highest Good); and that it relies on God's wisdom to argue for a connection between virtue and happiness (cf. Kant CPrR, 5: p. 131 n.: '[God] is thus the holy lawgiver (and creator), the beneficent ruler (and sustainer), and the just judge.').

Hegel then turns to a detailed critique of the moral world-view, in the section entitled 'Dissemblance or Duplicity'; passing judgement on Kant in a way that Kant himself had passed judgement on others, he declares that '[t]he moral world-view is … a "whole nest" of thoughtless contradictions' (PS: §617, p. 374). In particular, he tries to show that in fact we are in a stronger position than merely possessing the 'hopes' the Kantian puts forward, but that Kant's framework makes it impossible for him to acknowledge this. The result, Hegel suggests, is that the Kantian moralist has a view of morality that is divorced from the need for concrete action, so that (like the one adopted by the French revolutionaries discussed in the previous section) this outlook 'can produce neither a positive work nor a deed'.

Thus, as regards the first postulate, the Kantian treats 'the harmony of morality and Nature … [as] an *implicit* harmony, not explicitly for actual consciousness, not present; on the contrary, what is present is rather only the contradiction of the two' (PS: §618, p. 375). But, Hegel argues, we can do more than just *postulate* the harmony of morality and nature: in fact, every time we act morally in the world, we can see nature conforming to our will and thus showing itself to be in harmony with morality, not as a mere postulate but as a reality:

> Action, therefore, in fact directly fulfils what was asserted could not take place, what was supposed to be merely a postulate, merely a

beyond. Consciousness thus proclaims through its deed that it is not in earnest in making its postulate, because the meaning of the action is really this, to make into a present reality what was not supposed to exist in the present.

(PS: §618, p. 375)

Hegel then considers a Kantian response, that though I may find it possible to realize particular moral goods, this does not show that the ultimate moral goal of the Highest Good is realizable in nature. But, Hegel argues, this Kantian response is revealing, for it shows that for the Kantian what makes the Highest Good unrealizable is not so much nature, as that it takes more than the limited efforts of individuals to bring it about; but if *this* is so, then it is not clear why we should bother acting morally at all, and just rely instead on the hope that the Highest Good will mysteriously come about by itself:

Consciousness starts from the idea that, *for it*, morality and reality do not harmonize; but it is not in earnest about this, for in the deed the presence of this harmony becomes *explicit for it*. But is not in earnest even about the deed, since the deed is something individual; for it has such a high purpose, the *highest good*. But this again is only a dissemblance of the facts, for such dissemblance would do away with all action and all morality. In other words, consciousness is not, strictly speaking, in earnest with *moral* action: what it really holds to be most desirable, to be the Absolute, is that the highest good be accomplished, and that moral action be superfluous.

(PS: §621, p. 377)

In essence, then, Hegel's objection to the first postulate is quite simple: the Kantian starts from a basic dualism of morality and nature, and this blinds him to the fact that enough of our moral goals are achieved to make continued moral action rational; but once this fact is admitted, we are no longer obliged to treat the 'agreement [of the world] with moral purposiveness' as a mere postulate, in the way that Kant tries to do. The Kantian moralist cannot see this, however, with the result (Hegel claims) that he fails to be 'in earnest' when it comes to the value of moral action.

As regards the second postulate, Hegel poses a dilemma for the Kantian. On the one hand, he argues, the Kantian cannot treat the morally pure will as one with *no* desires and inclinations, because otherwise it would be impossible to explain its capacity for action. On the other hand, the Kantian could see the morally pure will as possessing desires and inclinations, but that these are *in conformity with* the dictates of morality; but then, if the Kantian is right to take the natural subject as phenomenal and the moral subject as noumenal, why should we think that this conformity should *ever* arise, as the different realms have different structures? Thus, while the second postulate seems to hold out some hope of overcoming the dualism of duty and inclination in an infinite beyond, Kant's actual position would show such hope to be misguided: 'the harmony [of morality and sense-nature] is beyond consciousness in a nebulous remoteness where nothing can any more be accurately distinguished or comprehended; for our attempts just now to comprehend this unity failed' (PS: §622, p. 378). Now, Hegel argues, this result will not really bother the Kantian, because in fact he sees morality as consisting in just this never-ending struggle between duty and inclination, as without this struggle the virtuous individual could not show that he is capable of resisting the perpetual threat of temptation:

> Morality is both the *activity* of this pure purpose, and also the consciousness of rising above sense-nature, of being mixed up with sense-nature and struggling against it. That consciousness is not in earnest about the perfection of morality is indicated by the fact that consciousness itself shifts it away into *infinity*, i.e. asserts that the perfection is never perfected.
>
> (PS: §622, p. 378)

Finally, as regards the third postulate, Hegel raises two objections. First, against the idea that God sanctifies our specific duties and so makes them obligatory, Hegel argues that this is incompatible with the commitment to moral autonomy, which is fundamental to the Kantian position, and to Kant's insistence that 'we shall not look upon actions as obligatory because they are commands of God, but shall regard them as divine commands because we have an inward obligation to them' (Kant CPR: A819/B847). Thus, the Kantian cannot appeal to God to overcome the tension between pure and specific duties:

> The moral self-consciousness ... holds these *many* duties to be unessential; for it is concerned only with the one pure duty, and the *many* have no truth *for it* in so far as they are *specific* duties. They can therefore have their truth only in another being and are made sacred – which they are *not* for the moral consciousness – by a holy lawgiver. But this again is only a dissemblance of the real position. For the moral self-consciousness is its own Absolute, and duty is absolutely only what *it knows* as duty. But duty it knows only as pure duty; what is not sacred for it is not sacred in itself, and what is not in itself sacred, cannot be made sacred by the holy being.
>
> (PS: §626, p. 380)

Hegel's second objection concerns the possibility of conceiving God as a moral agent, acting under an imperative of pure duty, while we carry out our specific duties. Hegel's claim is that such 'a purely moral being' is an 'unreal abstraction in which the concept of morality, which involves thinking of pure duty, willing, and doing it, would be done away with' (PS: §628, p. 381). In other words, it is hard to conceive of God, as a being lacking in any specific attachments and as existing outside the world, as having any moral agency within it: God just appears to be altogether beyond the moral situation. Thus, while the Kantian moralist thinks that we are not capable of fully developed moral agency because we are 'affected by sense-nature and Nature opposed to it', it is not clear that God is capable of moral agency either, since 'the *reality* of pure duty is its *realization* in Nature and sense'; but God is 'above the *struggle* with Nature and sense' (PS: §628, p. 381), and so outside the realm in which moral action takes place. Once again, therefore, Hegel claims that the Kantian has a difficulty in relating the reality of moral action with his conception of the moral will.

CONSCIENCE

From this critique of the moral consciousness, Hegel moves to a kind of ethical outlook that he calls *conscience*, which sets out to escape the aporias that beset morality. Conscience thus rejects 'the internal divisions which gave rise to the dissemblance [of morality], the division between the in-itself and the self, between pure duty qua pure purpose, and reality qua a Nature and sense opposed to pure purpose' (PS: §634, p. 385). Conscience thus has none of the (feigned) self-doubts that beset morality (cf. Fichte 2005: 165: 'Conscience never errs and cannot err ...'). It takes itself to know how to act in particular cases, and does not feel any tension between pure and specific duties, 'for the fact is that pure duty consists in the empty abstraction of pure thought, and has its reality and its content only in a specific reality, in a reality which is the reality of a consciousness itself, and consciousness not as a mere "thought-thing" but as an individual' (PS: §637, pp. 386–87); nor does conscience feel its 'natural self' as a check to such knowledge or moral action. Likewise, it does not worry about whether or not nature will frustrate its goals, because what matters to it is that others see it has at least *tried* to act well: 'What is done with the conviction of duty is, therefore, at once something that has standing and a real existence. There is, then, no more talk of good intentions coming to nothing, or of the good man faring badly' (PS: §640, p. 388).

Nonetheless, Hegel argues that the situation for conscience is not as straightforward as it claims, and it too involves elements of dissemblance. For, first, conscience holds that it can determine what is right in particular concrete situations by thinking through the consequences of its possible actions. But how can it claim to have a full understanding of what those consequences might be, given the complexity involved? For 'it does not possess that full acquaintance with *all* the attendant circumstances which is required, and ... its pretence of conscientiously weighing all the circumstances is vain' (PS: §642, p. 390). Similarly, conscience only denies that the real situation involves a clash of moral duties because it thinks it can rely on its 'gut feelings' to tell it what it ought to do. Conscience defends this position by arguing that depending on one's point of view, it is possible to see almost anything as a morally legitimate action, so that only such 'gut feelings' can really count in the end: '[Conscience] places in duty, as the [empty] universal in-itselfness, the content that it takes from natural individuality; for the content is one that is present within itself' (PS: §646, p. 393). However, the individual cannot be sure that others will share his moral intuitions, and thus cannot be sure how he will be judged by them. Conscience therefore asks to be judged merely on its conscientiousness: that is, whether it was acting correctly by its *own* lights:

> Whether the assurance of acting from a conviction of duty is *true*, whether what is done is actually a *duty* – these questions or doubts have no meaning when addressed to conscience.
>
> To ask whether the assurance is true would presuppose that the inner intention is different from the one put forward, i.e. that what the individual self wills, can be separated from duty ... But this distinction between the universal consciousness and the individual self is just what has been superseded, and the supersession of it *is* conscience. The self's immediate knowing that is certain of itself is law and duty.
>
> (PS: §654, pp. 396–97)

At first, the inwardness of conscience brings great consolation, as it appears to the agent that he can now make it impossible for others not to recognize his 'moral genius' (PS: §655, p. 397), because he can make sure that at the very least they acknowledge his good intentions:

> The spirit and substance of their association are this assurance of their conscientiousness, good intentions, the rejoicing over their moral purity, and the refreshing of themselves in the glory of knowing and uttering, of cherishing and fostering, such an excellent state of affairs.
>
> (PS: §656, p. 398)

However, the individual comes to see that the best way to secure his reputation for integrity in the eyes of others is to refrain from acting, as action might lead to a misinterpretation of his motives; the 'moral genius' thus becomes the 'beautiful soul':

> It lives in dread of besmirching the splendour of its inner being by action and an existence; and, in order to preserve the purity of its

> heart, it flees from contact with the actual world, and persists in its
> self-willed impotence to renounce its self which is reduced to the
> extreme of ultimate abstraction.
>
> (PS: §658, p. 400)

(For a useful study that puts Hegel's discussion of the beautiful
soul in its intellectual context, see Norton 1995.)

Faced with the 'emptiness' of the beautiful soul, conscience
realizes that it must act; but it still sees itself as morally authoritative, so that there is an inevitable conflict between individual
consciousnesses, and between individuals and the universal qua
established moral order: 'As a result, the antithesis of individuality to other individuals, and to the universal, inevitably
comes on the scene, and we have to consider this relationship and
its movement' (PS: §659, p. 400). As a result, the individual who
acts from conscience will look evil to others who abide by the
established moral order, because he refuses to act in accordance
with the duties laid down by that order; the individual will also
be accused of hypocrisy, because he claims to be interested in
acting morally while at the same time flouting the moral rules:

> In contrast to this internal determination [of conscience] there thus
> stands the element of existence or universal consciousness, for which
> the essential element is rather universality, duty; while individuality, on
> the other hand, which in contrast to the universal is for itself, counts
> only as a superseded moment. For the consciousness which holds
> firmly to duty, the first consciousness counts as *evil*, because of the
> disparity between its *inner being* and the universal; and since, at the
> same time, this first consciousness declares its action to be in con-
> formity with itself, to be duty and conscientiousness, it is held by the
> universal consciousness to be *hypocrisy*.
>
> (PS: §660, p. 401)

In fact, however, Hegel argues, there is little to choose between
these two forms of consciousness. In condemning the individual
conscience, the dutiful majority show themselves to be more
interested in criticizing others than in acting themselves, while
their accusation of hypocrisy betrays a mean-minded spirit, blind

to the moral integrity of the moral individualist: 'No man is a hero to his valet; not, however, because the man is not a hero, but because the valet – is a valet' (PS: §665, p. 404). The moral individualist thus comes to see that its critic has much in common with itself, and that both are equally fallible: it therefore 'confesses' to the other, expecting the other to reciprocate. However, at first the other does not do so, remaining 'hard hearted': it thus *itself* becomes a 'beautiful soul', taking up a position of deranged sanctimoniousness (PS: §§668–69, pp. 406–7).

With this evident failure, the 'hard heart' is forced to reconcile itself with the moral individualist, as each recognizes the one-sidedness of its position, and hence overcomes it. In this insight (and the move from hard-heartedness to forgiveness it brings), Hegel sees the attainment of a properly dialectical standpoint of mutual recognition, a moment of 'being at home' that constitutes the realization of Spirit:

> The reconciling *Yea*, in which the two 'I's let go their antithetical *existence*, is the *existence* of the 'I' which has expanded into a duality, and therein remains identical with itself, and, in its complete externalization and opposite, possesses the certainty of itself: it is God manifested in the midst of those who know themselves in the form of pure knowledge.
>
> (PS: §671, p. 409)

With this abrupt reference to God, Hegel completes his discussion of Spirit in this chapter, and gives himself a bridge to the discussion of religion in the next, where a number of remaining dialectical tensions remain to be played out.

CONTENT SUMMARY

TRUE SPIRIT: ETHICAL LIFE

§§438–43 (pp. 263–66)   Transition from Reason to Spirit, seen as ethical life.

§§444–63 (pp. 266–78)   Presentation of ethical life as it appeared in the Greek world, as involving a positive

SPIRIT THAT IS CERTAIN OF ITSELF: MORALITY

§§596–615 (pp. 364–74)   A similarly abstract view of freedom underlies the Kantian conception of the moral subject, who is set apart from the natural order, leading to a division between inclination and duty, happiness and morality, which Kant tries to soften with his postulates.

§§616–31 (pp. 374–83)   Hegel argues that Kant's strategy here cannot succeed, where the various postulates are shown to be unsustainable, given Kant's fundamental dualism.

§§632–57 (pp. 383–99)   The discussion now turns to conscience as an ethical guide, which sees freedom in the ability of the individual to decide for himself how to act; but such individualism becomes overweening, as it refuses to accept criticism from others, or that it can do wrong.

§658 (pp. 399–400)   In order to avoid such criticism, the individual becomes a 'beautiful soul', who refuses to act for fear of appearing to do wrong in the eyes of others.

§§659–71 (pp. 400–409)   Seeing that this way out is unacceptable, the individual acts and allows himself to be judged by others, where each comes to see the other as equally fallible and in need of forgiveness.

6

THE DIALECTIC OF RELIGION
(PHENOMENOLOGY, C. (CC.) RELIGION)

NATURAL RELIGION

As we have already seen, among the many dichotomies belonging to modern consciousness that Hegel wishes to transcend, there is the dichotomy of faith and reason, which rests on an opposition between God and man, feeling and intellect, religion and philosophy. Hegel observes that we have already witnessed this dichotomy at several points in the *Phenomenology*, when considering the Unhappy Consciousness, Greek ethical life, and the Enlightenment (PS: §§672–76, pp. 410–11). In his discussion of the Enlightenment, and its apparent victory over faith in the chapter on Spirit, Hegel clearly foreshadowed our return to religion in this current chapter: 'we shall see whether Enlightenment can remain satisfied; that yearning of the troubled Spirit which mourns over the loss of its spiritual world lurks in the background' (PS: §573, p. 349). The instability of the Enlightenment's world-view, and its inability to bring us satisfaction, have been demonstrated, and this has been filled out in his discussion of the unstable place of God within the Kantian framework of 'Morality'. It is now therefore time to return to religion to see how faith can be reintegrated into a less one-sided philosophical outlook, in which the opposition between the sheerly transcendent and the utterly worldly is overcome:

> There is indeed one Spirit of both, but its consciousness does not embrace both together, and religion appears as a part of existence, of conduct and activity, whose other part is the life lived in its real world. As we now know that Spirit in its own world and Spirit conscious of itself as Spirit, or Spirit in religion, are the same, the perfection of religion consists in the two becoming identical with each other.
>
> (PS: §678, p. 412)

Hegel's aim in this chapter, therefore, is to show what this 'perfection of religion' might look like, and how it can be reached by religious thought. The latter must be radically different from the kind of religious belief targeted by the Enlightenment, where faith was supposedly proved by scripture (which was then shown to be historically inaccurate), to be based around artefacts and relics (which were then shown to be no more than natural objects), and to involve a transcendent deity (which then became unknowable). Hegel takes himself to have demonstrated how the attempt by the Enlightenment to put religious consciousness aside was disastrous; he now sets out to show how religion may be conceived in a way that makes this negative stance unnecessary, so that religious belief may be incorporated within philosophy, and not excluded from it. He therefore offers here a reconstruction or interpretation of the development of religion, to show how religious thinking may be seen as converging on rather than departing from the insights so central to the rationalistic philosophical consciousness of the modern world. This chapter therefore has a more definite cultural–historical and chronological character than the previous ones. It should be said, however, that this attempt by Hegel to 'swing religious consciousness into full support of a scientific interpretation of human life' (Harris 1983: 302) has proved highly controversial, as some have taken it to compromise the original Enlightenment project, whilst others have seen it as an inevitable distortion of the proper religious outlook. In so far as both of these responses involve what Hegel would have seen as one-sided conceptions of philosophy and faith respectively, their persistence is an example of the ease with which consciousness can become polarized in this way.

Hegel's strategy for overcoming this polarization is to consider the development of religious consciousness, from 'natural religion' to 'religion in the form of art' to 'revealed religion',[1] thereby hoping to show that far from alienating us from the world and standing opposed to rationalism, religion when properly developed expresses just this philosophical outlook, albeit in a non-philosophical form. He therefore attempts to show how religious consciousness must come to adopt a faith that upholds rather than rejects a rational view of the world, so that in the end the struggle between the Enlightenment and religious belief is not a battle that either side needs to fight, as when properly developed each can incorporate the other. Put another way: Hegel hopes to show that the kind of rationalistic picture that philosophy leads to need not bring an end to religion, since the same picture is implicitly present within religious consciousness itself. He therefore considers the underlying telos in the evolution of religious consciousness in order to establish that in its highest form it can be made compatible with philosophy, and is not intrinsically opposed to it, as the militantly atheistic thinkers of the Enlightenment (and especially of the French Enlightenment) had supposed.

In beginning with 'natural religion', Hegel takes himself to be considering religion in its simplest or most 'immediate' form, where there is no separation between man and nature, and thus where nature itself is divinized, first in the form of light, and then in the form of plants and animals. In light-religion, light is taken to be a creative force that brings the world into being out of darkness, and which the individual therefore venerates. This light-force lacks any determination, however, and appears insubstantial in comparison to the material world. Religious consciousness then sees the deity in plant and animal form, where in the latter the gods take on the most primitive aspect of selfhood (seen earlier in the transition from life to Desire), in the warring of animal gods with each other, reflecting the struggle for supremacy between different tribal groups. However, as society moves from this division into tribes to the emergence of empire and the stability this brings, 'Spirit enters into another shape' (PS: §690, p. 421), where individuals' conception of God reflects their transition from warriors to agriculturalists, who now see themselves as relating to the divine through their work.

This process gives rise to the 'artificer' or master-craftsman, whose task is to fabricate objects of religious significance, so that divinity then no longer exists in a purely given or natural form. At first, the master-craftsman only creates objects that have a geometrical shape, but the abstraction of these objects renders them unsatisfying to religious consciousness, so that the craftsman begins to make objects in plant and animal shapes, until they finally assume human form. At this level, however, the statues of gods that the craftsman creates cannot communicate to us in human terms; when this limitation is transcended, and the divine is seen as sharing our language, the artisan is no longer a craftsman, but an artist, in so far as the gods he creates now come to have an *expressive* function.

RELIGION IN THE FORM OF ART

In moving from 'natural religion' to 'religion in the form of art', Hegel makes clear that we are now considering the religious outlook of ethical Spirit, which (as we have seen) Hegel took to be exemplified by the Greeks. As previously, Hegel presents us with a picture that emphasizes the attractions but also the limitations of this ethical Spirit. Hegel makes clear that at the level of its religious consciousness, it represents a higher achievement than everything that has gone before, something that is made possible by the social form of the *polis*:

> [Spirit] is for them neither the divine, essential Light in whose unity the being-for-self of self-consciousness is contained only negatively, only transitorily, and in which it beholds the lord and master of its actual world; nor is it the restless destruction of hostile peoples, nor their subjection to a caste-system which gives the semblance of

> organization of a completed whole, but in which the universal free-
> dom of the individuals is lacking. On the contrary, this Spirit is the
> free nation in which hallowed custom constitutes the substance of all,
> whose actuality and existence each and everyone knows to be his own
> will and deed.
>
> (PS: §700, p. 425)

However, Hegel reminds us here that the harmony he associates
with the *polis* is unstable, and its eventual dissolution is reflected
in the 'absolute art' of Greek tragedy, in which religion in the form
of art culminates, prior to the point at which 'Spirit transcends art
in order to gain a higher representation of itself' (PS: §702, p. 426).

As we have seen, Hegel takes the turning-point from natural
religion to religion in the form of art to involve a shift away from
man's relation to nature, to man's relation to the *polis*, so that the
gods now embody the state (as did the goddess Athena, for
example), rather than natural phenomena:

> These ancient gods, first-born children of the union of Light with
> Darkness, Heaven, Earth, Ocean, Sun, the Earth's blind typhonic Fire,
> and so on, are supplanted by shapes which only dimly recall those
> Titans, and which are no longer creatures of Nature, but lucid, ethical
> Spirits of self-conscious nations.
>
> (PS: §707, p. 428)

However, although the gods now take on human form and are
intrinsically related to the human community, it is at first difficult for the religious artist to bring the people together with
these gods, when religious art takes on a sculptural form. At this
stage, Hegel argues, the artist aspires to be merely a vehicle or
instrument for the divinities, who tries to set aside his own crea-
tivity and simply be inspired by them; but he is also aware that
he has laboured to create the statues, and so that he is also present
in what he has made, standing between the people and their
gods. Thus, although the worshippers may feel that the statue he
has cast has made the gods present among them, the artist knows
that he has created a mere representation, as he was unable to
'forget himself' in it.

Rather than seeing its gods as mute, therefore, the religious community needs to make its divinities *speak*, so that they may be worshipped not only in sculptural form, but also through *hymns*, in which the writer may see himself as simply transcribing the words of the gods:

> The work of art therefore demands another element of its existence, the god another mode of coming forth than this ... This higher element is Language – an outer reality that is immediately self-conscious existence ... The god, therefore, who has language for the element of his shape is the work of art that is in its own self inspired, that possesses immediately in its outer existence the pure activity which, when it existed as a Thing, was in contrast to it.
>
> (PS: §710, pp. 429–30)

Hegel contrasts this use of the hymn to the role of the oracle in religious cultures, where in the oracle the divinity speaks in an alien tongue, reflecting the fact that the oracle was used to settle contingent matters (like whether it would be good to travel) which were not covered by the laws of the gods (which everyone knew without having to consult the oracle). However, although the hymn marks an advance over the oracle, the worshippers nonetheless came to feel that it only makes the god present to them in an impermanent way (in contrast to the permanence of the statue): we therefore move to a further form of religious life, of the *cult*, which attempts to overcome this defect by bringing speech and statuary together, as the worshippers sing hymns before the statues in order to welcome and receive their gods.

In order for this to take place, the worshippers attempt to purify themselves and overcome their bodily selves (for they do not yet see evil as residing in the soul). They therefore sacrifice their material possessions, although paradoxically this sacrifice is also a prelude to a feast, which 'cheats the act [of sacrifice] out of its negative significance' (PS: §718, p. 434). The cult attempts to resolve this tension by instead devoting itself to constructing holy buildings, where the creative individuality of the artist at the level of sculptural art is no longer so intrusive: 'this action is not the individual labour of the artist, this particular aspect of it being dissolved in universality' (PS: §719, p. 435). Nonetheless, the temples hereby created now come to serve more as places where the city can parade and display its wealth and power.

In this phase of religious development, consciousness has a joyous and affirmative relation to the divine, which is reflected in the feasting of the worshippers: 'In this enjoyment, then, is revealed what that divine risen Light really is; enjoyment in the mystery of its being' (PS: §722, p. 437). However, the cult merely relates to the divine as nature: 'its self-conscious life is only the mystery of bread and wine, of Ceres and Bacchus, not of the other, the strictly higher, gods whose individuality includes as an essential moment self-consciousness as such' (PS: §724, p. 438). In the games and processions the gods continue to be represented in human form, in the athletic champion who is a kind of living statue, and simultaneously a repository of national pride.

However, religious consciousness comes to feel that it cannot properly represent its gods in this way, in terms of the 'corporeal individuality' of the handsome warrior. It therefore turns from the plastic arts to literary forms: to the epic, tragedy, and comedy.

In the epic, the gods are seen to guide the actions and destiny of the heroes portrayed in the story, as a controlling agency:

> They are the universal, and the positive, over against the *individual self* of mortals which cannot hold out against their might; but the universal self, for that reason, hovers over them and over this whole world of picture-thinking to which the entire content belongs, as the irrational void of Necessity – a mere happening which they must face as beings without a self and sorrowfully, for these *determinate* natures cannot find themselves in this purity.
>
> (PS: §731, p. 443)

In tragedy, by contrast, the individuals appear more in control of their destiny in relation to the gods: they are '*self-conscious* human beings who *know* their rights and purposes, the power and the will of their specific nature and know how to *assert* them' (PS: §733, p. 444). Hegel argues that this difference is reflected in the fact that whereas in the epic the narrator is the 'minstrel' who stands outside the story, in tragedy the hero or heroine speaks for him or herself, and hence the actor plays a part *in* the drama. Nonetheless, a sense of powerlessness in relation to the gods is reflected by the chorus, which 'clings to the consciousness of an *alien fate* and produces the empty desire for ease and comfort, and feeble talk of appeasement' (PS: §734, p. 445). What tragedy really reveals, however, is the split within ethical substance itself, between family and state, feminine and masculine, and the blindness of each side to its other, symbolized in the way the gods mislead the tragic heroes: 'The action, in being carried out, demonstrates their unity in the natural downfall of both powers and both self-conscious characters' (PS: §740, p. 448). Because of the role of character in tragedy, the religious consciousness no longer thinks of these gods as agents directing the lives of the heroes; but instead the divine is viewed as fate. Hegel remarks that '[t]his Fate completes the depopulation of Heaven ... The expulsion of such shadowy, insubstantial picture-thoughts which was demanded of the philosophers of antiquity thus already begins in [Greek] Tragedy' (PS: §741, p. 449).

This process continues further in comedy, as the representation of the gods using masks can be used to reveal that behind it all is just another actor. The gods therefore become merely abstract Platonic universals, mocked by Aristophanes in the *Clouds*, as religious consciousness no longer sets the divine apart from itself:

> It is the return of everything universal into the certainty of itself which, in consequence, is this complete loss of fear and of essential being on the part of all that is alien. This self-certainty is a state of spiritual well-being and of repose therein, such as is not to be found anywhere outside of this Comedy.
>
> (PS: §747, pp. 452–53)

THE REVEALED RELIGION

Hegel now sets out to show how consciousness cannot rest satisfied with the kind of purely secular outlook we have reached, but now moves back to a more overtly religious outlook and a conception of the divine that represents an advance on anything we have witnessed hitherto. He puts this in the following terms: so far, we have moved from the doctrine that 'Absolute Being is substance' (which gives priority to God as a self-subsistent and independent reality), to 'The Self as absolute Being' (which gives priority to humanity as having the kind of subjectivity that God is seen to lack); we must now move to the final stage of religion, in which 'Absolute Being is subject' (where God will be seen as achieving self-consciousness *through* humanity, so that neither side takes undialectical precedence over the other).

Hegel makes the transition from the happy consciousness of Greek comedy to the unhappy consciousness of Roman Stoicism and Scepticism by focusing on the inevitable 'disenchantment' of the world that the former brings in its wake, as consciousness comes to feel what it means to say 'God is dead':

> Trust in the eternal laws of the gods has vanished, and the Oracles, which pronounced on particular questions, are dumb. The statues are now only stones from which the living soul has flown, just as the hymns are words from which belief has gone. The tables of the gods provide no spiritual food and drink, and in his games and festivals man no longer recovers the joyful consciousness of his unity with the divine. The works of the Muse now lack the power of the Spirit, for the Spirit has gained its certainty of itself from the crushing of gods and men.
>
> (PS: §753, p. 455)

Hegel argues that once this position has been reached, religious consciousness can never find itself in a 'return' to natural religion or art–religion, and that religious belief must therefore take another form. Only by encountering God in the shape of a human being can religious consciousness recover itself, and thereby take us beyond other previous varieties of religious experience:

> The Self of existent Spirit has, as a result, the form of complete immediacy; it is posited neither as something thought or imagined, nor as something produced, as is the case with the immediate Self in natural religion, and also in the religion of Art; on the contrary, this God is sensuously and directly beheld as a Self, as an actual individual man; only so *is* this God self-consciousness.
>
> (PS: §758, p. 459)

In taking this form, religious consciousness has come to treat the divine as something *revealed* or *manifest*; God has now become another subject, knowable to us as sharing in our natures: 'The divine nature is the same as the human, and it is this unity that is beheld' (PS: §759, p. 460). At the same time, God remains a substance, for in becoming human He remains unconditioned and absolute; indeed, it is only by becoming human that He *can be* unconditioned and absolute, because otherwise He would be set over against us in a purely transcendent realm: 'The absolute Being which exists as an actual self-consciousness seems to have come down from its eternal simplicity, but by thus *coming down* it has in fact attained for the first time to its own highest essence' (PS: §760, p. 460). Thus, Hegel argues, only in the revealed form can we truly conceive of the divine as absolute. This is why Christianity constitutes the highest form of religious consciousness: 'The hopes and expectations of the world up till now had pressed forward solely to this revelation, to behold what absolute Being is, and in it to find itself' (PS: §761, p. 461). As we shall see, Hegel takes this to coincide with his own philosophical outlook, according to which such 'hopes and expectations' are fulfilled in much the same way, so that here the tension between religion and philosophy is finally and in principle overcome. (For a useful general discussion of Hegel's final position, see Houlgate 1991: 176–232.)

However, before this point can be reached, the revealed religion must deal with the following difficulty: how can God, incarnated in a particular individual, nonetheless share His nature with us all, as distinct individuals? – 'i.e. Spirit as an individual Self is not yet equally the universal Self, the Self of everyone' (PS: §762, p. 462). To resolve this problem, the divine must give up its immediate incarnation, and be resurrected, so that the religious community can see that its existence is more than 'this objective individual' (PS: §763, p. 462); God is thus now conceived of as Holy Spirit. Nonetheless, Hegel argues, it is hard for the religious consciousness not to hark back to the incarnation, and to see it as the exclusive basis of its faith; but, he suggests, this will leave it 'still burdened with an unreconciled split into a Here and a Beyond' (PS: §765, p. 463), since it realizes that the time of this incarnation cannot be fully recovered. The religious consciousness forgets, however, that the real lesson of the resurrection is to show that the incarnation is not in itself significant, as God is *always* present in the life of the community of believers when He is recognized as such:

> What results from this impoverishment of Spirit, from getting rid of the idea of the community, and its action with regard to its idea, is not the Notion, but rather bare externality and singularity, the historical manner of the manifestation of its immediacy and the non-spiritual recollection of a supposed individual figure and of its past.
>
> (PS: §766, p. 463)

Hegel therefore shows how mistaken it is for religious consciousness to get involved in purely historical questions about Christ's life, of the sort typically raised by the Enlightenment.

Hegel then turns to the doctrine of the Trinity itself to see how far it too reflects a perspective compatible with his philosophical standpoint. He argues that this doctrine shows how this form of religious thought has already succeeded in transcending the distinctions between essence and appearance, reason and world, in precisely the way that is required if it is to be appropriated by speculative philosophy; however, it still does not make this advance in properly conceptual terms, but only in its characteristic 'picture-thinking', in an externally 'representational' form. It therefore talks in terms of God the Father and God the Son, and of God creating the world, and of the Fall. Hegel argues that faith is inclined to understand these doctrines in literal terms, which gives rise to inevitable difficulties. In fact their true significance is essentially philosophical, implicitly reflecting an insight into the way in which reason is realized in this world. So, regarding the idea of creation, Hegel comments: 'This "creating" is picture-thinking's word for the Notion itself in its absolute movement' (PS: §774, p. 467). Hegel thus sees a parallel between his philosophical claim that reality is informed by reason, and the Christian idea of the creation, whereby God instantiates Himself in the world. Likewise, the story of the Fall conveys the way in which the thinking subject comes to feel alienated from the world, once he tries to reflect on it, and forfeits his immediate absorption in nature:

> Immediate existence suddenly turns into thought, or mere self-consciousness into consciousness of thought; and, moreover, because the thought stems from immediacy or is *conditioned* thought, it is not pure knowledge, but thought that is charged with otherness and is, therefore, the self-opposed thought of Good and Evil. Man is pictorially thought of in this way: that it once *happened*, without any necessity, that he lost the form of being at one with himself through plucking the fruit of the tree of knowledge of Good and Evil, and was expelled from the state of innocence, from Nature which yielded its fruits without toil, and from Paradise, from the garden with its creatures ... Such a form of expression as 'fallen' which, like the expression 'Son', belongs, moreover, to picture-thinking and not to the Notion, degrades the moments of the Notion to the level of picture-thinking or carries picture-thinking over into the realm of thought.
>
> (PS: §775, p. 468)

Thus, by separating out the 'rational content' of religion from its 'representational form' (cf. LHP: I, p. 79/ILHP: 141), Hegel hoped to show how many of the issues that preoccupied religion's Enlightenment critics (concerning the mechanics of the creation, or God's relation to his Son, for example), were not *real* issues, but simply problems that arose in relation to the form in which religious belief cloaked its underlying speculative ideas, ideas which could then be given a less mystifying expression in philosophical thought.

Turning once again to the story of the crucifixion and resur-rection, Hegel argues that Christianity ought to be a religion in which the divine is seen as living within the spiritual commu-nity, and thus as lacking any wholly transcendent element: 'The death of the Mediator is the death not only of his *natural* aspect or of his particular being-for-self, not only of the already dead husk stripped of its essential Being, but also of the *abstraction* of the divine Being' (PS: §785, p. 476). However, Hegel argues that it is hard for the Christian community to do away with all aspects of transcendence in its religious thought, so it therefore continues to hold that full rational insight, which Hegel sees as the imperative behind religious consciousness, is only to be gained in the 'beyond'. It therefore remains for philosophy to show how this insight can be gained in the here and now:

> The world is indeed *implicitly* reconciled with the divine Being; and regarding the divine Being it is known, of course, that it recognizes the object as no longer alienated from it but as identical with it in its love. But for self-consciousness, this immediate presence still has not the shape of Spirit. The Spirit of the community is thus in its immediate consciousness divided from its religious consciousness, which declares, it is true, that *in themselves* they are not divided, but this merely *implicit* unity is not realized, or has not yet become an equally absolute being-for-self.
>
> (PS: §787, p. 478)

CONTENT SUMMARY

NATURAL RELIGION

§§672–83 (pp. 410–16)   A look back at the way in which religion has figured in the discussion up to now (in the Unhappy Consciousness, Greek ethical life, etc.), and the need to find an adequate place for religion within modern thought as part of Spirit.

§§684–98 (pp. 416–24)   The simplest and most immediate form of religious life is natural religion, where the divine is seen in natural phenomena and processes; but as societies develop, the gods are given a more human form, through the work of craftsmen who create images of them, leading to 'religion in the form of art'.

RELIGION IN THE FORM OF ART

§§699–713 (pp. 424–32)   From representing the gods in sculptural form, the gods are given the capacity for *language*, to be communicated with through hymns and oracles.

§§714–26 (pp. 433–39)   This gives rise to religious worship in the form of cults, but communication with the gods remains opaque.

§§727–47 (pp. 439–53)   A greater clarity is achieved through the use of drama, which first takes an epic, then tragic, then comedic form, where in the latter the gods are not venerated but mocked, putting religion under threat.

THE REVEALED RELIGION

§§748–87 (pp. 453–78)   Rather than dying, however, the divine is now conceived of in a new, more philosophically sophisticated shape, as capable of taking on a human form, as revealed or manifest to us, rather than as unknowable and transcendent.

7

PHILOSOPHY AS DIALECTIC
(*PHENOMENOLOGY*, C. (DD.)
ABSOLUTE KNOWING)

ABSOLUTE KNOWING

In the previous chapter, we saw that for Hegel it made sense to claim that there might be common ground between religion and philosophy, in so far as both in their highest form (as Christianity and Hegelianism respectively) will allow us to find satisfaction in the world and to be 'at home'. However, while in Christianity the idea of this satisfaction finds expression in the stories and myths of religious representation, in philosophy this idea is given a more literal meaning, once the aporias that prevent us comprehending the world in a rational form are resolved. Hegel calls this kind of rational insight 'absolute knowing', and the form of consciousness that achieves it he calls 'absolute Spirit':

> The *content* of this picture-thinking [at the level of religion] is absolute Spirit; and all that now remains to be done is to supersede this mere

form, or rather, since this belongs to *consciousness as such*, its truth
must already have yielded itself in the shape of consciousness.

(PS: §788, p. 479)

At the end of the *Phenomenology*, it is now clear to consciousness
how this absolute knowing is to be achieved. For it now understands that it has failed to find satisfaction in the world because it
has come to the world in the wrong way, adopting limited conceptions that must be made more complete: absolute knowing
therefore relates to the idea of complete or unimpaired rational
cognition of the world, rather than to knowledge of some non-
worldly entity ('the absolute'). Hegel thus briefly sketches ways in
which consciousness must learn to bring these limited conceptions together, recapitulating the various stages that the dialectic
has already taken. He begins with Consciousness and he argues
that it should now be apparent to us, as phenomenological
observers, that the standpoints adopted by consciousness (Sense-
certainty, Perception, and Understanding) were one-sided, and
that the truth lies in seeing how no one of them does justice to
the way in which individuality, particularity, and universality are
related in the object:

> Thus the object is in part *immediate* being or, in general, a Thing –
> corresponding to immediate consciousness; in part, an othering of
> itself, its relationship or *being-for-an-other*, and *being-for-itself*, i.e.
> determinateness – corresponding to perception; and in part *essence*,
> or in the form of a universal – corresponding to the Understanding. It
> is, as a totality, a syllogism or the movement of the universal through
> determination to individuality, as also the reverse movement from
> individuality through superseded individuality, or through determina-
> tion, to the universal. It is, therefore, in accordance with these three
> determinations that consciousness must know the object as itself.
>
> (PS: §789, p. 480)

Now, it is not immediately clear from the *Phenomenology* what this
conception of individuality, particularity, and universality as
applied to our thinking about objects involves: but on my reading this is not surprising, because we should expect this positive

account to be elaborated elsewhere, in the *Logic* (as indeed it is: see EL: §§160–212, pp. 223–74. For further discussion, see Stern 1990: 54–76, and Winfield 1991: 51–58). The *Phenomenology* is thus a *via negativa* for consciousness, showing how anything less than this complex conception will fail, and bringing to light the dialectical limitations that have brought about this failure. It has therefore served its essentially pedagogical and motivational function, of leading us on to the *Logic*, where the positive doctrine is systematically elaborated in terms of pure categories and thought-forms.

Likewise, Hegel discusses the various standpoints of Self-Consciousness, Reason, and Spirit, reminding us how each on its own proved to be incomplete and that what is now required is to find a way of unifying them into a more complex whole:

> These are the moments of which the reconciliation of Spirit with its own consciousness proper is composed; by themselves they are single and separate, and it is solely their spiritual unity that constitutes the power of this reconciliation. The last of these moments is, however, necessarily this unity itself and, as is evident, it binds them all into itself.
>
> (PS: §793, p. 482)

As Hegel makes clear, the role of the *Phenomenology* has been to put these 'single and separate' moments alongside one another, to show where each is inadequate when taken on its own: 'Our *own* act here has been simply to *gather together* the separate moments, each of which in principle exhibits the life of Spirit in its entirety' (PS: §797, p. 485).

Hegel then goes on to consider what makes the standpoint of consciousness at the end of the *Phenomenology* distinctive, as it prepares to undertake Science: that is, a reflective examination of its categories in an attempt to overcome the kind of one-sided positions we have just traversed. For such a Science to be possible, consciousness must have come to see, through a process of self-examination, that it can arrive at a view of the world that will make the world fully intelligible, where until then it has appeared alien to consciousness. Thus Science, by taking us through the categories corresponding to the limited forms of consciousness portrayed in the *Phenomenology*, can help us to achieve the kind of dialectical outlook that absolute knowing requires. By showing us how these categories have operated when instantiated in various world-views, the *Phenomenology* therefore constitutes 'the Science of Knowing in the sphere of appearances' (PS: §808, p. 493); its preparatory role having been completed, we are now ready to move to the more abstract level of the *Logic*, where these categories can be examined in their own right:

> Spirit, therefore, having won the Notion, displays its existence and movement in this ether of its life and is *Science*. In this, the moments of its movement no longer exhibit themselves as specific *shapes of consciousness*, but – since consciousness's difference has returned into the Self – as *specific Notions* and as their organic self-grounded movement.
> (PS: §805, p. 491)

In this way, Hegel prepares us for his transition within the system, from the 'shapes of consciousness' of the *Phenomenology*, to the 'specific Notions' (the concepts or categories) of the *Logic*, and thus for Science in its pure and abstract form, 'in this ether of its life'.

CONTENT SUMMARY

ABSOLUTE KNOWING

§§788–97 (pp. 479–85) A recapitulation of what has gone before, and has led us to this point.

§§798–808 (pp. 485–93) Consciousness has now reached the outlook of absolute knowing, the development of which is reflected in the history of Spirit, as it has led to this absolute standpoint, from which philosophy as science can be finally articulated.

CONCLUSION

Perhaps because Hegel was himself a historicist, who believed that 'each individual is ... a *child of his time*; thus philosophy, too, is *its own time comprehended in thoughts'* (PR: Preface, p. 21), it is customary for commentators on his work to conclude by asking how far his thought has significance merely in its own historical context, and how much of it continues to be relevant for us. For many of Hegel's works, including the *Phenomenology*, it has been suggested that though we may admire them, we cannot now take them in the way Hegel himself intended them to be taken, as our perspective is crucially and fundamentally different from his (post-Darwin, post-Marx, post-Auschwitz, post-modern, or whatever): we must therefore distinguish clearly between the 'rational kernel' and the 'mystical shell' (K. Marx 1906: 25), between what is 'living' and what is 'dead' in Hegel's thought (Croce 1915). How much of the *Phenomenology*, then, should we conclude is lost to us in this way?

Some will claim that we cannot now take the *Phenomenology* seriously as a whole, precisely because the central Hegelian ideas around which it is constructed – such as 'Spirit', 'absolute idealism', and 'absolute knowing' – are too extraordinary to have plausible currency in modern philosophical consciousness. These are seen as concepts rooted in parts of Hegel's background that are least accessible to us (his Romanticism, Christian mysticism, or rationalistic Platonism), and which led Hegel to adopt a position in the *Phenomenology* and elsewhere that is incredible in the modern context (cf. Taylor 1975: 537–46). On this view, while there may still be things we can learn from the *Phenomenology* – in its critique of other thinkers, for example, or as a historical analysis of the cultural and philosophical origins of modernity – we cannot hope to recapture its underlying argument for a positive doctrine in so far as it intrinsically involves these problematic notions.

It may be, however, that such a historicist approach does Hegel a disservice, in failing to interpret properly Hegel's understanding of these key ideas, and making them appear more peculiar than they really are: certainly many current commentators now offer so-called 'non-metaphysical' readings of terms like 'Spirit' and 'Idea' that bring them much closer to contemporary perspectives (where Spirit is understood in terms of intersubjectivity, for example: see Williams 1987). And even if these readings are dismissed as merely *re*-readings or reconstructions, it could also be argued that these concepts play a far less central role in Hegel's thinking than might at first appear. Thus, for example, in the account I have offered above of the *Phenomenology*, I hope to have shown that it is possible to follow Hegel's text without any very rich conception of Spirit being required, even if this rich conception was the one he actually held. We can learn from Hegel, even if what we learn is not everything he actually taught.

However, even if it is admitted that the *Phenomenology* is not historically inaccessible to us in this way as an independent text, it has often been claimed that Hegel's system as a whole remains alien to us, and that this will cut us off from the *Phenomenology* at least in so far as we try (as I have done) to integrate it into the system in general, and the *Logic* in particular. Thus, many have claimed that for the *Phenomenology* to remain 'living', it must be divorced from the first book of the *Encyclopedia*, which is assuredly 'dead'. Reasons for rejecting the *Logic* out of hand in this way vary, but two are commonplace: the first is that it is a product of essentialist metaphysics which attempts to deduce being from essence, the world from thought; and the second is that the dialectical method it employs sets it at odds with the principles of logic (such as the law of non-contradiction) on which modern logical theory relies (cf. Wood 1990: 1–6). Given this damning indictment of the *Logic*, the commentator on the *Phenomenology* would appear to face a stark choice: either take Hegel at his word and attempt to integrate the two texts, while robbing the latter of its vitality; or try to avoid this, but at the cost of depriving the *Phenomenology* of its apparent rationale and organizing scheme.

Now, here is not the place to attempt to offer a more positive account of the *Logic*, but obviously this would be one way out of the dilemma that has just been posed. For, once again, many commentators would hold that the *Logic* itself is neither so 'metaphysical' and essentialist, nor so bizarre in its methodology, as it is here assumed to be: in that case, the *Phenomenology* is not necessarily moribund even when its relationship to the *Logic* is taken seriously. As I hope to have shown, giving the *Phenomenology* an introductory role to the *Logic* conceived of as a dialectical investigation of categories shows it to be more than just a collection of observations on philosophical history, or on political and social theory, or on the problems of modernity: because I see no reason why the *Logic* interpreted this way should be 'dead' to us, I have not felt afraid to associate these two texts directly with one another.

A third historicizing argument to be considered concerns not the alien nature of the concepts Hegel employs in the *Phenomenology*, nor of the other parts of the system with which the *Phenomenology* can be linked, but rather the *goal* of his whole project, and the underlying outlook and aspirations which that goal expresses. It is this, perhaps more than anything else, that may be felt to separate us from Hegel: in his claim that 'to him who looks at the world rationally the world looks rationally back', and in his desire to enable us to feel 'at home', Hegel may seem profoundly out of touch with contemporary sensibilities. (See Geuss 1999 for a helpful and lucid account of how thinkers such as Schopenhauer, Nietzsche, and Adorno came to reject this view.) To us, the goal itself may appear troubling in its apparent quietism and conservatism, while Hegel's hopes that it could be achieved may seem naive, or foolish, or plain self-deluding; and, even if the goal and the hopes are accepted, Hegel's suggestion that *philosophy* (and not science, or art, or religion, or politics on their own) can accomplish such aims may seem absurd, and little more than a function of his overblown ambitions for his own chosen career as a 'systematic' philosopher.

This objection is a large one, and perhaps more difficult to assess than it initially appears. For, once again, Hegel's position can be presented in a way that may avoid some of these concerns (cf. Hardimon 1994: 15–41), while it could also be argued that the faith in reason and progress that Hegel's project is said to embody is not entirely lost to us (although perhaps his grandiose conception of philosophy is: see Stern 1999). Fortunately, there is no need to resolve these issues here, because while Hegel's aim as a whole may be one of 'reconciliation', and while this may well seem unrealizable or even undesirable to us, it does not in my view affect the value of the *Phenomenology*, whose negative role has been to show just how hard this reconciliation is to achieve, and what obstacles stand in our way. We can therefore learn a good deal from Hegel's critique of what he sees as one-sided claims that aspire to provide satisfaction for consciousness in the *Phenomenology*, while reserving judgement on whether he himself can avoid these shortcomings in the positive programme he builds on this approach in the system proper. (In this respect, Adorno's words offer a permanent challenge to the Hegelian project: 'Dialectics serves the end of reconcilement … but none of the reconcilements claimed by [Hegel's] absolute idealism – and no other kind remained consistent – has stood up, whether in logic or in politics and history' (Adorno 1973: 6–7).)

Of course, this is not to deny that certain aspects of the *Phenomenology* make it very much a work of its time, so that parts of it are of merely historical interest; but for such a dense and in many ways idiosyncratic work, this is the case surprisingly rarely (for example, even in the Observing Reason section, where Hegel's focus is obviously on the scientific outlook of his period, the *problem* he is interested in is one we can still take seriously and reinterpret in our own terms). And of course, a historicist critique of any work has its own dangers: for, as has so often happened with Hegel, despite the repeated suggestion that his time has irrevocably passed (by Marxist materialists, by post-modernists, or by analytic philosophers, for example), he has repeatedly returned to speak to us once again, in ways that were previously unimagined. It seems likely, therefore, that as long as Hegel's problems remain our problems, it is to the living present rather than the dead past that the *Phenomenology* will continue to belong.

8

THE RECEPTION OF THE *PHENOMENOLOGY*

Having offered an account of the *Phenomenology* as I understand it, I now offer a brief account of how it has been received by others, and the influence it has exerted. This, too, is a fascinating story, which reveals not only the curious place of the work within Hegel's oeuvre, but also the curious structure and style of the work itself. For, as we have seen, one central interpretative issue hinges on how the *Phenomenology* is related to the rest of Hegel's system, where at different times the *Phenomenology* has been read as self-standing, and thus either as largely irrelevant or as Hegel's most important text, depending on whether the rest of the system has been in or out of favour; alternatively, attempts have been made to see the *Phenomenology* as integral to everything else. Likewise, the *Phenomenology* itself has been treated by some as a unified text, but by others as an uneven and disjointed work, where some parts can then be taken seriously and the rest ignored. At the same time, many interpreters have been tempted to find some section which might hold the 'key' to the book as a whole, and indeed to Hegel's entire enterprise – such as the master/slave dialectic, or his treatment of the Unhappy Consciousness, or his analysis of the French Revolution. Finally, the reception of the *Phenomenology* is of course bound up with Hegel's reception more generally, which itself is a complex affair. His reputation has waxed and waned several times, while the overall picture of his philosophy has undergone major changes. As we have discussed previously, the explanation for such divergent readings may be said to lie with the dialectical nature of Hegel's thought itself, as well as of course relating to the different political, historical, and philosophical contexts of his many interpreters.

As mentioned at the outset (p. 6), initial reaction to the *Phenomenology* was somewhat muted and unenthusiastic, as readers struggled both to understand the book, and to see how it differed from Hegel's earlier, apparently more Schellingian writings – with Schelling himself (angered by the Preface) wishing one correspondent and future reviewer luck at disentangling it (see Pinkard 2000a: 257). The book certainly did not provide Hegel with the instant career advancement that he so badly needed at the time; indeed, its first edition failed to sell out. It was really the publication of the *Science of Logic* that established his reputation, in part because its final instalment coincided with his move to Heidelberg in 1816 to take up his first professorship, with the *Encyclopedia* then to follow in its various editions, as Hegel moved to Berlin in 1818. It is thus not surprising that, in the assimilation of Hegel's ideas during his lifetime and immediately thereafter, the *Phenomenology* was largely eclipsed in favour of his subsequent writings – particularly when, as we have seen, the *Phenomenology* appeared to be partially incorporated into the third book of the *Encyclopedia* on the *Philosophy of Spirit*, and its role as an 'introduction' was seemingly brought into doubt by Hegel himself (see p. 9). So, for example, when one of Hegel's followers, Georg Andreas Gabler, took the unusual step of writing a work relating to the *Phenomenology* in 1827, he focused on those parts that overlapped with the *Philosophy of Spirit* and neglected to discuss the rest (see Gabler 1827). Likewise, in his collection of sympathetic essays published in 1840 that reflect many of the current debates, Hegel's official biographer Karl Rosenkranz gives no special discussion to the *Phenomenology*, concentrating only on the systematic triad of logic–nature–spirit (see Rosenkranz 1840). Meanwhile, the concerns of many of the 'Hegelian school' lay elsewhere, in ethics, politics, law, religion, and the history of philosophy, for example; and while such matters are of course central to the *Phenomenology* as we have seen, they are also discussed in subsequent parts of the system or the related lectures, some-times at greater length and arguably with greater clarity – so it is not surprising that these other works were the focus of discussion and interpretation among Hegel's more immediate students and disciples (see Bonsiepen 1979 for an overview).

Whilst it is wrong to classify all the members of the 'Hegelian school' together in the same way, as their outlooks diverged on the issues that concerned them, it is nonetheless fair to say that they were united by a commitment to Hegel's systematic ambitions and thus the promise of his mature philosophy, which was seen to depend mainly on writings that came after the *Phenomenology*. Not for the last time, and ironically enough, it was only when Hegel's systematic ambitions came under attack from the younger gen-eration of so-called 'Left Hegelians', that the *Phenomenology* was taken more seriously, as perhaps providing an *alternative* to the Hegel of the *Encyclopedia* and the *Philosophy of Right*, which were seen as irredeemably idealist, theological, and conservative. Whilst other Left Hegelians such as David Strauss and Bruno Bauer focused mainly on religious and political issues (Strauss calling the *Phenomenology* 'the alpha and omega of Hegel's works' (Strauss 1851: 53)), others like Ludwig Feuerbach, Karl Marx, and Friedrich Engels raised more general concerns; and here they were in part echoing criticisms of Hegel made by the later Schelling, who emerged after Hegel's death as a major opponent, albeit from a religiously conservative perspective that they abhorred. A key issue here concerned the famous beginning of the *Logic* and its supposedly 'presuppositionless' starting point of pure being (cf. White 1983: 15–41; Bowie 1993: 127–77; Houlgate 1999); when this was deemed unsatisfactory, it then raised the question whether the *Phenomenology* might provide some sort of better presuppositionless 'grounding' for the *Logic* instead, given its method of immanent critique. With this problem in mind, Feuerbach came to consider the *Phenomenology* in his 'Towards a Critique of Hegelian Philosophy' of 1839, to look in turn at the beginning of that text, and specifically Hegel's treatment of sense-certainty. Feuerbach argues, however, that this will not help Hegel's cause, as (he claims) far from being a form of internal or immanent critique that does not beg any questions against its opponent, Hegel in fact takes for granted the idealism he wants to prove, making this beginning no better than that of the *Logic*, which it in fact presupposes (see Feuerbach 1839: 116–18). However, as well as this negative assessment, it is clear that the *Phenomenology* had a positive impact on Feuerbach's own thinking, especially on *The Essence of Christianity*, where his treatment of religion in part echoes Hegel's treatment of religious themes in the *Phenomenology* itself.

A similar mixture of negative and positive elements can be found in Marx's posthumously published 'Economic and Philosophical Manuscripts' of 1844. Thus, he shared Feuerbach's suspicion of the systematic role of the *Phenomenology* and its relation to the *Logic*; nonetheless, he admired its *critical* content as an analysis of the *aporia* of the modern world:

> The *Phenomenology* is therefore concealed and mystifying criticism, criticism which has not attained self-clarity; but in so far as it grasps the *estrangement* of man – even though men appear only in the form of mind – *all* the elements of criticism are concealed within it, and often *prepared* and *worked out* in a way that goes beyond Hegel's own point of view. The 'unhappy consciousness', the 'honest consciousness', the struggle of the 'noble and base consciousness', etc., these separate sections contain the *critical* elements – but still in estranged form – of entire spheres, such a religion, the state, civil life and so forth.
>
> (K. Marx 1975: 385/Stern (ed.) 1993c: I, 168)

Marx's observations were also highly significant for the mention he appeared to make of the master/slave dialectic and of its themes of alienation and of work – although he criticizes Hegel from his materialist perspective by saying that '[t]he only labour Hegel knows and recognizes is *abstract mental* labour' (K. Marx 1975:

386/Stern (ed.) 1993c: 169; see Arthur 1986 for further discussion). These private notes of course had little impact at the time when they were written, but when they came to be published in 1932 they influenced a whole generation of Marxist and leftist readers of Hegel, for both their positive and negative comments (cf. O'Neill (ed.) (1996)). It is clear from Marx's writings, as well as those of Engels, that they appreciated Hegel's attempts to reveal the dialectical difficulties in the positions he discusses in the *Phenomenology* (for example, the analysis of Kant's ethics, and of utilitarianism), as well as its proto-historical structure – while they also wanted to transform its underlying aims and outlook for their own purposes.

These early debates concerning both the *Phenomenology*, as well as the *Logic* and the system more generally, also get to the heart of the issues we have discussed in previous chapters, particularly Hegel's attempt to overcome the dialectical tension between universality and individuality. The question raised by these early critics (including Søren Kierkegaard, who had also been influenced by Schelling), was whether in relating these two categories as he does, Hegel can avoid reducing the latter to the former, and thus escape an idealism in which the specific is overcome by the general, the person by the social whole, matter by form, being by thought, and so on. This concern runs like a thread from this period to later opponents such as Jacques Derrida and Gilles Deleuze (see Stern 2009: 345–70). An ultimate assessment of Hegel on this issue, and whether he can avoid these suspicions, must depend on an examination not just of the *Phenomenology*, but also the rest of his writings; but as we have seen, the *Phenomenology* is crucial in setting the issue up, where it has been felt that even the way this is done should give us concern: for example, in 'Towards a Critique of Hegelian Philosophy', Feuerbach argues that Hegel's treatment of sense-certainty favours general concepts over the particularity of individuals, so that these then are never adequately dealt with in Hegel's system.

In part through the critique of Hegel mounted by Schelling, Feuerbach and others, and in part through the rise of alternative schools and figures (such as materialism, positivism, neo-Kantianism, and hermeneutics), orthodox Hegelianism was eclipsed in

Germany by the 1860s and 1870s. At the same time, however, Hegel's star was rising in other parts of Europe and in America, where his reception and that of the *Phenomenology* then continued in a different context. Nonetheless, the pattern we have found in Germany is repeated here too, where Hegel's more loyal followers largely turned for inspiration to the *Encyclopedia* system and to the *Logic* in particular, rather than to the *Phenomenology*. Thus, for example, when the Italian Augusto Vera tried to popularize Hegel's ideas in France with his *Introduction à la Philosophie de Hegel* of 1855 he did not mention the *Phenomenology*, while after the hiatus of the Franco-Prussian war, when Lucien Herr and Georges Noël returned to Hegel in the 1890s, their emphasis was largely on the *Logic* (see Vera 1855; Herr 1894; Noël 1897). Likewise in Britain, the *Phenomenology* was hardly referred to in James Hutcheson Stirling's *The Secret of Hegel*, which was the first appreciable study of Hegel's thought in English (see Stirling 1865); and J. M. E. McTaggart wrote several commentaries relating to Hegel's *Logic*, but no commentary on the *Phenomenology*.

The same pattern is repeated in the initial phases of Hegel's reception in America; but in 1906, Josiah Royce delivered his posthumously published lectures on 'Aspects of Post-Kantian Idealism', which broke new ground by laying greater stress on the *Phenomenology* than the *Logic*, and using it to argue for a less conservative reading of Hegel. It is worth quoting Royce at some length, as it reveals the relative neglect of the text at this time, and how Royce hoped it could be used to change current perceptions of Hegel and his thought:

> Because it has become customary for the modern historians of philosophy to judge Hegel by his later works, and because the political conservatism of his Berlin period and the dictatorial manner that he then assumed rendered him unpopular to the generation of German liberals whose influence culminated in the year 1848, the *Phaenomenologie* has remained unduly neglected. Few of the textbooks of the history of philosophy give it much more than a perfunctory summary. [Rudolf] Haym in his book *Hegel und seine Zeit* [1857] discusses the work, but with an austere lack of sympathy for what was most characteristic about it. [Wilhelm] Windelband in his *History of Modern*

Philosophy [1892; English translation 1893] speaks of it much more sympathetically, but characterizes it, not altogether unjustly, as the most difficult treatise in the history of philosophy ... Of all the brief summaries of the book in the histories of philosophy, the sketch which [Eduard] Zeller gives in his *Geschichte der deutschen Philosophie seit Leibnitz* [1873, 2nd edn 1875] is to my mind the best. The account of [Karl] Rosenkranz in his *Life of Hegel* [1844] is decidedly valuable, although I feel that Rosenkranz himself regards the book as a little too much from the point of view of its relation to Hegel's later system.

(Royce 1919: 137–38/Stern (ed.) 1993c: II, 182–83)

As this last sentence intimates, Royce is radical in holding that as an introduction to that later system, the *Phenomenology* 'must certainly be called a failure'; instead, he reads it as a 'study of human nature, as it is expressed in various individual and social types', as well as an 'application of the dialectical method, and a very important series of reflections on the problems of idealistic thought' (see Royce 1919: 138–40/Stern (ed.) 1993c: II, 184). He does not consider the suggestion that this may be precisely the sort of introduction that Hegel has in mind. Royce thus gives the *Phenomenology* a kind of significance and priority that few earlier had seen fit to attribute to it, as offering 'a sort of biography of the world-spirit', in the manner of *Wilhelm Meister*, Goethe's celebrated *Bildungsroman* or journey of education (Royce 1919: 147–49/Stern (ed.) 1993c: II, 189–90).

An equally bold reassessment of the merits of the text can be found in France a couple of decades later, but in a manner that was to have a more lasting impact, with the publication in 1929 of Jean Wahl's *Le Malheur de la Conscience dans la Philosophie de Hegel* (2nd edn Wahl 1951). In this work, Wahl attempted to uncover a side to Hegel's thought that was darker, more Romantic, and less rationalistic than had previously been noticed, and to cast fresh light on the whole direction of his philosophy. He was helped towards this reinterpretation by the publication of Hegel's early writings by Hermann Nohl in 1907 (translated as ETW), which had already brought about some re-evaluation of Hegel's thought in Germany; this material meant that rather than being seen merely as the ladder to the *Encyclopedia* system that was then to be kicked away, the *Phenomenology* could be viewed instead as the culmination of the insights of the young Hegel, insights that were then to some extent ossified and made more academic as he came to develop 'the system'. These early writings revealed to Wahl that Hegel's real preoccupations and concerns were close to those of a Christian existentialist like Kierkegaard, a fact that had been obscured by the speculative approach of the later *Encyclopedia*. Wahl was therefore led to look anew at the *Phenomenology*, treating it not merely as a prolegomenon to the *Logic*, but as the highest expression of Hegel's troubled vision. At the centre of his reading Wahl placed Hegel's treatment of the Unhappy Consciousness, in which (he argued) this sense of loss was epitomized. Thus, though Wahl himself was not prepared to call Hegel an existentialist, his influential study of the *Phenomenology* showed how existentialist themes could be uncovered in Hegel's thought, and in this text in particular. The importance of Hegel's Jena writings in relation to the *Phenomenology* was also underlined by Alexandre Koyré (see Koyré 1934), who translated some of this material into French.

In the wake of Wahl's study, the Hegel renaissance in France was taken further and given greater impetus by the work of Alexandre Kojève and Jean Hyppolite. Kojève gave an important series of seminars on the *Phenomenology* from 1933 to 1939 at the École Pratique des Hautes Études, which was attended by many who were to become leading luminaries of French intellectual life, as well as influential interpreters of Hegel in their own right, including Maurice Merleau-Ponty, Eric Weil, Georges Bataille, and Jacques Lacan. The text of these seminars was published in 1947 (see Kojève 1969 for an abridged translation), and it remains one of the most challenging readings of Hegel's thought. Equally important were the efforts of Hyppolite, who published the first volume of his magisterial translation of the *Phenomenology* in 1939 and the second in 1941, and in 1946 completed his influential commentary on the text (translated in Hyppolite 1974).

Kojève made the master/slave dialectic the key to his treatment, into which he wove both Heideggerian and Marxist themes. He uses as an epigraph to his lectures a comment from

Marx's 'Economic and Philosophical Manuscripts' concerning the significance Hegel gives to labour, and takes himself to be following Marx in identifying the work of the slave as an essential moment in self-objectification. At the same time, like Heidegger he emphasizes the slave's experience of death, and his recognition of finitude, out of which the slave also feels liberation from the natural world. (Similar themes, inspired by Kojève, can be found in Bataille's essay of 1955, translated as Bataille 1990.) Moreover, drawing on both Heidegger and Marx, Kojève argues that for Hegel history began with a sense of otherness, and can end in the universal satisfaction of the desire for recognition that shapes the master/slave dialectic, putting a stop to our urge to negate and overcome all externality. This emphasis on the theme of desire and recognition has gone on to be seen as one of the key contributions of the *Phenomenology*, and again one that perhaps relates more to the early Hegel than the later systematic project; for example, it forms the background to the discussions of 'the problem of the Other' in Jean-Paul Sartre and Simone de Beauvoir, as well as Lacan's psychoanalytic theory of the desiring subject (see Sartre 1958: 221–302, Beauvoir 1974: 64–65, Lacan 2007: 75–81). Kojève's approach continues to have an influence on recent commentators, for example Fukuyama 1992 and Jameson 2010.

For many readers of Hegel, however, Kojève's interpretation has seemed too idiosyncratic to pass as a plausible reading, whatever its merits as a piece of philosophizing in its own right, an attitude summed up in Jean Wahl's observation that 'it is quite false but very interesting' (see Wahl 1975: 383; cf. also Wahl 1955: 93). Hyppolite's approach is rather more judicious and closer to the text, while he too is influenced in his reading by existentialism and Marx. Like Wahl, he treats the Unhappy Consciousness as a fundamental theme of the *Phenomenology*, and allows for parallels with Kierkegaard. At the same time, Hyppolite emphasizes Hegel's foreshadowing of Marx's account of alienation, and agrees with Kojève that recognition is capable of overcoming the tension between self and other; however, his focus is more on the chapter on forgiveness and reconciliation at the end of the 'Spirit' section than on the master/slave dialectic. In his later works, Hyppolite gives greater weight to the *Logic* than hitherto; he holds, however, that there is a tension between this return to the *Logic* and metaphysics, and what he takes to be the more humanistic, anthropological method of the *Phenomenology*, a tension which he sees as fundamental to Hegel's thought.

Outside France but around the same time, the Hungarian intellectual Georg Lukács was also led to re-examine the place of the *Phenomenology*. Like Wahl, he did so in the light of the emergence of Hegel's early writings, while like Kojève, he was also influenced by the publication of Marx's 'Economic and Philosophical Manuscripts'. Even before the latter were known, already in his 1923 classic *History and Class Consciousness* (translated as Lukács 1968), Lukács had commented on '[t]he contradictions in method between the *Phenomenology* and the system' (Lukács 1968: xlv); thus, as has been noted, while he 'did not specifically argue for the primacy of the *Phenomenology* over other works by Hegel' in this text, 'he might as well have' (Pinkard 2010: 122). Lukács's position on this is made much clearer and more explicit in the later study on *The Young Hegel*, first published in 1948 (translated as Lukács 1975). Here the *Phenomenology* receives extensive discussion, particularly the themes of alienation and labour, which were seen as underexplored materialist elements within Hegel's idealist outlook. And within the later tradition of critical theory, while no commentary or detailed study of the *Phenomenology* came to be written by the leading protagonists, figures such as Theodor W. Adorno, Jürgen Habermas, and Axel Honneth are all marked by the themes of dialectic, alienation, recognition, labour, sociality, enlightenment, and modernity that appear in this text. At the same time, in the face of mounting criticisms of Hegel's 'totalizing' thought by French critics such as Derrida and Deleuze, the *Phenomenology* continued to be seen as perhaps presenting a place in Hegel's work where such problems could be escaped, before the system itself is broached. Moreover, influenced by Heidegger's earlier analysis of the *Phenomenology* itself as an essentially Cartesian text that served to 'subjectivize' Being, this work then became a focus for critique by writers in this tradition (see Heidegger 1970, which discusses the Introduction to the *Phenomenology*, and was first published in 1950; and Heidegger

1994, which was given as lecture course in 1930/31 and first published in 1980).

Many of these questions and issues concerning the *Phenomenology* continue to be debated; but there are also some distinctive aspects to its contemporary reception which deserve mention, three of which are particularly evident in the current English-language literature in particular. First, one relatively new theme in relation to the text has been to emphasize its *epistemological* dimension, and how Hegel's immanent and dialectical method might be used to resolve various sceptical challenges, most particularly from the ancient sceptics, especially the so-called 'problem of the criterion' and the 'problem of equipollence': that is, how we can devise a standard or criterion for knowledge without already taking it for granted that we *have* such knowledge; and how we can respond to the sceptic who claims that beliefs opposing ours can be supported with as much justification as our own, making it impossible rationally to hold onto either point of view (see K. R. Westphal 1989 and 2003, Forster 1989 and 1998: 126–92, Heidemann 2008). More generally, epistemological issues are also at the centre of interpretations of Hegel that take him to be offering a form of idealism that will enable him to overcome any sceptical gap between mind and world, a gap that seemed to remain even in Kant's transcendental idealism in so far as this still leaves us with no knowledge of things as they are in themselves (cf. Pippin 1989: 91–171, Rockmore 1997). Second, instead of reading Hegel as just in dialogue with figures like Marx and Kierkegaard, Hegel is now frequently read in the light of the work of Wilfrid Sellars as well as pragmatists like John Dewey and C. S. Peirce. So, for example, Hegel's treatment of sense-certainty can be taken as akin to Sellars's attack on the 'myth of the given'; at the same time, Hegel's turn from the 'I' to the 'we' and thus to Spirit is seen as foreshadowing Sellars's focus on the 'space of reasons' and of norms as involving an essentially social dimension, with no grounding outside our various historical practices, which are protected from relativism by their developmental and dialectical relation to their predecessors (see Pinkard 1994, Brandom 2002: 178–234, Redding 2007, Pippin 2008, esp. 210–38). Similar themes arguably also relate Hegel to pragmatism, together with his anti-Cartesianism, anti-dualism, and anti-reductionism, so important aspects of the *Phenomenology* are now seen in a pragmatist light (see Rorty 1998, K. R. Westphal 2003, Pinkard 2007, Stern 2009: 209–326). Third, topics within the *Phenomenology*, including desire, recognition, alienation, and also particularly his discussion of *Antigone*, have made this text a matter of debate by feminist philosophers, which has given rise to a focus on these Hegelian concerns from the perspective of issues to do with gender in ways that were previously only explored by Simone de Beauvoir (see Mills (ed.) 1996, and Hutchings 2003).

Thus, as Hegel above all philosophers would no doubt expect and approve of, the *Phenomenology* continues to be seen anew in different times, whilst also giving rise to a core of central debates and controversies, as will always surely remain the case with this most enigmatic and multi-faceted of philosophical masterpieces.

Notes

1 THE *PHENOMENOLOGY* IN CONTEXT

1 While a private tutor in Berne, Hegel had translated and written a commentary on a political pamphlet by Jean-Jacques Cart, which was published anonymously in 1798, after Hegel had left his position in Berne and taken up a new one in Frankfurt.

2 There is no proper synonym for *Geist* in English, and it may be translated equally as 'spirit' or 'mind' as it has connotations of both. I will generally use 'spirit', as this is the rendering used in Miller's English translation of the *Phenomenology*, which is the one I refer to in the text.

3 'Science' here is the translation of the German term '*Wissenschaft*'. It is important to realize that there is a distinction in German that is often overlooked in English between '*Wissenschaft*' (meaning science as simply a body of organized knowledge) and '*Naturwissenschaft*' (meaning natural science as this term is applied to physics, chemistry, and biology). In claiming that his philosophy constitutes a science, therefore, Hegel was merely claiming that it is systematic, not that it bears any more direct comparison with these empirical modes of investigation into the natural world.

4 Cf. Nozick 1981: 8–10:

> Many philosophical problems are ones of understanding how something is or can be possible. How is it possible for us to have free will, supposing that all actions are causally determined? Randomness, also, seems no more congenial; so how is free will (even) possible? ... How is it possible that motion occurs, given Zeno's arguments? How is it possible for

something to be the same thing from one time to another, through change? ... The form of these questions is: how is one thing possible, given (or supposing) certain other things? Some statements r_1, ... ,r_n are assumed or accepted or taken for granted, and there is a tension between these statements and another statement p; they appear to exclude p's holding true. Let us term the r_i *apparent excluders* (of p). Since the statement p also is accepted, we face the question of how p is possible, given its apparent excluders ... To see how p can be true (given these apparent excluders) is to see how things fit together. This philosophical understanding, finding harmony in apparent tension and incompatibility, is, I think, intrinsically valuable.

5 As with the *Phenomenology*, so with the *Logic* any reading is controversial. My approach here is broadly in line with what have been called 'category theory' readings of the *Logic*, though in a more metaphysical form than this sometimes takes, because the category theory in question is not merely transcendental and concerned with our conceptual scheme, but rather with the categories of being as such. For helpful brief characterizations of these issues, with further references, see Wartenberg 1993: 123–24 and Redding 2010: §2.

6 'Notion' or 'concept' are the terms used in English translations for the German word *Begriff*. 'Concept' is the more natural translation, but 'notion' is also used, partly to convey the fact that Hegel uses this as a technical term. Neither translation captures the fact that the noun in German relates to the verb *begreifen*, which itself relates to *greifen*, meaning to grasp or encompass, hence conveying something of the way in which the categories of universal, particular, and individual include one another under the overarching unity of *der Begriff*.

7 For a helpful overview of how Hegel came to see the tension between universality and particularity as of central philosophical importance, beginning with the clash between the 'universalism' of his Enlightenment education and the 'particularism' of the culture of the Duchy of Württemberg in which he grew up, see Pinkard 1997 and Pinkard 2000a: 198–99, 469–70, and 478–79.

8 Cf. Roberts 1988: 78:

> The recurring motif in Hegel, which guides notions like negation and continuity, or consciousness and its other, is the opposition *and the union* of individuality and generality. The individual is material singularity, the *hic et nunc*; the general is concept, rule, law, prescription. For 'reality', whether it be the reality of experience, of morality, or of politics, *both* sides must play their part. A thing is not only the example of a genus, it is a singular piece of matter. A person is not merely a function, he or she is a living flesh-and-blood individual. A political leader is not merely the representative of a group, he or she is an entirely unique character with unique fears and hopes. But, beyond either of the two sides, the reality of change is a unity, the unity of freedom, practice and reason.

9 Hegel himself highlights the polemical role of the Preface in his publicity announcement for the *Phenomenology* that appeared in various periodicals in 1807 (see Forster 1998: 613):

In the preface the author explains his views concerning what seem to him to be the needs of philosophy at its present standpoint, and in addition concerning the presumption and nonsense of philosophical formulas which currently injures the dignity of philosophy, and generally concerning what is essential in philosophy and its study.

2   THE DIALECTIC OF THE OBJECT

1 In this latter remark regarding the contrast between apprehension and comprehension, Hegel is in fact characterizing our proper attitude to the form of consciousness we are examining, rather than sense-certainty itself: but, because Hegel is claiming we must conduct ourselves in the same way as the consciousness we are observing, it may be inferred that he also meant to characterize sense-certainty itself in this way.

3   THE DIALECTIC OF THE SUBJECT

1 In his translation, Miller uses 'Lordship and Bondage' here, but 'Mastership and Servitude' or 'Master and Slave' have become more usual in English accounts of this section, perhaps in order to avoid the misleading sexual connotations of Miller's rendering of '*Knechtschaft*', which means bondsman merely in the sense of servant, farmhand, or vassal.

4   THE DIALECTIC OF REASON

1 Hegel was not alone in suggesting that both the unified position of the Greeks and the more atomistic perspective of individualistic Reason are both one-sided, and that some synthesis of the two is required: cf. Schiller 1967: 234:

> Are not those three stages which we can distinguish in all empirical knowledge likely to hold approximately for the general development of human culture?
>
> (1) The object stands before us as a whole, but confused and fluid.
> (2) We separate particular characteristics and distinguish; our knowledge is now *distinct*, but isolated and limited.
> (3) We unite what we have separated, and the whole stands before us again, no longer confused, however, but illuminated from all sides.
>
> The Greeks found themselves in the first of these three phases. We find ourselves in the second. The third, therefore, we may still hope for, and when it comes we shall no longer yearn for the Greeks to return.

2 The term 'ethical life' is the now standard English translation of the German term *Sittlichkeit*, which derives from *Sitte*, meaning 'custom', a kind of habitual

mode of conduct followed by a social group and regarded as setting down the rules for decent behaviour. Hegel characteristically distinguished between *Sittlichkeit* and *Moralität* (morality), which he associated with Kant, and saw as an individualistic ethic, arrived at by reason and conscience (cf. PR: §33, p. 63 and §150, p. 195).

6 THE DIALECTIC OF RELIGION

1 As Harris 1997: II, p. 649 points out, 'revealed' is somewhat inaccurate as a translation for the third form of religious consciousness, as the German word used by Hegel is not '*geoffenbart*', but '*offenbar*', which is more like 'manifest' or 'made evident': that is, in this form of religion what is important is that nothing about God is hidden, not that here religious faith is founded on revelation. For ease of reference, I have kept to the Miller translation, but this caveat should be kept in mind when the terminology of 'revealed religion' is used.

FURTHER READING

For reasons of space and accessibility, detailed suggestions for further reading relating to each chapter are only given to works available in English. A short guide to the literature in German and French is provided in the last section. For more extensive bibliographies of works on the *Phenomenology*, see Harris 1997: II, pp. 795–868, Stewart (ed.) (1998), 479–503, and Stewart 2000: 527–52.

THE *PHENOMENOLOGY* IN CONTEXT

ON HEGEL'S LIFE AND WORKS

The best and most recent intellectual biography of Hegel is Pinkard 2000a. For a detailed and magisterial study of the development of Hegel's thought up until the publication of the *Phenomenology*, see Harris 1972 and Harris 1983; for a synopsis see Harris 1993. Lukács 1975 remains a classic treatment. For an accessible account of the intellectual and cultural issues shaping philosophical debate in Hegel's period, see Beiser 1987.

GENERAL STUDIES OF HEGEL'S SYSTEM

The following works provide accounts of Hegel's thought as a whole and the place of the *Phenomenology* within it that are useful for the beginning student: Beiser 2005, Houlgate 1991, Houlgate 2001, Redding 2010, Roberts 1988: 68–121, Rockmore 1993, Singer 1983, Soll 1969, Speight 2008, Stern 1998. For Hegel's terminology, Inwood 1992 and Magee 2010 are helpful resources.

For more detailed and advanced studies see Findlay 1958, Inwood 1983, Kaufmann 1965, Pinkard 1988, Pippin 1989, Redding 1996, Rosen 1974, Stern 1990, Taylor 1975.

STUDIES OF THE *PHENOMENOLOGY*

The following works offer studies of the *Phenomenology* as a whole that are useful to the beginning student: Dudeck 1981, Franco 1999: 81–119, Harris 1995, Houlgate 2013, Krasnoff 2008, Norman 1981, Pinkard 1999, Pinkard 2000b, Pippin 1993, Pippin 2006, Rockmore 1997, Solomon 1993, Verene 2007.

For more advanced and detailed studies see Findlay 1977, Flay 1984, Forster 1998, Harris 1997, Heidegger 1994, Hyppolite 1974, Kain 2005, Kainz 1976 and 1983, Kojève 1969, Lauer 1976, Loewenberg 1965, Pinkard 1994, Russon 2004, Simpson 1998, Solomon 1983, Stewart 1995, K. R. Westphal 1989 and 2003, and M. Westphal 1998b.

ON THE PREFACE AND THE INTRODUCTION

The Preface and the Introduction are discussed fully in Dudeck 1981: 17–82, Harris 1997: I, pp. 30–207, Kainz 1976: 54–61, Lauer 1976: 23–40 and 270–300, Loewenberg 1965: 1–22, Rockmore 1997: 6–36, Solomon 1983: 237–318, Verene 2007: 1–24, and M. Westphal 1998b: 1–58. Norman 1981: 9–28 and Stewart 2000: 32–52 discuss the Introduction but not the Preface.

For specialist studies see Adelman 1984, Gillespie 1984: 63–84, Heidegger 1970, Kaufmann 1965: 363–459, Lamb 1980: 3–41, W. Marx 1975, Sallis 1977, Schacht 1972, Stepelevich 1990, and K. R. Westphal 1998b.

THE DIALECTIC OF THE OBJECT

The Consciousness chapter is discussed in Dudeck 1981: 63–91, Flay 1984: 29–80, Harris 1995: 22–34, Harris 1997: I, pp. 208–315, Heidegger 1994: 45–128, Houlgate 2013: 31–82, Hyppolite 1974: 77–142, Kain 2005: 25–38, Kainz 1976: 61–82, Krasnoff 2008: 77–92, Lauer 1976: 46–89, Loewenberg 1965: 23–74, Norman 1981: 29–45, Pinkard 1994: 20–45, Pippin 1989: 116–42, Rockmore 1997: 37–58, Simpson 1998: 1–40, Solomon 1983: 319–424, Stewart 2000: 53–103, Verene 2007: 41–54, M. Westphal 1998b: 59–120.

For specialist studies of the Consciousness chapter as a whole, see Taylor 1972, K. R. Westphal 2009a.

For specialist studies of the 'Sense-certainty' section, see Craig 1987: 205–19, De Nys 1978, deVries 1988a and 2008, Dulckheit 1986, Lamb 1978, Soll 1976, Stewart 1996, and K. R. Westphal 2000.

For specialist studies of the 'Perception' section, see Stewart 1996, Vaught 1986, K. R. Westphal 1998a, and M. Westphal 1998a.

For specialist studies of the 'Force and the Understanding' section, see De Nys 1982, Flay 1970, Gadamer 1976a, and Murray 1972.

THE DIALECTIC OF THE SUBJECT

The Self-Consciousness chapter is discussed in Dudeck 1981: 93–119, Flay 1984: 81–112, Harris 1995: 35–46, Harris 1997: I, pp. 316–446, Heidegger 1994: 129–48, Houlgate 2013: 83–123, Hyppolite 1974: 143–215, Kain 2005: 39–68, Kainz 1976: 82–98, Krasnoff 2008: 93–112, Lauer 1976: 90–124, Loewenberg 1965: 75–112, Norman 1981: 46–66, Pinkard 1994: 46–78, Pippin 1989: 143–71, Rockmore 1997: 59–79, Rosen 1974: 151–82, Shklar 1976: 57–69, Simpson 1998: 40–74, Solomon 1983: 425–70, Stewart 2000: 104–64, Verene 2007: 55–70, M. Westphal 1998b: 121–38.

For specialist studies see Adelman 1980, Bernstein 1984, Burbidge 1978, Chiereghin 2009, Duquette 1994, Gadamer 1976b, Honneth 2008, G. A. Kelly 1965, Kojève 1969: 3–70, McDowell 2006, Neuhouser 1986 and 2009, Pippin 2011, Rauch and Sherman 1999: 55–160, Redding 2008, Stern 2012a, Wahl 1951, Williams 1992: 141–90.

THE DIALECTIC OF REASON

The Reason chapter is discussed in Dudeck 1981: 121–84, Flay 1984: 113–61, Harris 1995: 47–60, Harris 1997: I, pp. 447–623 and II, pp. 1–146, Houlgate 2013: 123–45, Hyppolite 1974: 219–320, Kain 2005: 69–130, Kainz 1976: 98–133, Lauer 1976: 125–76, Loewenberg 1965: 113–84, Norman 1981: 67–85, Pinkard 1994: 79–134, Rockmore 1997: 80–110, Shklar 1976: 96–141, Solomon 1983: 401–13 and 480–534, Stewart 2000: 165–287, Verene 2007: 71–90.

For specialist studies of Hegel on the issue of idealism see Ameriks 1991, Stern 1990 and 2008, Wartenberg 1993, and K. R. Westphal 1989.

For specialist studies of the 'Observing Reason' section, see Dahlstrom 2007, Ferrini 2009, Lamb 1980: 98–164, and Quante 2008.

For specialist studies of Hegel's discussion of physiognomy and physiology see Acton 1971, MacIntyre 1972a, and von der Luft 1987.

For specialist studies of Hegel's discussion of 'the spiritual animal kingdom' see Pinkard 2009 and Shapiro 1979.

For specialist studies of Hegel's critique of Kant's ethics see Ameriks 1987, D. C. Hoy 1989 and 2009, Korsgaard 1996, Lottenbach and Tenenbaum 1995, Sedgwick 1988a and 1988b, Shklar 1974, Stern 2012b, Walsh 1969, K. R. Westphal 1995, and Wood 1989, 1990: 127–43, and 1993.

THE DIALECTIC OF SPIRIT

The Spirit chapter is discussed fully in Dudeck 1981: 185–244, Flay 1984: 163–226, Harris 1995: 61–79, Harris 1997: II, pp. 147–520, Houlgate 2013: 145–73, Hyppolite 1974: 320–528, Kain 2005: 131–212, Kainz 1983: 1–107, Lauer 1976: 177–229, Loewenberg 1965: 185–287, Norman 1981: 86–104, Pinkard 1994: 135–220, Rockmore 1997: 111–54, Shklar 1976: 142–208, Simpson 1998: 75–98, Solomon 1983: 534–79, Stewart 2000: 288–383, Verene 2007: 71–90, M. Westphal 1998b: 121–86.

For specialist studies of Hegel's discussion of *Antigone* see J. B. Hoy 2009, Hutchings 2003: 80–111, Mills 1986, Pietercil 1978, and Steiner 1984.

For specialist studies of Hegel's discussion of the Enlightenment see Hinchman 1984, Pinkard 1997, Rosen 1974: 183–228, Stern 1993a, Stolzenberg 2009, and Wokler 1997.

For specialist studies of Hegel's discussion of the French Revolution see Beck 1976, Comay 2010, Habermas 1973, Harris 1977, Honneth 1988, Hyppolite 1969, Nusser 1998, Ripstein 1994, Ritter 1982, Schmidt 1998, Smith 1989, Suter 1971, and Wokler 1998.

For specialist treatments of the 'Morality' section, see Beiser 2009, Friedman 1986, Gram 1978, D. C. Hoy 1981, Jamros 1994: 82–127, Robinson 1977, and K. R. Westphal 1991.

THE DIALECTIC OF RELIGION

The Religion chapter is discussed fully in Dudeck 1981: 245–70, Flay 1984: 227–48, Harris 1995: 80–91, Harris 1997: II, pp. 521–707, Houlgate 2013: 173–85, Hyppolite 1974: 529–72, Kain 2005: 213–16, Kainz 1983: 125–71, Lauer 1976: 230–55, Loewenberg 1965: 292–353, Pinkard 1994: 221–68, Rockmore 1997: 155–78, Solomon 1983: 580–635, Stewart 2000: 384–454, M. Westphal 1998b: 187–210, Williams 1992: 221–52.

For specialist studies see De Nys 1986, Devos 1989, di Giovanni 2009, Jamros 1994: 128–260, Lewis 2008, Schöndorf 1998, and Vieillard-Baron 1998.

PHILOSOPHY AS DIALECTIC

The Absolute Knowing chapter is discussed fully in Dudeck 1981: 271–84, Flay 1984: 249–68, Harris 1995: 92–97, Harris 1997: II, pp. 708–63, Houlgate 2013: 185–9, Hyppolite 1974: 573–606, Kain 2005: 217–33, Kainz 1983: 172–86, Lauer 1976: 256–69, Loewenberg 1965: 354–71, Rockmore 1997: 179–94, Solomon 1983: 635–41, Stewart 2000: 455–68, Verene 2007: 91–98, M. Westphal 1998b: 211–30, Williams 1992: 253–84.

For specialist studies see Burbidge 1998, de Laurentiis 2009, De Vos 1989, Devos 1998, Flay 1998, Houlgate 1998, Kojève 1969: 150–68, Ludwig 1989, Lumsden 1998, Miller 1978, and Williams 1998.

THE RECEPTION OF THE *PHENOMENOLOGY*

There is no study of the reception of the *Phenomenology* specifically, but for accounts of the reception of Hegel's philosophy generally, which include some discussion of the *Phenomenology*, see Pinkard 2010, Sinnerbrink 2007, and Stern and Walker 1998. There are also more specialist studies that consider the reception of Hegel within particular national contexts: for Germany see Bubner 1981, Löwith 1964 and Toews 1980; for France see Baugh 2003, Butler 1999, Descombes 1980, Gutting 2011: 24–49, M. Kelly 1992, Poster 1975: 3–35, Rockmore 1995: 27–39, Roth 1988; for Britain see Bradley 1979 and Mander 2011: 17–19 and 40–51; for Denmark see Stewart 2007; for Italy see Jacobitti 1981 and Nuzzo 1998; and for America see Easton 1966, Flower and Murphy 1977, and Watson 1980.

TEXTS ON THE *PHENOMENOLOGY* IN GERMAN AND FRENCH

Important biographical material relating to the genesis and background of the *Phenomenology* can be found in Rosenkranz 1844. (For a partial translation see SEL: 254–65.) Fulda 1965 and 1966, Haering 1929 and 1934, and Pöggeler 1961, 1966, and 1973 contain classic discussions of the *Phenomenology*, and particularly its relation to the rest of Hegel's system and later thought. More recent studies in German include Becker 1971, Claesges 1981, Fink 1977, Heinrichs 1974, Kähler and Marx 1992, Kimmerle 1978, W. Marx 1986, Scheier 1980, Siep 2000, and Vieweg and Welsch (eds) (2008). For commentaries in French see Labarrière 1968, and Labarrière and Jarczyk 1987 and 1989.

BIBLIOGRAPHY

WORKS BY HEGEL AND KANT

'Aphorisms from Hegel's Wastebook', translated by S. Klein, D. L. Roochnik, and G. E. Tucker, *Independent Journal of Philosophy*, 3, 1979: 1–6. (This is a partial translation: for the full text see 'Aphorismen aus Hegels Wastebook', in *Jenaer Schriften, Theorie Werkausgabe*, edited by E. Moldenhauer and K. M. Michel, 20 vols and index, Frankfurt am Main: Suhrkamp, 1969–71, II, pp. 540–67.)

The Berlin Phenomenology, edited and translated by M. J. Petry, Dordrecht: D. Reidel, 1981.

The Critical Journal of Philosophy, 'Introduction: On the Essence of Philosophical Criticism Generally, and Its Relationship to the Present State of Philosophy', translated by H. S. Harris, in *Between Kant and Hegel: Texts in the Development of Post-Kantian Idealism*, translated by G. di Giovanni and H. S. Harris, Albany: SUNY Press, 1985, pp. 272–91.

The Difference Between Fichte's and Schelling's System of Philosophy, translated by H. S. Harris and W. Cerf, Albany: SUNY Press, 1977.

Hegel's Logic: Part One of the Encyclopedia of the Philosophical Sciences, translated by W. Wallace, 3rd edn, Oxford: Oxford University Press, 1975.

Hegel's Philosophy of Nature (Part Two of the *Encyclopedia of the Philosophical Sciences*), edited and translated by M. J. Petry, 3 vols, George Allen & Unwin: London, 1970.

Hegel's Philosophy of Mind: Part Three of the Encyclopedia of the Philosophical Sciences, translated by W. Wallace and A. V. Miller, Oxford: Oxford University Press, 1971.

Early Theological Writings, translated by T. M. Knox, Chicago: University of Chicago Press, 1948.

Elements of the Philosophy of Right, edited by A. W. Wood, translated by H. B. Nisbet, Cambridge: Cambridge University Press, 1991.

Faith and Knowledge, translated by W. Cerf and H. S. Harris, Albany: SUNY Press, 1977.

Hegel: The Letters, translated by C. Butler and C. Seiler, Bloomington: Indiana University Press, 1984.

Introduction to the Lectures on the History of Philosophy, translated by T. M. Knox and A. V. Miller, Oxford: Oxford University Press, 1985.

Lectures on the Philosophy of World History; Introduction: Reason in History, translated by H. B. Nisbet, Cambridge: Cambridge University Press, 1975.

Jenaer Systementwürfe I: Das System der speculativen Philosophie, edited by K. Düsing and H. Kimmerle, Hamburg: Felix Meiner Verlag, 1986; translated in SEL (see below).

Jenaer Systementwürfe II: Logik, Metaphysik, Naturphilosophie, edited by R.-P. Horstmann, Hamburg: Felix Meiner Verlag, 1982; partially translated in *The Jena System, 1804–1805*, translated by J. W. Burbidge and G. di Giovanni, Montreal: McGill-Queen's University Press, 1986.

Jenaer Systementwürfe III: Naturphilosophie und Philosophie des Geistes, edited by R.-P. Horstmann, Hamburg: Felix Meiner Verlag, 1987; partially translated in *Hegel and the Human Spirit: A Translation of the Jena Lectures on the Human Spirit 1805–6*, translated by L. Rauch, Detroit: Wayne State University Press, 1983.

Hegel's Aesthetics: Lectures on Fine Art, translated by T. M. Knox, 2 vols, Oxford: Oxford University Press, 1975.

Lectures on the History of Philosophy, translated by E. S. Haldane and F. H. Simson, 3 vols, London: K. Paul, Trench, Trübner, 1892–96; reprinted London: University of Nebraska Press, 1995.

Lectures on the Philosophy of Religion, translated by E. B. Speirs and J. B. Sanderson, New York: Humanities Press, 1962.

Natural Law: The Scientific Ways of Treating Natural Law, Its Place in Moral Philosophy, and Its Relation to the Positive Sciences of Law, translated by T. M. Knox, Philadelphia, PA: University of Pennsylvania Press, 1975.

'Notizen und Aphorismen 1818–31', in *Berliner Schriften 1818–1831, Theorie Werkausgabe*, edited by E. Moldenhauer and K. M. Michel, 20 vols and index, Frankfurt am Main: Suhrkamp, 1969–71, XI, pp. 556–74.

Phenomenology of Spirit, translated by A. V. Miller, Oxford: Oxford University Press, 1977.

The Philosophy of History, translated by J. Sibree, New York: Dover, 1956.

Political Writings, edited by L. Dickey and H. B. Nisbet, translated by H. B. Nisbet, Cambridge: Cambridge University Press, 1999.

Reason in History: A General Introduction to the Philosophy of History, translated by R. S. Hartman, Indianapolis: Bobbs-Merrill, 1953.

'The Relationship of Scepticism to Philosophy', translated by H. S. Harris, in *Between Kant and Hegel: Texts in the Development of Post-Kantian Idealism*, translated by G. di Giovanni and H. S. Harris, Albany: SUNY Press, 1985, pp. 311–62.

'*System of Ethical Life*' *(1802/3) and '*First Philosophy of Spirit*' (Part III of the System of Speculative Philosophy 1803/4)*, edited and translated by H. S. Harris and T. M. Knox, Albany: SUNY Press, 1979.

Science of Logic, translated by A. V. Miller, London: George Allen & Unwin, 1969.

In the case of those works that include material from student notes, if the text referred to is taken from these notes, this is indicated by adding a 'Z' to the paragraph number (e.g. EL: §158Z). In cases where a reference comes from two different translations of the same text, this is indicated by putting a '/' between the references (e.g. ILPWH: 29/RH: 13).

The following works by Kant are cited in this volume:

The Critique of Practical Reason
The Critique of Pure Reason
Groundwork of the Metaphysics of Morals
What Real Progress Has Metaphysics Made In Germany Since the Time of Leibniz and Wolff?

References are given to the volume and page number of the Berlin Academy Edition of Kant's writings (which can be found in the margins of most translations of these works), except in the case of the *Critique of Pure Reason*, which is cited in the standard form, relating to the pagination of the A (first) and B (second) editions.

OTHER WORKS

Acton, H. B. (1971), 'Hegel's Conception of the Study of Human Nature', in *Royal Institute of Philosophy Lectures, Vol. 4: 1969–70: The Proper Study* (Brighton: Harvester Press), 32–47; reprinted in Inwood (ed.) (1985): 137–52.

Adelman, H. (1980), 'Of Human Bondage: Labour, Bondage, and Freedom in the *Phenomenology*', in Verene (ed.) (1980): 119–35; reprinted in O'Neill (ed.) (1996): 171–86; and in Stewart (ed.) (1998): 155–71.

——(1984), 'Hegel's *Phenomenology*: Facing the Preface', *Idealistic Studies*, 14: 159–70.

Adorno, T. W. (1973), *Negative Dialectics*, trans. E. B. Ashton, London: Routledge.

Ameriks, K. (1987), 'The Hegelian Critique of Kantian Morality', in B. den Ouden and M. Mouen (eds) (1987); reprinted in his (2000) *Kant and the Fate of Autonomy*, Cambridge: Cambridge University Press, 309–37.

——(1991), 'Hegel and Idealism', *The Monist*, 74: 386–402; reprinted in Stern (ed.) (1993c), III: 522–37.

——(2000a), 'Introduction: Interpreting German Idealism', in Ameriks (ed.) (2000b): 1–17.

——(ed.) (2000b), *The Cambridge Companion to German Idealism*, Cambridge: Cambridge University Press.

Arthur, C. J. (1986), *Dialectics of Labour: Marx and his Relation to Hegel*, Oxford: Blackwell.

Austin, J. L. (1962), *Sense and Sensibilia*, Oxford: Oxford University Press.
Bataille, G. (1990), 'Hegel, Death and Sacrifice', trans. J. Strauss, in A. Stoekl (ed.), *On Bataille*, Yale French Studies no. 78: 9–28; reprinted in Stern (ed.) (1993c): II, 383–99.
Baugh, B. (2003), *French Hegel: From Surrealism to Postmodernism*, New York: Routledge.
Baxter, D. (1996), 'Bradley on Substantive and Adjective: The Complex-Unity Problem', in Mander (ed.) (1996): 1–24.
Beauvoir, S. de (1974), *The Second Sex*, trans. and ed. H. M. Parshley, New York: Vintage.
Beck, L. W. (1976), 'The Reformation, the Revolution, and the Restoration in Hegel's Political Philosophy', *Journal of the History of Philosophy*, 14: 51–61.
Becker, W. (1971), *Hegels Phänomenologie des Geistes: Eine Interpretation*, Stuttgart: Kohlhammer.
Beiser, F. C. (1987), *The Fate of Reason: German Philosophy from Kant to Fichte*, Cambridge, MA and London: Harvard University Press.
——(2005), *Hegel*, London: Routledge.
——(2009), ' "Morality" in Hegel's *Phenomenology of Spirit*', in K. R. Westphal (ed.) (2009b): 209–25.
——(ed.) (1993), *The Cambridge Companion to Hegel*, Cambridge: Cambridge University Press.
——(ed.) (2008), *Hegel and Nineteenth-Century Philosophy*, Cambridge: Cambridge University Press.
Bernstein, J. M. (1984), 'From Self-Consciousness to Community: Act and Recognition in the Master-Slave Relationship', in Pelczynski (ed.) (1984): 14–39.
Blanshard, B. (1984), 'Bradley on Relations', in Manser and Stock (eds) (1984): 211–26.
Bonsiepen, W. (1979), 'Erste zeitgenössiche Rezensionen der *Phänomenologie des Geistes*', *Hegel-Studien*, 14: 9–38.
Bowie, A. (1993), *Schelling and Modern European Philosophy*, London: Routledge.
Bradley, F. H. (1930), *Appearance and Reality*, ninth impression (corrected), Oxford: Oxford University Press.
Bradley, J. (1979), 'Hegel in Britain: A Brief Survey of British Commentary and Attitudes', *Heythrop Journal*, 20: 1–24 and 163–82.
Brandom, R. B. (2002), *Tales of the Mighty Dead: Historical Essays in the Metaphysics of Intentionality*, Cambridge, MA: Harvard University Press.
Brooks, T. (ed.) (2012), *Hegel's Philosophy of Right: Essays on Ethics, Politics and Law*, Oxford: Wiley-Blackwell.
Bubner, R. (1981), *Modern German Philosophy*, Cambridge: Cambridge University Press.
Burbidge, J. W. (1978), '"Unhappy Consciousness" in Hegel', *Mosaic* 11: 67–80; reprinted in his (1992) *Hegel on Logic and Religion: The Reasonableness of Christianity*, Albany: SUNY Press, 105–18; and in Stewart (ed.) (1998): 192–209.
——(1998), 'Absolute Acting', *The Owl of Minerva*, 30: 103–18.
Butler, J. (1999), *Subjects of Desire: Hegelian Reflections in Twentieth-Century France*, paperback edn, New York: Columbia University Press.
Chiereghin, F. (2009), 'Freedom and Thought: Stoicism, Skepticism, and Unhappy Consciousness', in K. R. Westphal (ed.) 2009b: 55–71.

Claesges, U. (1981), *Darstellung des erscheinenden Wissens: Systematische Einleitung in Hegels Phänomenologie des Geistes*, Bonn: Bouvier.

Comay, R. (2010), *Mourning Sickness: Hegel and the French Revolution*, Stanford: Stanford University Press.

Craig, E. J. (1987), *The Mind of God and the Works of Man*, Oxford: Oxford University Press.

Croce, B. (1915), *What is Living and What is Dead of the Philosophy of Hegel*, trans. D. Ainslie, London: Macmillan.

——(1941), *History as the Story of Liberty*, trans. S. Sprigge, London: George Allen & Unwin.

Dahlstrom, D. O. (2007), 'Challenges to the Rational Observation of Nature in the *Phenomenology of Spirit*', *The Owl of Minerva*, 38: 35–56.

de Laurentiis, A. (2009), 'Absolute Knowing', in K. R. Westphal (ed.) (2009b): 246–64.

Deligiorgi, K. (ed.) (2006), *Hegel: New Directions*, Chesham: Acumen.

den Ouden, B. and Mouen, M. (eds) (1987), *New Essays on Kant*, New York: Peter Lang.

De Nys, M. J. (1978), '"Sense-Certainty" and Universality: Hegel's Entrance into the *Phenomenology*', *International Philosophical Quarterly*, 18: 445–65; reprinted in Stern (ed.) (1993c), III: 108–30.

——(1982), 'Force and Understanding: The Unity of the Object of Consciousness', in M. Westphal (ed.) (1982): 57–70.

——(1986), 'Mediation and Negativity in Hegel's Phenomenology of Christian Consciousness', *Journal of Religion*, 66: 46–67; reprinted in Stewart (ed.) (1998): 401–23.

Descartes, R. (1985), 'Rules for the Direction of the Mind', in *The Philosophical Writings of Descartes*, trans. J. Cottingham, R. Stoothoff, and D. Murdoch, 2 vols, Cambridge: Cambridge University Press: I, 7–78.

Descombes, V. (1980), *Modern French Philosophy*, trans. L. Scott-Fox and J. M. Harding, Cambridge: Cambridge University Press.

De Vos, L. (1989), 'Absolute Knowing in the *Phenomenology*', in Wylleman (ed.) (1989): 231–70.

Devos, R. (1989), 'The Significance of Manifest Religion in the *Phenomenology*', in Wylleman (ed.) (1989): 195–229.

——(1998), 'How Absolute is Hegel's Absolute Knowing?', *The Owl of Minerva*, 30: 33–50.

deVries, W. A. (1988a), 'Hegel on Reference and Knowledge', *Journal of the History of Philosophy*, 26: 297–307.

——(1988b), *Hegel's Theory of Mental Activity*, Ithaca and London: Cornell University Press.

——(1991), 'The Dialectic of Teleology', *Philosophical Topics*, 19: 51–70.

——(2008), 'Sense-Certainty and the "This-Such"', in Moyar and Quante (eds) (2008): 63–75.

di Giovanni, G. (2009), 'Religion, History and Spirit in Hegel's *Phenomenology of Spirit*', in K. R. Westphal (ed.) (2009b): 226–45.

Donougho, M. (1989), 'The Woman in White: On the Reception of Hegel's *Antigone*', *The Owl of Minerva*, 21: 65–89.

Dudeck, C. V. (1981), *Hegel's 'Phenomenology of Mind': Analysis and Commentary*, Washington: University Press of America.

Dulckheit, K. (1986), 'Can Hegel Refer to Particulars?', *The Owl of Minerva*, 17: 181–94; reprinted in Stewart (ed.) (1998): 105–21.

Duquette, D. (1994), 'The Political Significance of Hegel's Concept of Recognition', *Bulletin of the Hegel Society of Great Britain*, 29: 38–54.

Easton, L. (1966), *Hegel's First American Followers: The Ohio Hegelians*, Athens, OH: Ohio University Press.

Emmanuel, S. M. (ed.) (2001), *The Blackwell Guide to the Modern Philosophers: From Descartes to Nietzsche*, Oxford: Blackwell.

Ferrini, C. (2009), 'Reason Observing Nature', in K. R. Westphal (ed.) (2009b): 92–135.

Feuerbach, L. (1839), 'Towards a Critique of Hegelian Philosophy', trans. Z. Hanfi; reprinted in Stern (ed.) (1993c): I, 100–130.

Fichte, J. G. (2005), *The System of Ethics, According to the Principles of the Wissenschaftslehre*, trans. and ed. by Daniel Breazeale and Günter Zöller, Cambridge: Cambridge University Press.

Findlay, J. N. (1958), *Hegel: A Re-examination*, London: Allen and Unwin.

——(1977), 'Analysis of the Text', in *Hegel's Phenomenology of Spirit*, trans. A. V. Miller, Oxford: Oxford University Press, 495–592.

Fink, E. (1977), *Hegel: Phänomenologische Interpretationen der Phänomenologie des Geistes*, Frankfurt: Klostermann.

Flay, J. C. (1970), 'Hegel's "Inverted World"', *Review of Metaphysics*, 23: 662–78; reprinted in Stern (ed.) (1993c): III, 148–61; and in Stewart (ed.) (1998): 138–54.

——(1984), *Hegel's Quest For Certainty*, Albany: SUNY Press.

——(1998), 'Absolute Knowing and the Absolute Other', *The Owl of Minerva*, 30: 69–82.

Fleischmann, E. (1971), 'The Role of the Individual in Pre-revolutionary Society: Stirner, Marx, and Hegel', in Pelczynski (ed.) (1971): 220–29.

Flower, E. and Murphy, M. G. (1977), *A History of Philosophy in America*, New York: Capricorn and Putnam.

Forster, M. N. (1989), *Hegel and Skepticism*, Cambridge, MA: Harvard University Press.

——(1998), *Hegel's Idea of a 'Phenomenology of Spirit'*, Chicago: University of Chicago Press.

Franco, P. (1999), *Hegel's Philosophy of Freedom*, New Haven and London: Yale University Press.

Friedman, R. Z. (1986), 'Hypocrisy and the Highest Good: Hegel on Kant's Transition from Morality to Religion', *Journal of the History of Philosophy*, 24: 503–22.

Fukuyama, F. (1992), *The End of History and the Last Man*, London: Penguin.

Fulda, H.-F. (1965), *Das Problem einer Einleitung in Hegels Wissenschaft der Logik*, Frankfurt: Klostermann.

——(1966), 'Zur Logik der Phänomenologie von 1807', *Hegel-Studien*, Beiheft 3: 75–101; reprinted in Fulda and Henrich (eds) (1973): 391–422.

Fulda, H-F. and Henrich, D. (eds) (1973), *Materialen zu Hegels 'Phänomenologie des Geistes'*, Frankfurt: Suhrkamp.

Gabler, G. A. (1827), *Kritik des Bewusstseins: Eine Vorschule zu Hegel's Wissenschaft der Logik*, Leiden: A. H. Adriani.

Gadamer, H-G. (1976a), 'Hegel's "Inverted World"', in his *Hegel's Dialectic: Five Hermenutical Studies*, trans. P. Christopher Smith, New Haven and London: Yale University Press, 35–53; reprinted in Stern (ed.) (1993c): III, 131–47.

——(1976b), 'Hegel's Dialectic of Self-Consciousness', in his *Hegel's Dialectic: Five Hermenutical Studies*, trans. P. Christopher Smith, New Haven and London: Yale University Press, 54–74; reprinted in O'Neill (ed.) (1996): 149–70.

Geuss, R. (1999), 'Art and Theodicy', in his *Morality, Culture, and History: Essays on German Philosophy*, Cambridge: Cambridge University Press, 78–115.

Gillespie, M. A. (1984), *Hegel, Heidegger, and the Ground of History*, Chicago and London: University of Chicago Press.

Glendinning, S. (ed.) (1999), *The Edinburgh Encyclopedia of Continental Philosophy*, Edinburgh: Edinburgh University Press.

Gram, M. S. (1978), 'Moral and Literary Ideals in Hegel's Critique of "The Moral World-View"', *Clio*, 7: 375–402; reprinted in Stewart (ed.) (1998): 307–33.

Gutting, G. (2011), *Thinking the Impossible: French Philosophy since 1960*, Oxford: Oxford University Press.

Guyer, P. (2000), *Kant on Freedom, Law, and Happiness*, Cambridge: Cambridge University Press.

Habermas, J. (1973), 'Hegel's Critique of the French Revolution', in his *Theory and Practice*, trans. John Viertel, Boston: Beacon Press, 121–41.

Haering, T. L. (1929), *Hegel: Sein Wollen und Sein Werke*, Leipzig: Tuebner; reprinted Aalen: Scientia, 1963.

——(1934), 'Die Enstehungsgeschichte der Phänomenologie', in B. Wigersma (ed.) (1934): 118–38.

Hardimon, M. O. (1994), *Hegel's Social Philosophy: The Project of Reconciliation*, Cambridge: Cambridge University Press.

Harris, H. S. (1972), *Hegel's Development I: Toward the Sunlight (1770–1801)*, Oxford: Oxford University Press.

——(1977), 'Hegel and the French Revolution', *Clio*, 7: 5–18.

——(1983), *Hegel's Development II: Night Thoughts (Jena 1801–6)*, Oxford: Oxford University Press.

——(1993), 'Hegel's Intellectual Development', in Beiser (ed.) (1993): 25–51.

——(1995), *Hegel: Phenomenology and System*, Indianapolis: Hackett.

——(1997), *Hegel's Ladder*, 2 vols, Indianapolis: Hackett.

Haym, R. (1857), *Hegel und seine Zeit*, Berlin: Rudolf Gaertner; reprinted Darmstadt: Wissenschaftliche Buchgesellschaft, 1962.

Heidegger, M. (1970), *Hegel's Concept of Experience*, trans. J. G. Gray, New York: Harper & Row.

——(1994), *Hegel's 'Phenomenology of Spirit'*, trans. P. Emad and K. Maly, Bloomington: Indiana University Press.

Heidemann, D. (2008), 'Substance, Subject, System: The Justification of Science in Hegel's *Phenomenology of Spirit*', in D. Moyar and M. Quante (eds) 2008: 1–20.

Heine, H. (1986), *Religion and Philosophy in Germany*, trans. J. Snodgrass, Albany: SUNY Press.

Heinrichs, J. (1974), *Die Logik der Phänomenologie des Geistes*, Bonn: Bouvier.

Herman, B. (1993), *The Practice of Moral Judgment*, Cambridge, MA: Harvard University Press.

Herr, L. (1894), 'Hegel', *La Grande Encyclopédie*, 19: 997–1003; reprinted in his *Choix d'Écrits*, Paris: Les Éditions Ridier, 1932, vol. 2: 109–40.

Hinchman, L. P. (1984), *Hegel's Critique of the Enlightenment*, Gainesville: University Press of Florida.

Honneth, A. (1988), 'Atomism and Ethical Life: On Hegel's Critique of the French Revolution', *Philosophy and Social Criticism*, 14: 359–68.

——(1995), *The Struggle for Recognition: The Moral Grammar of Social Conflict*, trans. J. Anderson, Cambridge: Polity Press.

——(2008), 'From Desire to Recognition: Hegel's Account of Human Sociality', in Moyar and Quante (eds) (2008): 76–90.

Houlgate, S. (1991), *Freedom, Truth and History: An Introduction to Hegel's Philosophy*, London: Routledge.

——(1998), 'Absolute Knowing Revisited', *The Owl of Minerva*, 30: 51–68.

——(1999), 'Schelling's Critique of Hegel's *Science of Logic*', *Review of Metaphysics*, 53: 99–128.

——(2001), 'G. W. F. Hegel', in Emmanuel (ed.) (2001): 278–305.

——(2013), *Hegel's 'Phenomenology of Spirit'*, London: Bloomsbury.

Hoy, D. C. (1981), 'Hegel's Morals', *Dialogue*, 20: 84–102.

——(1989), 'Hegel's Critique of Kantian Morality', *History of Philosophy Quarterly*, 6: 207–32.

——(2009), 'The Ethics of Freedom: Hegel on Reason and Law-Giving and Law-Testing', in K. R. Westphal (ed.) (2009b): 153–71.

Hoy, J. B. (2009) 'Hegel, *Antigone*, and Feminist Critique: The Spirit of Ancient Greece', in K. R. Westphal (ed.) (2009b): 172–89.

Hume, D. (1978), *A Treatise of Human Nature*, 2nd edn, ed. L. A. Selby-Bigge and P. H. Nidditch, Oxford: Oxford University Press.

Hutchings, K. (2003), *Hegel and Feminist Philosophy*, Cambridge: Polity.

Hyppolite, J. (1969), 'The Significance of the French Revolution in Hegel's *Phenomenology*', in his *Studies on Marx and Hegel*, trans. J. O'Neill, London: Heinemann, 35–69.

——(1974), *Genesis and Structure of Hegel's 'Phenomenology of Spirit'*, trans. S. Cherniak and J. Heckman, Evanston: Northwestern University Press.

Inwood, M. (1983), *Hegel*, London: Routledge.

——(1992), *A Hegel Dictionary*, Oxford: Blackwell.

——(ed.) (1985), *Hegel*, Oxford: Oxford University Press.

Jacobitti, E. E. (1981), *Revolutionary Humanism and Historicism in Modern Italy*, New Haven: Yale University Press.

James, W. (1909), *A Pluralistic Universe*, London: Longmans, Green, & Co., 83–130; reprinted in Stern (ed.) (1993c): II, 208–24.

Jameson, F. (2010), *The Hegel Variations: On the 'Phenomenology of Spirit'*, London: Verso.

Jamros, D. P. (1994), *The Human Shape of God: Religion in Hegel's 'Phenomenology of Spirit'*, New York: Paragon House.

Jebb, R. C. (1902), 'Introduction', *The Antigone of Sophocles*, ed. R. C. Jebb, abridged by E. S. Shuckburgh, Cambridge: Cambridge University Press, xi–xxx.

Kähler, K. and Marx, W. (1992), *Die Vernunft in Hegels Phänomenologie des Geistes*, Frankfurt: Klostermann.

Kain, P. J. (2005), *Hegel and the Other: A Study of the 'Phenomenology of Spirit'*, Albany: SUNY Press.

Kainz, H. P. (1976), *Hegel's 'Phenomenology', Part I: Analysis and Commentary*, Tuscaloosa: University of Alabama Press; reprinted Athens, OH: Ohio University Press, 1988.

——(1983), *Hegel's 'Phenomenology', Part II*, Athens, OH: Ohio University Press.

Kaufmann, W. (1965), *Hegel: Reinterpretation, Texts, and Commentary*, London: Weidenfeld and Nicolson.

——(1971), 'Hegel's Ideas about Tragedy', in Steinkraus (ed.) (1971): 201–20.

Kelly, G. A. (1965), 'Notes on Hegel's "Lordship and Bondage"', *Review of Metaphysics*, 19: 780–802; reprinted in his (1978) *Retreat from Eleusis: Studies in Political Thought*, Princeton: Princeton University Press, 29–54; and in O'Neill (ed.) (1996), 253–72; and in Stern (ed.) (1993c): III, 162–79; and in Stewart (ed.) (1998): 172–91.

Kelly, M. (1992), *Hegel in France*, Birmingham: Birmingham Modern Languages Publications.

Kimmerle, G. (1978), *Sein und Selbst: Untersuchung zur kategorialen Einheit von Vernunft und Geist in Hegels Phänomenologie des Geistes*, Bonn: Bouvier.

Kojève, A. (1969), *Introduction to the Reading of Hegel*, abridged, trans. J. H. Nichols, New York: Basic Books.

Koyré, A (1934), 'Hegel à Iéna', *Revue d'histoire et de philosophie religiuese*, reprinted in his *Études d'histoire de la pensée philosophiques*, Paris: Armand Colin, 1961, 135–73.

Korsgaard, C. M. (1996), 'Kant's Formula of the Universal Law', in her *Creating the Kingdom of Ends*, Cambridge: Cambridge University Press, 77–105; reprinted from *Pacific Philosophical Quarterly*, 1985, 66: 24–47.

Krasnoff, L. (2008), *Hegel's 'Phenomenology of Spirit': An Introduction*, Cambridge: Cambridge University Press.

Labarrière, P.-J. (1968), *Structures et mouvement dialectique dans la Phénoménologie de l'Esprit de Hegel*, Paris: Aubier.

Labarrière, P.-J. and Jarczyk, G. (1987), *Hegel: Les premiers combats de la reconnaissance, maîtrise et servitude dans la Phénoménologie de Hegel*, Paris: Aubier.

——(1989), *Hegel: Le malheur de la conscience ou l'accès à la raison: Liberté de l'autoconscience: stoicisme, scepticisme et la conscience malheureuse: Texte et commentaire*, Paris: Aubier.

Lacan, J. (2007), *Écrits*, trans. B. Fink, New York: W. W. Norton.

Lamb, D. (1978), 'Hegel and Wittgenstein on Language and Sense-Certainty', *Clio*, 7: 285–301.

——(1980), *Hegel: From Foundation to System*, The Hague: Nijhoff.

Lauer, Q. J. (1976), *A Reading of Hegel's 'Phenomenology of Spirit'*, New York: Fordham University Press.

Lewis, T. A. (2008), *Religion and Demythologization in Hegel's 'Phenomenology of Spirit'*, in Moyar and Quante (eds) (2008): 192–209.

Locke, J. (1975), *An Essay Concerning Human Understanding*, ed. P. H. Nidditch, Oxford: Oxford University Press.

Loewenberg, J. (1965), *Hegel's 'Phenomenology': Dialogues on the Life of Mind*, La Salle, IL: Open Court.

Lottenbach, H. and Tenenbaum, S. (1995), 'Hegel's Critique of Kant in the *Philosophy of Right*', *Kant Studien*, 86: 211–30.

Löwith, K. (1964), *From Hegel to Nietzsche: The Revolution in Nineteenth-Century Thought*, trans. D. E. Green, New York: Columbia University Press.

——(1971), 'Mediation and Immediacy in Hegel, Marx and Feuerbach', in Steinkraus (ed.) (1971): 119–41.

Ludwig, W. D. (1989), 'Hegel's Conception of Absolute Knowing', *The Owl of Minerva*, 21: 5–19.

Lukács, G. (1968), *History and Class Consciousness*, trans. R. Livingstone, London: Merlin Press.

——(1975), *The Young Hegel*, trans. R. Livingstone, London: Merlin Press.

Lumsden, S. (1998), 'Absolute Knowing', *The Owl of Minerva*, 30: 3–32.

Lunteren, F. von (1993), 'Eighteenth-Century Conceptions of Gravitation', in Petry (ed.) (1993): 343–66.

McDowell, J. (2006), 'The Apperceptive I and the Empirical Self: Towards a Heterodox Reading of "Lordship and Bondage" in Hegel's *Phenomenology*', in Deligiorgi (ed.) (2006): 33–48.

McGinn, C. (1993), *Problems in Philosophy: The Limits of Inquiry*, Oxford: Blackwell.

MacIntyre, A. (1972a), 'Hegel on Faces and Skulls', in MacIntyre (ed.) (1972b): 219–36; reprinted in Stewart (ed.) (1998): 213–24.

——(ed.) (1972b), *Hegel: A Collection of Critical Essays*, New York: Anchor Books.

Magee, G. A. (2010), *The Hegel Dictionary*, London: Continuum.

Mander, W. J. (ed.) (1996), *Perspectives on the Logic and Metaphysics of F. H. Bradley*, Bristol: Thoemmes Press.

——(2011), *British Idealism: A History*, Oxford: Oxford University Press.

Manser, A. and Stock, G. (eds) (1984), *The Philosophy of F. H. Bradley*, Oxford: Oxford University Press.

Marcuse, H. (1955), *Reason and Revolution: Hegel and the Rise of Social Theory*, 2nd edn, London: Routledge & Kegan Paul.

Marx, K. (1906), *Capital*, vol. 1, trans. E. Aveling and S. Moore, New York: Modern Library.

——(1975), 'Economic and Philosophical Manuscripts', trans. R. Livingstone and G. Benton, in *Early Writings*, Harmondsworth: Penguin, 279–400.

Marx, W. (1975), *Hegel's 'Phenomenology of Spirit': A Commentary on the Preface and Introduction*, trans. P. Heath, New York: Harper and Row.

——(1986), *Das Selbstbewusstsein in Hegels Phänomenologie des Geistes*, Frankfurt: Klostermann.

Miller, M. H. (1978), 'The Attainment of the Absolute Standpoint in Hegel's *Phenomenology*', *Graduate Faculty Philosophy Journal*, 7: 195–219; reprinted in Stewart (ed.) (1998): 427–43.

Mills, P. J. (1986), 'Hegel's *Antigone*', *The Owl of Minerva*, 17: 131–52; reprinted in Mills (ed.) (1996): 59–88; and in Stewart (ed.) (1998): 243–71.

——(ed.) (1996), *Feminist Interpretations of G. W. F. Hegel*, University Park, PA: The Pennsylvania State University Press.

Moyar, D. and M. Quante (eds) (2008), *Hegel's 'Phenomenology of Spirit': A Critical Guide*, Cambridge: Cambridge University Press.

Murray, D. (1972), 'Hegel: Force and Understanding', in Vesey (ed.) (1972): 163–73.

Nagel, T. (1986), *The View from Nowhere*, Oxford: Oxford University Press.

Neuhouser, F. (1986), 'Deducing Desire and Recognition in the *Phenomenology of Spirit*', *Journal of the History of Philosophy*, 24: 243–62.

——(2000), *Foundations of Hegel's Social Theory: Actualizing Freedom*, Cambridge, MA and London: Harvard University Press.

——(2009), 'Desire, Recognition, and the Relation Between Bondsman and Lord', in K. R. Westphal (ed.) (2009b): 55–71.

Neuser, W. (1993), 'The Concept of Force in Eighteenth-Century Mechanics', in Petry (ed.) (1993): 383–98.

Nietzsche, F. (1974), *The Gay Science*, trans. W. Kaufmann, New York: Random House.

Noël, G. (1897), *La Logique de Hegel*, Paris: Germer Ballière et Cie.

Norman, R. (1981), *Hegel's 'Phenomenology': A Philosophical Introduction*, Brighton: Harvester Press.

Norton, R. E. (1995), *The Beautiful Soul: Aesthetic Morality in the Eighteenth Century*, Ithaca and London: Cornell University Press.

Nozick, R. (1981), *Philosophical Explanations*, Oxford: Oxford University Press.

Nussbaum, M. (1986), *The Fragility of Goodness*, Cambridge: Cambridge University Press.

Nusser, K. (1998), 'The French Revolution and Hegel's *Phenomenology of Spirit*', trans. J. Stewart, in Stewart (ed.) (1998): 282–306.

Nuzzo, A. (1998), 'An Outline of Italian Hegelianism (1832–1998)', *The Owl of Minerva*, 29: 165–205.

O'Neill, J. (ed.) (1996), *Hegel's Dialectic of Desire and Recognition*, Albany: SUNY Press.

Pelczynski, Z. A. (ed.) (1971), *Hegel's Political Philosophy*, Cambridge: Cambridge University Press.

——(ed.) (1984), *The State and Civil Society*, Cambridge: Cambridge University Press.

Petry, M. J. (ed.) (1993), *Hegel and Newtonianism*, Dordrecht: Kluwer.

Pietercil, R. (1978), 'Antigone and Hegel', *International Philosophical Quarterly*, 18: 289–310.

Pinkard, T. (1988), *Hegel's Dialectic: The Explanation of Possibility*, Philadelphia, PA: Temple University Press.

——(1994), *Hegel's 'Phenomenology': The Sociality of Reason*, Cambridge: Cambridge University Press.

——(1997), 'Romanticized Enlightenment? Enlightened Romanticism? Universalism and Particularism in Hegel's Understanding of the Enlightenment', *Bulletin of the Hegel Society of Great Britain*, 35: 18–38.

——(1999), 'History and Philosophy: Hegel's *Phenomenology of Spirit*', in Glendinning (ed.) (1999): 57–68.

——(2000a), *Hegel: A Biography*, Cambridge: Cambridge University Press.

——(2000b), 'Hegel's *Phenomenology* and *Logic*: An Overview', in Ameriks (ed.) (2000b): 161–79.

——(2007), 'Was Pragmatism the Successor to Idealism?', in C. Misak (ed.), *The New Pragmatism*, Oxford: Oxford University Press, 142–68.

——(2009), 'Shapes of Active Reason: The Law of the Heart, Retrieved Virtue, and What Really Matters', in K. R. Westphal (ed.) (2009b): 136–52.

——(2010), 'Hegelianism in the Twentieth Century', in D. Moran (ed.), *The Routledge Companion to Twentieth Century Philosophy*, Abingdon: Routledge, 118–47.

Pippin, R. B. (1989), *Hegel's Idealism: The Satisfactions of Self-Consciousness*, Cambridge: Cambridge University Press.

——(1993), 'You Can't Get from Here to There: Transition Problems in Hegel's *Phenomenology of Spirit*', in Beiser (ed.) (1993): 52–85.

——(2006), 'Recognition and Reconciliation: Actualized Agency in Hegel's Jena *Phenomenology*', in Deligiorgi (ed.) (2006): 125–42.

——(2008), *Hegel's Practical Philosophy: Rational Agency as Ethical Life*, Cambridge: Cambridge University Press.

——(2011), *Hegel on Self-Consciousness: Desire and Death in the 'Phenomenology of Spirit'*, Princeton: Princeton University Press.

Pöggeler, O. (1961), 'Zur Deutung der Phänomenologie des Geistes', *Hegel-Studien*, 1: 255–94; reprinted in Pöggeler (1973): 170–230.

——(1966), 'Die Komposition der Phänomenologie des Geistes', in *Hegel-Studien*, Beiheft 3: 27–74; reprinted in Fulda and Henrich (eds) (1973): 329–90.

——(1973), *Hegels Idee einer Phänomenologie des Geistes*, Freiburg and Munich: Karl Alber.

Poster, M. (1975), *Existential Marxism in Postwar France: From Sartre to Althusser*, Princeton: Princeton University Press.

Quante, M. (2008), '"Reason Apprehended Irrationally": Hegel's Critique of Observing Reason', in Moyar and Quante (eds) (2008): 91–111.

Rauch, L. and Sherman, D. (1999), *Hegel's Phenomenology of Self-Consciousness*, Albany: SUNY Press.

Redding, P. (1996), *Hegel's Hermeneutics*, Ithaca and London: Cornell University Press.

——(2007), *Analytic Philosophy and the Return of Hegelian Thought*, Cambridge: Cambridge University Press.

——(2008), 'The Independence and Dependence of Self-Consciousness: The Dialectic of Lord and Bondsman in Hegel's *Phenomenology of Spirit*', in Beiser (ed.) (2008): 94–110.

——(2010), 'Georg Wilhelm Friedrich Hegel', *The Stanford Encyclopedia of Philosophy (Fall 2010 Edition)*, Edward N. Zalta (ed.), available online: http://plato.stanford.edu/archives/fall2010/entries/hegel/.

Riley, P. (1995), 'Rousseau's General Will: Freedom of a Particular Kind', in Wokler (ed.) (1995): 1–28.

Ripstein, A. (1994), 'Universal and General Wills: Hegel and Rousseau', *Political Theory*, 22: 444–67.

Ritter, J. (1982), *Hegel and the French Revolution*, trans. R. D. Winfield, Cambridge, MA and London: MIT Press.

Roberts, J. (1988), *German Philosophy: An Introduction*, Cambridge: Polity Press.

Robinson, J. (1977), *Duty and Hypocrisy in Hegel's 'Phenomenology of Mind'*, Toronto and Buffalo: University of Toronto Press.

Rockmore, T. (1993), *Before and After Hegel: A Historical Introduction to Hegel's Thought*, Berkeley: University of California Press.

——(1995), *Heidegger and French Philosophy: Humanism, Antihumanism and Being*, London: Routledge.

——(1997), *Cognition: An Introduction to Hegel's 'Phenomenology of Spirit'*, Berkeley: University of California Press.

Rorty, R. (1998), 'Dewy Between Hegel and Darwin', in his *Truth and Progress: Philosophical Papers volume 3*, Cambridge: Cambridge University Press, 290–306.

Rosen, S. (1974), *G. W. F. Hegel: An Introduction to the Science of Wisdom*, New Haven: Yale University Press.

Rosenkranz, K. (1840), *Kritische Erläuterungen des Hegelschen Systems*, Königsberg: Bornträger.

——(1844), *Georg Wilhelm Friedrich Hegels Leben*, Berlin: Duncker and Humblot; reprinted Darmstadt: Wissenschaftliche Buchgesellschaft, 1963.

Roth, M. (1988), *Knowing and History: Appropriations of Hegel in Twentieth Century France*, Ithaca: Cornell University Press.

Rousseau, J-J. (1991), *Émile*, trans. A. Bloom, London: Penguin.

——(1994), *The Social Contract*, trans. C. Betts, Oxford: Oxford University Press.

Royce, J. (1919), *Lectures on Modern Idealism*, ed. J. Loewenberg, New Haven and London: Yale University Press.

Russell, B. (1956), *Portraits from Memory and Other Essays*, London: George Allen & Unwin.

Russon, J. (2004), *Reading Hegel's 'Phenomenology'*, Bloomington: Indiana University Press.

Sallis, J. (1977), 'Hegel's Concept of Presentation: Its Determination in the Preface to the *Phenomenology of Spirit*', *Hegel-Studien* 12: 129–56; reprinted in his (1986), *Delimitations: Phenomenology and the End of Metaphysics*, Bloomington and Indianapolis: Indiana University Press, 40–62; and in Stewart (ed.) (1998): 25–51.

Sartre, J.-P. (1958), *Being and Nothingness*, trans. H. E. Barnes, London: Routledge.

Schacht, R. (1972), 'A Commentary on the Preface to Hegel's *Phenomenology*', *Philosophical Studies* 23: 1–31; reprinted in his (1975) *Hegel and After: Studies in Continental Philosophy Between Kant and Sartre*, Pittsburgh: University of Pittsburgh Press, 41–68.

Scheier, C.-A. (1980), *Analytischer Kommentar zu Hegels Phänomenologie des Geistes*, Freiberg and Munich: Alber.

Schiller, F. (1967), *On the Aesthetic Education of Man*, trans. E. M. Wilkinson and L. A. Willoughby, Oxford: Oxford University Press.

Schmidt, J. (1998), 'Cabbage Heads and Gulps of Water: Hegel on the Terror', *Political Theory*, 26: 4–32.

Schöndorf, H. (1998), 'The Othering (Becoming Other) and Reconciliation of God in Hegel's *Phenomenology of Spirit*', trans. J. Stewart, in Stewart (ed.) (1998): 375–400.

Schopenhauer, A. (1965), *On the Basis of Morality*, trans. E. F. J. Payne, Indianapolis: Bobbs-Merill.

Sedgwick, S. (1988a), 'Hegel's Critique of the Subjective Idealism of Kant's Ethics', *Journal of the History of Philosophy*, 26: 89–105.

——(1988b), 'On the Relation of Pure Reason to Content: A Reply to Hegel's Critique of Formalism in Kant's Ethics', *Philosophy and Phenomenological Research*, 49: 59–80.

Sellars, W. S. (1963), *Science, Perception and Reality*, London: Routledge & Kegan Paul.

Shapiro, G. (1979), 'Notes on the Animal Kingdom of the Spirit', *Clio* 8: 323–38; reprinted in Stewart (ed.) (1998): 225–39.

Shklar, J. N. (1974), 'The *Phenomenology*: Beyond Morality', *Western Philosophical Quarterly*, 27: 597–623; reprinted in Stern (ed.) (1993c): IV, 189–219.

——(1976), *Freedom and Independence: A Study of the Political Ideas of Hegel's 'Phenomenology of Mind'*, Cambridge: Cambridge University Press.

Siep, L. (1979), *Anerkennung als Prinzip der praktischen Philosophie. Untersuchungen zu Hegels Jenaer Philosophie des Geistes*, Freiburg: Alber.

——(2000), *Der Weg der Phänomenologie des Geistes: Ein einführender Kommentar zu Hegels 'Differenzschrift' und 'Phänomenologie des Geistes'*, Frankfurt: Suhrkamp.

Simpson, P. (1998), *Hegel's Transcendental Induction*, Albany: SUNY Press.

Singer, P. (1983), *Hegel*, Oxford: Oxford University Press.

Sinnerbrink, R. (2007), *Understanding Hegelianism*, Stocksfield: Acumen.

Smith, S. B. (1989), 'Hegel and the French Revolution: An Epitaph for Republicanism', *Social Research*, 56: 233–61.

Soll, I. (1969), *An Introduction to Hegel's Metaphysics*, Chicago: Chicago University Press.

——(1976), 'Charles Taylor's *Hegel*', *Journal of Philosophy*, 73: 697–710; reprinted in Inwood (ed.) (1985): 54–66.

Solomon, R. C. (1983), *In the Spirit of Hegel: A Study of G. W. F. Hegel's 'Phenomenology of Spirit'*, Oxford: Oxford University Press.

——(1993), 'Hegel's *Phenomenology of Spirit*', in Solomon and Higgins (eds) (1993): 181–215.

Solomon, R. C. and Higgins, K. M. (eds) (1993), *The Age of German Idealism* (Routledge History of Philosophy Vol. VI), London: Routledge.

Speight, A. (2008), *The Philosophy of Hegel*, Stocksfield: Acumen.

Steiner, G. (1984), *Antigones*, Oxford: Oxford University Press, 19–42; reprinted in Stern (ed.) (1993c): III, 180–99.

Steinkraus W. E. (ed.) (1971), *New Studies in Hegel's Philosophy*, New York: Holt, Rinhart & Winston.

Stepelevich, L. S. (ed.) (1990), *G. W. F. Hegel: Preface and Introduction to the 'Phenomenology of Mind'*, New York: Macmillan.

Stern, R. (1989), 'Unity and Difference in Hegel's Political Philosophy', *Ratio* (new series), 2: 75–88.

——(1990), *Hegel, Kant and the Structure of the Object*, London: Routledge.

——(1993a), 'General Introduction', in Stern (ed.) (1993c), I: 1–20.

——(1993b), 'James and Bradley on Understanding', *Philosophy*, 68: 193–209; reprinted in Stern 2009: 327–41.

——(1998), 'G. W. F. Hegel', in Teichman and White (eds) (1998), 18–37.

——(1999), 'Going Beyond the Kantian Philosophy: On McDowell's Hegelian Critique of Kant', *European Journal of Philosophy*, 7: 247–69.

——(2000), *Transcendental Arguments and Scepticism*, Oxford: Oxford University Press.

——(2008), 'Hegel's Idealism', in Beiser (ed.) (2008): 135–73; reprinted in Stern 2009: 45–76.

——(2009), *Hegelian Metaphysics*, Oxford: Oxford University Press.

——(2012a), 'Is Hegel's Master/Slave Dialectic a Refutation of Solipsism?', *British Journal for the History of Philosophy*, 20: 333–61.

——(2012b), 'On Hegel's Critique of Kant's Ethics: Beyond the "Empty Formalism" Objection', in Brooks (ed.) (2012): 73–99.

——(forthcoming), 'Taylor, Transcendental Arguments, and Hegel on Consciousness', *Bulletin of the Hegel Society of Great Britain*, 67.

——(ed.) (1993c), *G. W. F. Hegel: Critical Assessments*, 4 vols, London: Routledge.

Stern, R. and N. Walker (1998), 'Hegelianism', in E. Craig (ed.), *The Routledge Encyclopedia of Philosophy*, IV: 280–302.

Stewart, J. (1995), 'The Architectonic of Hegel's *Phenomenology of Spirit*', *Philosophy and Phenomenological Research*, 55: 747–76; reprinted in Stewart (ed.) (1998): 444–77.

——(1996), 'Hegel's Doctrine of Determinate Negation: An Example from "Sense-Certainty" and "Perception"', *Idealistic Studies* 26: 57–78.

——(2000), *The Unity of Hegel's 'Phenomenology of Spirit'*, Evanston: Northwestern University Press.

——(2007), *A History of Hegelianism in Golden Age Demark*, 3 vols, Copenhagen: Reitzel.

——(2008), 'Hegel's *Phenomenology* as a Systematic Fragment', in Beiser (ed.) (2008): 74–93

——(ed.) (1998), *The 'Phenomenology of Spirit' Reader*, Albany: SUNY Press.

Stillman, P. G. (ed.) (1987), *Hegel's Philosophy of Spirit*, Albany: SUNY Press.

Stirling, J. H. (1865), *The Secret of Hegel*, London: Longman, Roberts & Green, 2 vols; 2nd edn Edinburgh: Oliver & Boyd, 1898; reprinted Bristol: Thoemmes, 1990.

Stolzenberg, J. (2009), 'Hegel's Critique of the Enlightenment in "The Struggle of the Enlightenment with Superstition"', in K. R. Westphal 2009b: 190–208.

Strauss, D. F. (1851), *Christian Märklin: Ein Lebens- und Charakterbild aus der Gegenwart*, Manheim: Bassermann.

Suter, J.-F. (1971), 'Burke, Hegel, and the French Revolution', in Pelczynksi (ed.) (1971): 52–72.

Taylor, C. (1972), 'The Opening Arguments of the *Phenomenology*', in MacIntyre (ed.) (1972b): 157–87.

——(1975), *Hegel*, Cambridge: Cambridge University Press.

Teichman, J. and White, G. (eds) (1998), *An Introduction to Modern European Philosophy*, 2nd edn, Houndmills: Macmillan.

Toews, J. (1980), *Hegelianism: The Path Towards Dialectical Humanism, 1805–1841*, Cambridge: Cambridge University Press.

Valberg, J. J. (1992), *The Puzzle of Experience*, Oxford: Oxford University Press.

Vaught, C. G. (1986), 'Subject, Object, and Representation: A Critique of Hegel's Dialectic of Perception', *International Philosophical Quarterly*, 26: 117–29.

Vera, A. (1855), *Introduction à la Philosophie de Hegel*, Paris: A. Franck; 2nd edn Paris: Ladrange, 1864.

Verene, D. P. (2007), *Hegel's Absolute: An Introduction to Reading Hegel's 'Phenomenology of Spirit'*, Albany: SUNY Press.

——(ed.) (1980), *Hegel's Social and Political Thought*, Atlantic Highlands, NJ: Humanities Press/Brighton: Harvester Press.

Vesey, G. N. A. (ed.) (1972), *Royal Institute of Philosophy Lectures, Vol. 5: 1970–71: Reason and Reality*, London and Basingstoke: Macmillan.

Vickers, B. (1973), *Towards Greek Tragedy: Drama, Myth, Society*, London: Longman.

Vieillard-Baron, J.-L. (1998), 'Natural Religion: An Investigation of Hegel's *Phenomenology of Spirit*', trans. J. Stewart, in Stewart (ed.) (1998): 351–74.

Vieweg, K. and Welsch, W. (eds) (2008), *Hegels Phänomenologie des Geistes: Ein kooperativer Kommentar*, Frankfurt: Suhrkamp.

von der Luft, E. (1987), 'The Birth of Spirit for Hegel out of the Travesty of Medicine', in Stillman (ed.) (1987): 25–42.

Wahl, J. (1951), *Le malheur de la conscience dans la philosophie de Hegel*, 2nd edn, Paris: Presses Universitaires de France: 119–47; trans. R. Northey in Stern (ed.) (1993c): II, 284–310.

——(1955), 'À propos de l'introduction à la Phénoménologie de Hegel par A. Kojève', *Deucalion*, 5: 77–99.

——(1975), 'Interview', in L. Pitkethly, 'Hegel in Modern France (1900–1950)', unpublished PhD dissertation, University of London: 382–86.

Walsh, W. H. (1969), *Hegelian Ethics*, London: Macmillan.

Wartenberg, T. E. (1993), 'Hegel's Idealism: The Logic of Conceptuality', in Beiser (ed.) (1993): 102–29.

Watson, D. (1980), 'The Neo-Hegelian Tradition in America', *Journal of American Studies*, 14: 219–34.

Westphal, K. R. (1989), *Hegel's Epistemological Realism: A Study of the Aim and Method of Hegel's 'Phenomenology of Spirit'*, Dordrecht: Kluwer.

——(1991), 'Hegel's Critique of Kant's Moral World View', *Philosophical Topics*, 19: 133–76.

——(1993a), 'Hegel, Idealism, and Robert Pippin', *International Philosophical Quarterly*, 33: 263–72.

——(1993b), 'The Basic Context and Structure of Hegel's *Philosophy of Right*', in Beiser (ed.) (1993): 234–69.

——(1995), 'How "Full" is Kant's Categorical Imperative?', *Jahrbuch für Recht und Ethik/Annual Review of Law and Ethics*, 3: 465–509.

——(1998a), 'Hegel and Hume on Perception and Concept-Empiricism', *Journal of the History of Philosophy*, 33: 99–123.

——(1998b), 'Hegel's Solution to the Dilemma of the Criterion', in Stewart (ed.) (1998): 76–91; earlier version in *History of Philosophy Quarterly*, 5 (1988): 173–88.

——(2000), 'Hegel's Internal Critique of Naive Realism', *Journal of Philosophical Research*, 25: 173–229.

——(2003), *Hegel's Epistemology: A Philosophical Introduction to the 'Phenomenology of Spirit'*, Indianapolis: Hackett.

——(2009a), 'Hegel's Phenomenological Method and Analysis of Consciousness', in K. R. Westphal (ed.) (2009b): 1–36.

——(ed.) (2009b), *The Blackwell Guide to Hegel's 'Phenomenology of Spirit'*, Oxford: Wiley-Blackwell.

Westphal, M. (1998a), 'Hegel's Phenomenology of Perception', in Stewart (ed.) (1998): 122–37.

——(1998b), *History and Truth in Hegel's 'Phenomenology'*, 3rd edn, Bloomington: Indiana University Press.

——(ed.) (1982), *Method and Speculation in Hegel's 'Phenomenology'*, New Jersey: Humanities Press.

White, A. (1983), *Absolute Knowledge: Hegel and the Problem of Metaphysics*, Athens, OH: Ohio University Press.

Wigersma, B. (ed.) (1934), *Verhandlungen des dritten Hegelkongresses*, Tübingen: Mohr.

Williams, R. R. (1987), 'Hegel's Concept of *Geist*', in Stillman (ed.) (1987): 1–20; reprinted in Stern (ed.) (1993c): III, 538–54.

——(1992), *Recognition: Fichte, Hegel and the Other*, Albany: SUNY Press.

——(1998), 'Towards a Non-Foundational Absolute Knowing', *The Owl of Minerva*, 30: 83–102.

Winfield, R. D. (1991), *Freedom and Modernity*, Albany: SUNY Press.

Wittgenstein, L. (1968), *Philosophical Investigations*, 3rd edn, trans. G. E. M. Anscombe, Oxford: Blackwell.

Wokler, R. (1997), 'The French Revolutionary Roots of Political Modernity in Hegel's Philosophy, or the Enlightenment at Dusk', *Bulletin of the Hegel Society of Great Britain*, 35: 71–89.

——(1998), 'Contextualizing Hegel's Phenomenology of the French Revolution and the Terror', *Political Theory*, 26: 33–55.

——(ed.) (1995), *Rousseau and Liberty*, Manchester: Manchester University Press.

Wood, A. W. (1970), *Kant's Moral Religion*, Ithaca and London: Cornell University Press.

——(1989), 'The Emptiness of the Moral Will', *The Monist*, 72: 454–83; reprinted in Stern (ed.) (1993c): IV, 160–88.

——(1990), *Hegel's Ethical Thought*, Cambridge: Cambridge University Press.

——(1993), 'Hegel's Ethics', in Beiser (ed.) (1993): 211–33.

Wylleman, A. (ed.) (1989), *Hegel on the Ethical Life, Religion and Philosophy (1793–1807)*, Leuven and Dordrecht: Leuven University Press and Kluwer.

INDEX